Catching the Wind in a Net

THE RELIGIOUS VISION OF ROBERTSON DAVIES

CATCHING THE WIND IN A NET

The Religious Vision of Robertson Davies

DAVE LITTLE

ECW PRESS

CANADIAN CATALOGUING IN PUBLICATION DATA

Little, Dave, 1957–

Catching the wind in a net : the
religious vision of Robertson Davies

Includes bibliographical references and index.
ISBN 1-55022-264-3

1. Davies, Robertson, 1913– – Religion.
2. Religion in literature. I. Title.

PS8507.A67Z8 1996   C818'.5409   C95-932075-X
PR9199.3.D38Z8 1996

COVER: Nicholas Roerich, *Mother of the World*
© Nicholas Roerich Museum, New York.

This book has been published with the help of a grant from the Canadian Federation for the Humanities, using funds provided by the Social Sciences and Humanities Research Council of Canada, and with the assistance of grants provided by the Ontario Arts Council and The Canada Council.

Design and imaging by ECW Type & Art, Oakville, Ontario.
Printed by Imprimerie Gagné, Louiseville, Quebec.

Distributed by General Distribution Services,
30 Lesmill Road, Don Mills, Ontario M3B 2T6.

Published by ECW PRESS,
2120 Queen Street East, Suite 200
Toronto, Ontario M4E 1E2.

*To my wife
in appreciation
for her
patience and encouragement*

ACKNOWLEDGEMENTS

Catching the Wind in a Net would not have been written without the help of many people. From the day that I apprehensively approached him with the germ of an idea that later became this book, W.J. ("Bill") Keith has offered unqualified enthusiasm and support for the project. His careful proofreading and perceptive comments improved each chapter of my evolving manuscript. I am particularly grateful for his assistance with my discussion of the *felix culpa* that appears in chapter four. Judith Skelton Grant, whose expertise is amply apparent in her superb biography of Robertson Davies, also helped me refine some of my arguments about Davies's religious views and eliminate some of the infelicities in my prose style. Robert Lecker and the staff at ECW PRESS have ably shepherded the work before you through the various stages from manuscript to published book. I wish particularly to recognize Cynthia Sugars for her thorough copyediting of the manuscript. During the past year my friend and colleague Carole Reddekopp graciously managed much of my correspondence to and from ECW in Montreal.

Crucial financial assistance has been provided during both the writing and publishing of this work. The University of Toronto awarded me three open fellowships as I researched and wrote the manuscript. More recently, this book has been published with the help of a grant from the Canadian Federation for the Humanities, using funds provided by the Social Sciences and Humanities Research Council of Canada. My employer, the Saskatchewan Valley School Division, initially encouraged me to pursue academic endeavours when I requested a change and recently, after I had completed the manuscript and very badly needed employment, generously rehired me.

I also owe several personal acknowledgements. I am grateful to my parents, Kathy and Roy Little, because both encouraged their six children to take risks in life and offered unqualified support if the risk-taking happened to result in failure. My mother-in-law, Rosemary Eckert, opened her home and provided accommodation to my wife and me and our four lively children during the years that I researched and partially wrote this book in Toronto — canonization seems almost a foregone conclusion. Finally, my wife's encouragement and considerable personal sacrifice during the writing of this work sustained me during the trials inherent in the process. I therefore dedicate this volume to her.

CONTENTS

". . . the ancients . . . said a wise man could catch the wind in a net. . . . It was a metaphor for understanding what could be felt but not seen, but of course not many people understood." (The Rebel Angels 53–54)

O N E

A Brief Religious Biography

Robertson Davies was born in 1913 into a Presbyterian family. As choir leader of Saint James Presbyterian Church in Thamesville, Ontario, and later as Sunday School superintendent of Saint Andrews in Renfrew, his father Rupert was an active participant in church life (Peterman 3, 5). His mother, Florence McKay Davies, while " 'moralistic,' " was, according to her son,

> not of a religious temper, and was indeed somewhat anti-clerical; one of her favorite books, which she read and re-read, was *Elmer Gantry*. I think this may have been because she had been "preached against" in the Methodist Church in her girlhood — the parson named her with two other girls because they had been dancing, which Methodism did not countenance. So she left that church and became a Presbyterian, but never a very doctrinal one. (qtd. in Peterman 2–3)

Like several of Davies's fictional characters, his parents frequently, although "not very reverently," recited passages from the Bible: "One of my mother's favorite quotations was that about how the dog shall return again to its vomit and the hog to his wallowing in the mire" (*Conversations* 228).[1] Young Robertson attended Presbyterian Sunday School where he learned by rote, and then absorbed an exegesis of, the 107 questions of the Shorter Catechism ("Keeping Faith" 188, 190).

---

1 In fact, Urky McVarish uses this verse derisively in *The Rebel Angels* to ridicule the dying Ellermann for returning to campus (12). The scriptural sources for the numerous biblical citations and allusions present in Davies's fiction are identified in Appendix II.

The orthodox theoretical instruction at church and somewhat heterodox atmosphere at home were augmented by Davies's own awareness of the often bewildering forces operating in his community. For instance, the children with whom he associated

> seemed to me to have two characters: there's the character they showed at Sunday School and to superiors . . . and there was their dreadful brutality to animals and to anything or everybody who was very weak. . . . I saw people who were weak suffer frightfully. (*Conversations* 215)

Davies himself often became the victim of "a group of lurking Catholic kids who beat the socks off me" (*Conversations* 246). He also recognized that perpetrating cruelties was by no means the exclusive domain of his youthful peers, and many years later still recalled how Anna, an orphaned schoolmate of his, was regularly burned with a heated iron by "the good Christian, fine-souled, woman who had taken her in" (*Conversations* 215). The dwarf tailor's suicide after his humiliation in a cruel Masonic rite, depicted in *What's Bred in the Bone*, is Davies's rendering of an incident that occurred in the Renfrew of his youth (Peterman 4). Likewise, in *Fifth Business*, his portrayal of the enraged throng burning the Kaiser's effigy is based on his childhood experience of a very similar mob whose "fury almost frightened me to death" (qtd. in Grant, *Robertson Davies* 37).

Eventually, once he was "free to choose," Davies left the Presbyterian fold, but not as one of those "religious illiterates" who "have not examined what they say they do not believe." Instead, through diligently studying his catechism, he mastered the main doctrinal underpinnings of the denomination he finally rejected ("Keeping Faith" 190). He concluded that his parents' church could not provide the answers and consolation demanded both by his observations of a world in which the workings of strong, often irrational, passions were constantly evident, and by his own psychological predisposition toward feeling rather than logic (*Conversations* 83). The "intellectual" Presbyterians (*Fifth* 16) promulgated "a strikingly cold and unsympathetic faith. . . . [A]t an early age, church chilled me" (*Conversations* 136).

Conversely, the sacramental rituals of the Catholic and Anglican churches increasingly attracted him, but he felt "ill-suited by temperament to be a Roman Catholic" (*Conversations* 136), probably because its more authoritarian nature is at odds with his own independent disposition. Davies has stated that he is "essentially a cradle Protestant," meaning that he requires great latitude in spiritual matters (*Conversations* 192); indeed, in a newspaper article addressing Father Ronald Knox's conversion from the Anglican to the Roman Church, he notes sympathetically how Knox found life "under the eye of some members of the hierarchy, unfamiliar and somewhat foreign in tone" (*Enthusiasms* 81). In his twenties Davies consequently "plumped for the more easy-going Anglicans," to use his character's words from *What's Bred in the Bone* (181), and was confirmed at Christ Church, Oxford, "while there as a student and away from home, so it avoided disturbing my parents" (*Conversations* 136).

Yet the Anglican faith proved more of a stopping-off point than a final destination. After his conversion, he remained dissatisfied and began to examine religious issues, through first the works of Sigmund Freud, and then those of Carl Gustav Jung (Roper, "Robertson Davies" 33).

> I very quickly found that for my taste, investigation of religion by orthodox theological means was unrewarding. You never got down to brass tacks, or at least nothing that I ever read did so. You started off by assuming that certain things were true, and then you developed all kinds of splendid things on top of that. I wanted to see about the basic things, so I thought that I would have a look at people who had had a wrestle with these very, very basic things. . . . (*Conversations* 81)

Davies's post-conversion exploration of these psychologists intensified. The "turning point" came "at the age of about thirty-five," when he determined to pursue "some kind of really significant inner life" (*Conversations* 230–31) — one of those "basic things" alluded to, but not identified, above. He emphasizes the importance of this in a 1944 book review, which criticizes the author for not recognizing "that religion might be a deeply personal matter — an inner struggle in which man strives to reconcile the conflicting elements of his character by relating himself to a greater power" ("Laski's New Religion"). Studying Freud and Jung nourishes this "inner life" — organized religion does not:

> anything that becomes a mass movement is reduced by the mass. . . . I feel that your devotion to God has to be personal

and individual. To do it with a great gang who are really trying to get away from thinking about God but want to do a lot of good for the Boat People may be very fine but it's not a religion. It's an escape from a dire confrontation with whatever is beyond. (*Conversations* 192–93)

In 1958, at the age of forty-five, Davies rejected the "strongly reductive" Freud in favour of Jung, eschewing Freud's contention that "the whole structure of religion, including belief in God, was an illusion" (*One Half* 242). Jung's more benign views on faith and the existence of God proved to be decisively attractive to Davies, who, as time went on, "became convinced of the existence of another dimension of life without which I could not live as a free and courageous being" (*One Half* 243). In an obvious departure from accepted Anglican doctrine, he also accepted Jung's heterodox explanation of the role of evil in the world:

> Orthodox Christianity has always had for me the difficulty that it really won't come, in what is for me a satisfactory way, to grips with the problems of evil. It knows an enormous amount about evil, it discusses evil in fascinating terms, but evil is always the other thing: it is something which is apart from perfection, and man's duty is to strive for perfection. I could not reconcile that with such experience of life as I had, and the Jungian feeling that things tend to run into one another, that what looks good can be pushed to the point where it becomes evil, and that evil very frequently bears what can only be regarded as good fruit. . . . (*Conversations* 82)

Davies's initial approbation in 1958, which prompted a wider exploration of Jung's theology, had become, by 1971, an encompassing acceptance:

> "I not only accept [Jung's] views on religion but I've found them to be true in practice, which is something else.
> It's impossible to express his ideas in concise and brief forms. He makes it pretty clear that a man who recognizes no God is probably placing an inordinate value on himself." (*Conversations* 66)

Davies's ensuing statements indicate continuing approval of Jung's religious observations. Thus, the linear journey which began in his

Presbyterian boyhood and proceeded through his Anglican conversion changed direction in Davies's mid-life. Today, his personal quest generally begins from a Jungian centrepoint, which he uses as a basis to expand the circumference of his individual theology.

With Davies's rejection of institutionalized faiths, religion has clearly come to mean something other than a prescribed form of worship and a traditional creed:

> to be aware all the time, even if you haven't got your mind directly on it, of the existence of things which are infinitely greater than yourself, and in the face of which you and your desires and your hopes are trivial. I think it's very important, and that is what I mean by religion, a sense of the great things of life. (*Conversations* 95)

> [W]hen I say "religious" I mean immensely conscious of powers of which I can have only the dimmest apprehension, which operate by means that I cannot fathom, in directions which I would be a fool to call either good or bad. (*Conversations* 82)

Davies has embarked on a number of very specific explorations, each predicated on the general sense of greater and often incomprehensible powers contained in these definitions. His attempts to get down to what he calls "brass tacks" or "basic things" (*Conversations* 81), their Jungian antecedents, and their importance in his fiction form the focus of the following study.

T W O

Towards a Definition of God: In Praise of the Quest

"I never heard anyone suggest that Uncle Frank was religious."

"The word is greatly misunderstood in the turmoil of our day," said Darcourt, "but in so far as it means seeking to know, and to live, beneath the surfaces of life, and to be aware of the realities beneath the superficialities, you may take it from me that Francis was truly religious." (*The Lyre of Orpheus* 340–41)

Determining the metaphysical characteristics of God is a difficult and often fruitless endeavour. Recognizing this, in *The Varieties of Religious Experience* William James makes sport of philosophers who confidently feel themselves successful in this undertaking:

What is their deduction of metaphysical attributes but a shuffling and matching of pedantic dictionary-adjectives. . . . [T]he metaphysical monster which they offer to our worship is an absolutely worthless invention of the scholarly mind. (340)

Equally, James dismisses accounts that seek to delineate God in terms of His moral qualities: "It stands with them as ill as with the arguments for his existence" (341).

Given this context, one can understand the knotty problem faced by Robertson Davies whenever he is asked to outline his notion of the supreme deity. His unease is evident, for although he is usually expansive, he sometimes refuses to attempt a definition. In the 1976 Larkin-Stuart lectures, for instance, he states:

Defining God has always seemed to me a pompous and self-defeating exercise. I am content that God should encompass me:

I do not think it likely that I shall encompass Him. Where God
is concerned, I am the object, not the subject. (*One Half* 243)

Subsequently, in 1981, he told Tom Harpur that he hadn't "any
particular definition or view of what God is. . . . The fact of God
being all-encompassing ever-present is really about all that I can say
about it" (*Conversations* 209).

These seemingly definite refusals notwithstanding, he is elsewhere
much more forthcoming. Yet in these cases, too, he exhibits uncertainty, not in any single description of God but in the discrepancies
between his accounts. Although in the Larkin-Stuart lectures Davies
characterizes any attempt to define God a "pompous and self
defeating exercise," he soon shifts abruptly and describes not only
God but also the Devil:

> I have been suggesting the existence of a power of good and a
> power of evil external to man, and working through him as an
> agency — a God, in fact, infinitely greater than man can conceive,
> and a Devil vastly more terrible than even the uttermost terrors
> of human evil. (*One Half* 264)

A 1986 interview with Michael Hulse shows Davies somewhat
similarly asserting that "the Devil is just a metaphor for negative
forces that are at work in human destiny, as God is (generally) a
metaphor for the — on the whole — benevolent, though often
minatory, forces in human destiny" (*Conversations* 257).

Different from this notion of a powerful force for good which
operates in contrast to an evil counterpart is Davies's perspective on
the word *God* in "The Conscience of the Writer" (1968). Here, by
"using that name to comprehend all the great and inexplicable things
and the redemptive or destructive powers that lie outside human
command and understanding" (*One Half* 127), he posits a less
exclusively benevolent deity. In this essay he also associates God with
some form of retribution, emphasizing that in this world "God is not
mocked, and . . . a man reaps — only too obviously — what he has
sown" (131). Subsequently, during a 1975 conversation with Margaret Penman about the deity, Davies eschewed any concept of
distinctly separate forces of good and evil, arguing, instead, for a
Jungian description of God: "if you're going to have a really satisfactory notion of God, you must include evil in it because evil is a
part of the universe as we know it . . ." (*Conversations* 154).

Moments later, however, he deprecated this idea, maintaining that humans are not "in any position to sit in judgment on God and say that he's either all good or partly bad . . ." (154). His emphasis then changed again, when he associated God with a seemingly morally-neutral form of creative evolution:

> We're not God, and we don't know what he needs or how he's running things or anything, but we do know that we somehow or other got from a protoplasmal atomic globule to you and me sitting in this studio with a fascinating amount of wire devices around us which make it possible for a lot of people to listen to us, and that's not just a tiny step. . . . (*Conversations* 154–55)

Even that conversation with Tom Harpur, during which Davies claimed that he hadn't "any particular definition or view of what God is," soon became a medium for expressing just such a view. In response to Harpur's next question, "Do you think then of God as some immanent force within us rather than some deity over and above the universe?", he replied:

> As both. Simply to say immanent within us suggests God is somehow the property of mankind and/or of the animal king-dom, [sic] I think God is immanent in everything that we know. . . . The idea that God is solely and gloatingly concerned with mankind is very self-flattering. (*Conversations* 209)

Finally, in a 1989 letter to the Trinity College *Salterrae*, Davies provided yet another conception: "God is an incorrigible joker."

Davies's tentative and sometimes contradictory attempts to delin-eate the divine might well prompt readers to reject his views on the subject. Yet while some censure for his lack of consistency may be warranted, an outright dismissal would be grossly simplistic for several reasons. First, he is exploring an area that many people today avoid completely. As William James illustrates, this undertaking proves difficult even for those professional metaphysicians who accept the challenge; surely, then, a measure of forbearance is appropriate for Robertson Davies. Further, Davies's contradictory statements square with the example set by his mentor Carl Jung, whose declarations vary from "What God is in himself nobody knows" (*Collected* 18: 1595),[1] to the aforementioned reference

---

1 All references to Jung's *Collected Works* are to paragraph number.

(offered in Davies's interview with Margaret Penman) about the deity being both good and evil, to the more relativistic "That psychological fact which is the greatest power in your system is the god" (*Psychology* 98).

If we judge Davies by the standards evident in his fiction, we see that the characters who generally engage our sympathy do not possess the facile theological uniformity and complacency of, for example, the Reverend Amasa Dempster or Hulda Schnakenburg's parents. Instead, those we admire tend to be most like Davies himself — believing in God but exhibiting uncertainty about His specific attributes. Seldom, however, do Davies's characters falter in their ongoing exploration of this and other fundamental questions. For instance, Padre Ignatio Blazon spends much of his life seeking a (probably non-Christian) God who will teach him to be an old man. In *World of Wonders* Dunstan Ramsay posits contradictory visions of the deity as he strives to understand Him, and Simon Darcourt does the same in the Cornish trilogy. These examples point to an aesthetic *apologia* that offers the most cogent reason for sanctioning Davies's tentativeness and lack of complete consistency in his concept of the divine. Clearly he is able to offer compelling, energetic portraits both of the struggle to comprehend God and of the varied resulting views, because he, too, has laboured for this comprehension and has explored many of these positions as part of his own personal quest.

The first major instance of Davies exploiting the uncertain nature of God appears in *Leaven of Malice* and, as one might expect in the Salterton trilogy, the effect is largely comic. Employing a combination of Aristotelian and Old Testament nomenclature, Humphrey Cobbler expresses his apprehension about God's metaphysical qualities:

> "Sometimes I have a nightmare in which I dream that I have gone to heaven, and as I creep toward the Awful Throne I am blinded by the array of service-club buttons shining on the robe of the Ancient of Days. . . . I am in for an eternity of Social Disapproval. Wouldn't it be an awful sell for a lot of us — all the artists, and jokers, and strivers-after-better-things — if God turned out to be the Prime Mover of capitalist respectability?" (141)

Juxtaposed to Cobbler's anxiety is Miss Vyner's inert complacency: "She never thought about God, herself, but she had a sleeping regard

19

for Him, as a Being who thought very much as she herself did, though more potently. Dragging God into a conversation embarrassed her deeply" (141). More pernicious is what appears to be Norm Yarrow's transcendent religious search that has discovered its "Faith Focus" through which "doubts and fears and misgivings are sublimated in [a] vast Power" (136). Yet Norm's "sincere but modern scientific Faith" does not achieve its crescendo in a majestic, transcendent supreme being, as his reference to sublimation in a "vast Power" might indicate, but, instead, in the mundane notion of "getting engaged, of course" (135–36).

More so than in *Leaven of Malice*, Davies foregrounds the contrast between dynamic God-seeking and static God-confining characters in *A Mixture of Frailties*. For example, by virtue of his office as Monica Gall's one-time spiritual director, Sidney Beamis is a figure of greater significance in this novel than are his counterparts Miss Vyner and Norm Yarrow in the preceding book. As pastor of the Thirteenth Apostle Tabernacle, Beamis champions the bizarre, simplistic ontology of the original Thirteener, Myron Coffey. This doctrine easily dismissed the world of the senses as a diabolical illusion, affirming instead that we are "coaevals in the realm of the spirit, which was the only real realm"; thus, God is here, but we must first " 'make contact' " (42). Executing this inviting metaphysical exploit is possible only through prayer, the reading of scripture, and "leading a good life," which "Coffey explained . . . in terms of what he believed his mother's life to have been — unstinting service to others, simple piety, mistrust of pleasure, and no truck with thought or education beyond what was necessary to read the Good Book" (42). The satire directed against Beamis and the Thirteeners reaches its zenith with the disclosure that "All these wonders came to Coffey in a single week, culminating in a revelation that he was the Thirteenth Apostle, destined to spread the good news to mankind" (42).

In contrast to her one-time pastor and former congregation, Monica Gall, the novel's central character, experiences an ongoing lack of religious assurance. Yet Davies's treatment of her uncertainty differs from that which he accords Humphrey Cobbler's in *Leaven of Malice*, as hers is more thoroughly investigated and less comically depicted. Apprehension about the prospect of God wearing service-club buttons is replaced by a deeper fear, as the postvirginal, post-Thirteener Monica ponders the possibility of divine retribution for practising birth control (231–32). This typifies the confusion she suffers as she is compelled — often by music — to continue a search begun with her rejection of the narrow, but once-comfortable, doctrine of Beamis and the Thirteeners. Her experience of the "majestic faith" evoked by the *St. Matthew Passion* leaves her "overwhelmed" and "frightened" (234). *Water Parted* prompts

> a yearning toward all the vast, inexplicable, irrational treasury from which her life drew whatever meaning and worth it possessed. It was the yearning for — ? . . . [N]ot all the wise men in the world could ever tell her, but it would last until the end. (311)

This song confirms her sense of a power transcending surface realities but provides no description of "— ?"; thus, Monica's uncertainty continues and remains unresolved at the novel's conclusion.

I have been suggesting that in terms of defining the deity, those characters who most engage our sympathies share Davies's own certainty about God's existence, his uncertainty about God's specific characteristics, and his continual but evidently unsuccessful quest to make this uncertainty a certainty. To this hypothesis I must offer one exception: as a general rule, a character can be presumed to have an orthodox, circumscribed notion of God and still remain appealing to the reader if and only if he is an Anglican priest. The Salterton trilogy's Dean Jevon Knapp is one example of this; another is *The Manticore*'s Father Gervase Knopwood. Davies may feel that Anglican convictions are at least acceptable in so far as they provide enough theological latitude to permit a definition of God in very broad terms. Thus, in the Dean's case they permit a middle road somewhere between Monica's ultimate tentativeness and Beamis's rigid reductionism.

However, Davies manages the issue very carefully. One can only assume that by virtue of the Dean's office Knapp has a reasonably certain idea of God's nature — he never actually discusses the topic. Also, Davies's description of Knapp's cathedral as "a true dwelling-place of one of the many circumscribed, but not therefore ignoble, concepts of God" (373) is somewhat backhanded. Had he dispensed with the double negative, which makes the statement sound rather defensive, and instead written "circumscribed and therefore noble," one's sense of grudging acknowledgement here might have been diminished. Then, as though he has given away too much even with this concession, Davies concludes *A Mixture of Frailties* with the

Dean's sermon, one of the topics of which is the tremendous difficulty encountered in coming to know God. Our final sense of Knapp's beliefs might therefore be summarized as: circumscription if necessary, but not necessarily circumscription.

The difficulty of coming to know God, increasingly important as the Salterton trilogy progresses, forms a thematic focus of *Fifth Business*. Very early in this novel Davies stakes out the metaphysical terrain for the Deptford trilogy through his inclusion of W.V., the little girl in the *Child's Book of Saints*. Described by Dunstan Ramsay as "a little pill" (82), she offers two opposite and equally unacceptable positions about God's nature. The first is so epistemologically pessimistic that it would seem to preclude any sort of endeavour to know Him: W.V. "could always fling a bridge of flowers" over "insoluble mysteries" by declaring that " 'Our sense . . . is nothing to God's. . . . We are only little babies to Him; we do not understand Him at all' " (38). Then, with a baffling leap of logic (perhaps the privilege of the very young), she presents an opposing view of such reductionist certainty that further exploration would seem useless: " 'He is just a dear old Father' " (38). The search for the divine must obviously proceed between these two extremes. In fact, W.V.'s latter position has already been negated by young Dunstan Ramsay's Dantean experience of God; her former will be challenged by other characters in the trilogy who are confident that the effort to understand the deity can bear fruit — in other words, that "our sense" is *something* to God's.

In spite of his travails, Dunstan Ramsay does not harvest this fruit in *Fifth Business*. Continuing his quest in *World of Wonders*, he reflects: "I had sought God in my lifelong, unlikely (for a Canadian schoolmaster) preoccupation with . . . Saints. But all I had found in that lifelong study was a complexity that brought God no nearer" (42). Yet *Fifth Business* is not entirely "the account of a failed search for the divine," as George Woodcock characterizes it (43), since Ramsay's friend Padre Blazon partially prevails in his endeavour. D.J. Dooley aptly describes this priest as "a very unJesuitical Jesuit" (120) because his quest for the deity prompts him to move beyond the relative certainties of Catholic doctrine and explore heterodox religious ideas. As his search progresses, Blazon concludes that God, " 'who knows the good and evil of life,' " has a plan for humans, and that in implementing it He " 'is subtle, but He is not cruel' " (*Fifth* 177); still, the Padre continues to seek a God who will teach him to be an old man. At last, some time after his one-hundredth birthday, he proclaims partial success, yet he describes the divine in terms which preclude W.V.'s narrow reductionism: " 'He is the very best of company. Very calm, very quiet, but gloriously alive: we *do*, but He *is*' " (250).

In *The Manticore*, Davies's exploration of the nature of God takes a peculiar turn. Here, he reconsiders a notion of the divine that he had earlier mocked in *A Mixture of Frailties*. In that novel Pastor Beamis argues that "God was here: Christ was now," if only we could just " 'make contact' " (43). Father Gervase Knopwood, a much more sophisticated character from *The Manticore*, dispenses with the idea of "making contact" through simplistic notions of knowledge contained in the Bible and the basic piety and morality exemplified by anybody's mother. However, he does salvage Beamis's initial premise. Another of Davies's very appealing Anglican priests, Knopwood "expounded the Creed in tough terms. . . . Christianity was serious and demanding, but worth any amount of trouble. God is here, and Christ is now. That was his line" (135).

Knopwood appears to have derived this conclusion from his humanitarian work and substantial knowledge of art and philosophy. He invokes his never fully explicated belief to encourage his wards to recognize and examine their sins, and upon this tenet predicates his attempt to persuade David Staunton to reject the sensuous frivolity of his father. He warns the boy that " 'love as a high condition of honour' " will not disappear because " 'God is not dead.' " To underscore his point, Knopwood employs Davies's own words, " 'God is not mocked' " (188), leaving implicit the sentiment — from Galatians 6.7 — with which Davies explicitly concludes this statement in his essay "The Conscience of the Writer": "and a man reaps — only too obviously — what he has sown" (*One Half* 131). The youth, however, remains unconvinced and rejects Knopwood: "For him, God was here and Christ was now. . . . He thought God was not mocked. I seemed to see God being mocked, and rewarding the mocker with splendid success, every day of my life" (195–96).

Liesl, the novel's other mentor figure whose ethical precepts incorporate God, accepts as valid Knopwood's contention that "God is here and Christ is now," but argues for a more expansive interpretation. She asserts that "it's equally true to say 'Odin is here and Loki is now' " (268), which is less a positing of the metaphysical qualities of God, Christ, Odin, and Loki, than it is a means of urging David to emulate the heroes of Judaeo-Christian and Norse mythology: "The heroic world is all around us, waiting to be known" (268).

When Staunton protests that the days for heroism are over, she disagrees, encouraging him to "Be the hero of your own epic," an adjunct to her definition of the modern hero as "the man who conquers in the inner struggle" (268). To engender in David the feeling of awe necessary to initiate this struggle, she conducts him to a mountain cave which for millennia has been the site of religious meditation and worship. There, appropriately, she again invokes the deity, suggesting that God is found in the darkness and that He can provide strength (274, 276). However, she never makes clear whether she is now advocating a particular position vis-à-vis a transcendent power, or whether she is continuing to employ God as a means of exhorting her companion to mythic and heroic feats (or both). It is perhaps this ambiguity that saps either alternative of its potential for supplying David with the power that would effect his escape from the physical and psychological caves in which he lies trapped. Recollection of a heroic ancestor must serve instead.

Just as Liesl's notion of God is ambiguous, so, ultimately, is the contention — albeit raised in this novel by a credible character — that "God is here, and Christ is now." As Knopwood predicts, and David discovers at last through his friends at Sorgenfrei, " 'love as a high condition of honour' " has not disappeared from the world — but is that because " 'God is not dead' " (188)? If people reap what they have sown, and they surely do so in this book, is it really because " 'God is not mocked' "? Davies defers answering these questions until the next and final work in this trilogy.

In *World of Wonders*, Magnus Eisengrim presents his autobiography, considering the part the divine has played in his life. Knopwood's aphorisms, though never directly quoted, underlie the magician's life story. For the young kidnapped boy, existing at his lowest ebb as the sodomized workings of the machine Abdullah, God is certainly not mocked; in fact, through His perceived retribution He seems only too palpably "here":

> "Sometimes I thought the Lord hated me; sometimes I thought he was punishing me for — for just about everything that had ever happened to me, beginning with my birth; sometimes I thought he had forgotten me, but that thought was blasphemy, and I chased it away as fast as I could." (111)

Many years later, long after renouncing the particulars of his father's Baptist fundamentalism, Eisengrim retains a loosely circumscribed belief in a partly benign — instead of exclusively minatory — interventionist deity. In an echo of one of Davies's own descriptions of God as comprising the "redemptive or destructive powers that lie outside human command and understanding" (*One Half* 127), Eisengrim professes

> "a humble awareness of the Great Justice and the Great Mercy.
> . . . I don't monkey with what I think of as the Great Justice. . . .
> And I don't administer it. Something else — something I don't understand, but feel and serve and fear — does that. It's sometimes horrible to watch. . . . But part of the glory and terror of our life is that somehow, at some time, we get all that's coming to us." (313–14)

He substantiates his assertion by offering the proud Sir John Tresize's humiliation and Boy Staunton's grotesque death as examples of the Great Justice at work (313–14). This Dispenser of often harsh payment is unmistakably the logical elaboration of the solemn figure of God, barren of laughter and "above jokes," that Eisengrim had posited earlier in his narrative (40).

Dunstan Ramsay, the other character especially absorbed by questions of the divine, subsequently illustrates the magician's professed, but unexplored, notion of the Great Mercy. Yet he is only able to do this after a significant shift in his convictions, between *Fifth Business* and *World of Wonders*, has occurred. As Judith Skelton Grant remarks: "Dunstan moves beyond his earlier limited statement that one can say with certainty only that faith is a psychological reality [*Fifth* 200]. Now, with Magnus, Liesl, and Lind, he believes that God and the Devil exist" (*Robertson Davies* 48). What prompts this change remains enigmatic; the trilogy reveals only that it is the result neither of Ramsay's study of saints, nor of his verbatim recollection of the Westminster Confession's description of God (*World* 41–42). His ability to recite from the Presbyterian catechism underscores Ramsay's theological credentials, yet the list of abstractions that he recounts proves inadequate on a spiritual level since it provides no suitable accompanying procedure by which he might seek the divine (42).

Although Ramsay has come to believe in God, albeit by means that remain mysterious, he is not very successful in circumscribing Him, even very loosely or consistently. In reply to Eisengrim's question, " 'Doesn't God put a price on things?' ", he declares: " 'No. One of

his attributes is magnanimity. But the Devil is a setter of prices . . .' "
(57). Later, however, he posits God as the evident apportioner of
value. When Kinghovn speculates about his own innocent childhood, asking, " 'Which was the greater use in the world? That child,
so sweet and pure, or me, as I am now, not sweet and damned well
not pure?' ", Ramsay responds, " 'there is no answer . . . without
God' " (139). His uncertainty about the deity is also apparent in his
comment on God's forgiving grace; after quoting Robert Louis
Stevenson, " ' "In the law of God there is no statute of limitations" ', "
Ramsay adds, " 'Are we ever forgiven for the follies even of our
earliest years? That's something that torments me often' " (221–22).
   At best, all that he can provide with assurance, and this on the
novel's final page, is that illustration of what Eisengrim has briefly
referred to as the Great Mercy. Using more traditional nomenclature,
Ramsay tells Liesl that Magnus's appearance as a benevolent presence in her life was a direct result of God's intervention (316). Yet
even here he quickly notes the formidable difficulty in discerning the
workings of God from those of the Devil: " 'both speak so compellingly it's tricky work to know who's talking' " (316). Ramsay's
search, no longer to find God but to know Him, must continue.
   In the Cornish trilogy this exploration intensifies. *The Rebel
Angels*, like *Fifth Business*, in part chronicles a character's fruitless
quest for the divine. Yet, unlike Dunstan Ramsay, who in the course
of the Deptford trilogy comes to a firm, though general, belief in the
deity, John Parlabane is crushed by the failure of his endeavour.
Parlabane, perhaps the novel's most dynamic character, had first
attempted to limit the debilitating scepticism of his young adulthood
by seeking God through orthodox methods. After experiencing
initially " 'His great mercy' " when reconciled with an estranged
friend, and then suffering distress when " 'God tested [him] sternly' "
with that friend's abrupt death (69), Parlabane joins an Anglican
monastery. Yet the monastic routine, and presumably the commensurate God toward whom it is directed, proves too exclusively good
and thus unsatisfactory:

   "I became positively sick for the existentialist gloom, the malicious joy at the misfortunes of others, and the gallows-humour
   that gave zest to modern intellectual life outside the monastery.
   I was like a child who is given nothing but the most wholesome
   food; my soul yearned for unwholesome trash, to keep me
   somehow in balance." (73)

The pared-down deity that the ex-monk later offers to Maria Theotoky is devoid of the great mercy and stern testing that had so influenced him earlier. Parlabane now preserves God as some sort of bare minimum who simply and inexorably exists, and thus serves as the one metaphysical certainty in an otherwise unknowable world: " 'Scepticism is of this world, my darling, but God is not of this world. . . . Without God the sceptic is in a vacuum and his doubt, which is his crowning achievement, is also his tragedy' " (196). He also retains God as the figure who allows us to transcend an anthropomorphic universe: " 'when human reason refuses to admit vassalage to anything other than itself, life becomes tragedy. God is the factor that banishes that tragedy' " (196).

The repeated fear of "tragedy" notwithstanding, Parlabane's belief in even this bare-minimum deity soon vanishes. His subsequent actions in the novel suggest that chaotic, sceptical life he had led prior to his supposed embracing of a superior being; his heavy use of drugs, veiled threats of violence towards Maria, and ultimate suicide are much more characteristic of despair than any sort of theological optimism. He is particularly doubtful about God in his departure from this world, taking his leave " 'in search of the Great Perhaps' " (297). As Susan Stone-Blackburn so aptly concludes: "What damns Parlabane in Davies' eyes is his scepticism, his nay-saying; in his consistent denial of the meaning and worth of anything in life, he is the embodiment of evil. . . . Parlabane epitomizes emptiness" (99). It is an emptiness which even the ex-monk's prodigious vitality cannot negate.

Contrasted with Parlabane is that other tremendously dynamic figure, Mamusia Laoutaro. Davies never has these two characters meet, perhaps realizing that to depict tension of such magnitude would tax even his considerable artistic prowess: what the sceptic represents as a powerful spokesman for nay-saying, the gypsy mother is equally for affirmation, for yea-saying. Hers is a universe of order and purpose, so she assures Simon Darcourt: " 'Nothing is without meaning; if it were, the world would dash to pieces' " (225). She validates this assertion through her readings of tarot cards and by grounding her ethical conduct on a bedrock conviction of a superior power. Though she never directly reiterates Knopwood's assertion that "God is here," her loose circumscription of God is predicated upon it — much like Eisengrim's very similar notion of the Great Justice. When Clement Hollier asks her to curse Urky McVarish, she refuses in horror:

"to curse him I have to be very well in with — *What?* — if I am to escape without harm to myself. Because *What?* is very terrible. *What?* does not deal in the Sweet Justice of civilized man, but in Balance, which is not nearly so much concerned with man, and may seem terrible and evil to him. . . . When Balance decides the time has come to settle the scales awful things happen. Much of what we do not understand is Balance at work. . . . I do not want to call on *What?*, who lives down there in the darkness where Cancer dwells, and whose army is all the creatures of the dark, and the spirits of the suicides and all the terrible forces. . . ." (268)

Davies's terminology here re-emphasizes the immense difficulties involved in formulating anything more than a very general description of the deity or first principle. "*What?*" is, no doubt, a direct descendant of Monica Gall's unknown "— ?" (*Mixture* 311), a rendering of the unnamed administrator of the Great Justice whom Magnus Eisengrim feels, serves, and fears, but understands only vaguely (*World* 313).

In *A Mixture of Frailties* Pastor Beamis urges his congregation to "'make contact.'" But that which Davies depicts comically in this novel, he offers in earnest in *The Rebel Angels*. All that Mamusia can assert for certain about "*What?*" — aside from its dark penchant for Balance — is that making contact with it is only too easy. She warns Hollier: "'you have already cursed your enemy in your heart, and you have reached *What?* without me. Man, I fear for you!'" (269). Subsequent events, which indicate a certain rectification or balance at work, appear to justify her apprehension. The disgusting McVarish dies in a perverse manner, which effects the recovery of a coveted manuscript he had stolen; after discovering the grotesque fate of the man he had cursed, Hollier experiences what might be construed as retribution in the form of a mental and physical collapse. Whether these are actually the doings of Mamusia's "*What?*" is, in keeping with Davies's pattern not to circumscribe God too rigidly, finally left uncertain.

Because Mamusia's predictions may be accurate, her statement about "*What?*" is important in the novel, as is Parlabane's examination of and ultimate scepticism about God. In fact, as I argued at the outset of this chapter, Davies's own quest to know God has been well incorporated into his fiction and has paid solid artistic dividends. However, exceptions to this begin to appear in *The Rebel Angels*, where a lack of coherence becomes increasingly evident. Barbara Godard recognizes in this book some aspects of the anatomy (240), a form typified by an abundance of "abstract ideas and theories" and the "free play of intellectual fancy" (Frye, *Anatomy* 309, 310). Davies's choice of the anatomy, with its preponderance of these elements, does not of itself account for the reader's uneasy sense here that scholarly speculation has become divorced from aesthetic concerns; instead, this is the result of the inadequate integration into the story of the "great variety of subject-matter and a strong interest in ideas" which characterize the anatomy form (Frye, *Anatomy* 365). Recognizing this weakness in an early review, Sam Solecki avers that "between *The Manticore* and *The Rebel Angels* . . . the novels become increasingly static, cluttered with the flotsam of Davies' store of learning. . . . More than its immediate predecessors *The Rebel Angels* creaks under an excess of intellectual baggage" (31). To relate Solecki's general observations to our discussion of the deity, in *The Rebel Angels* credible characters casually proffer fascinating, though rather absolutist, statements about the nature of God; however, Davies often leaves these dead in the water, as interesting ideas in search of a story.

Improbably, it is Maria Theotoky who instructs Simon Darcourt, the expert on biblical apocrypha, about the rebel angels Samahazai and Azazel. After they betrayed His secrets to Solomon, God ejected these Promethean figures from heaven.

> "And did they mope and plot vengeance? Not they! They weren't sore-headed egotists like Lucifer. Instead they gave mankind another push up the ladder, they came to earth and taught tongues, and healing and laws and hygiene — taught everything — and they were often special successes with 'the daughters of men.'" (257)

My extratextual research indicates that Maria has given Darcourt an incomplete and somewhat false account. Far from being a hygienic presence in this world, Azazel was "the personification of uncleanness" ("Azazel"). Hardly the unequivocally benign influence that Maria suggests, he also taught men warfare and witchcraft (Mercatante 99). And Azazel was Luciferian!:

> In *The Apocalypse of Abraham* he is "lord of hell, seducer of mankind," and here his aspect, when revealed in its true form,

29

shows him to be a demon with 7 serpent heads, 14 faces, and 12 wings. Jewish legend speaks of Azazel as the angel who refused to bow down before Adam . . . when the 1st human was presented to [sic] God to the assembled hierarchs in Heaven. For such refusal, Azazel was thenceforth dubbed "the accursed Satan." (Davidson 63)

Both rebel angels were indeed, as Maria says, "special successes with the 'daughters of men,'" but as a result they "managed . . . to spawn some pretty horrendous and very unruly monsters," described as "mutant and ravaging giants" (Godwin 86, 70). The account of the progeny of Samahazai, also known as Samiazaz, Shemhazai, Shemjaza, and Semyaza, corroborates this: "According to *The Zohar* (Genesis) Semyaza's sons, Hiwa and Hiya, by one of Eve's daughters, were so mighty that they ate daily 1,000 camels, 1,000 horses, and 1,000 oxen" (Davidson 265).

Were we to overlook these matters, we might still expect Maria's account of these angels as teachers to be appropriate for a book about an institution of higher learning: "'surely it is the explanation of the origin of universities!'" (257). But Maria continues,

"God doesn't come out of some of these stories in a very good light, does He? Job had to tell Him a few home truths about His injustice and caprice; the Rebel Angels showed Him that hiding all knowledge and wisdom and keeping it for Himself was dog-in-the-manger behaviour. I've always taken it as proof that we'll civilize God yet." (257)

This is interesting and potentially evocative material. In addition to the further information she provides about the Rebel Angels, Maria reveals her familiarity with the Book of Job, and probably Jung's "Answer to Job," an intriguing commentary on God's behaviour in the biblical story. In this essay, Jung argues that a rather primitive, savage deity needs man to teach Him civilized conduct: God

can boast of his superior power and enact laws which mean less than air to him. Murder and manslaughter are mere bagatelles, and if the mood takes him he can play the feudal grand seigneur and generously recompense his bondslave for the havoc wrought in his wheat-fields. "So you have lost your sons and daughters? No harm done, I will give you new and better ones." (*Collected* 11: 597)

Later, realizing His limitations, God "indirectly acknowledg[es] that the man Job is morally superior to him and that therefore he has to catch up and become human himself" (11: 640). Maria's statement provides numerous possibilities about the nature of God, yet one looks in vain to see how they are manifest in the story. Not only are we never given a sense, Jungian or otherwise, of how we might "civilize God yet," but we also look in vain for the expected Jobian figure engaged in a confrontation with Him.[1] Ultimately, her ideas about the deity, tantalizing for their potential, remain awkwardly unassimilated in *The Rebel Angels*.

If Maria's instructing her instructor about biblical apocrypha stretches credulity, what is the reader to make of a Board-of-Trade type reinterpreting Genesis and enlightening Darcourt on a Gnostic gospel?

> " 'The Kingdom of the Father is spread upon the earth and men do not see it.' . . . *The Gospel of Thomas* [v. 113], and very juicy stuff. . . . Adam and Eve had learned how to comprehend the Kingdom of the Father, and their descendants have been hard at it ever since. That's what universities are about, when they aren't farting around with trivialities. Of course God was jealous; He was being asked to share some of His domain. I'll bet Adam and Eve left the Garden laughing and happy with their bargain; they had exchanged a know-nothing innocence for infinite choice."
> (312)

The reader's curiosity is piqued by Arthur's intriguing assertion; however, once again we wait fruitlessly to see how this will play out in the story. Nowhere do we see the figure of a jealous God, or, for that matter, an Adam or Eve who must gain knowledge only at the price of defying Him.

Simon Darcourt's notions of God constitute a special case and problem in *The Rebel Angels*. They are neither as immediately relevant as Mamusia's and Parlabane's, nor are they all ideas in search of a story as are Arthur's and Maria's. Darcourt is the Davies character who most resembles his creator in that he offers a number

---

1 That Davies is familiar with one contemporary example that he might have used as a model, for the latter phenomenon at least, is evident from his favourable review of Archibald MacLeish's *J.B.*; in this review he also commends Jung's "Answer to Job" ("Answer to Job").

of general, and sometimes contradictory, notions of God. However, as we have seen in the previous two trilogies, this lack of certainty need not be an aesthetic liability. What is awkward in this case is that Darcourt's concepts do not manifest themselves in a story line until two novels later.

He first describes himself "as a priest and a professor and . . . a man who was humble before God but not necessarily humble before his fellows" (56). Yet the reader is never certain what significance the presence of this humility-eliciting deity has for the novel, or indeed what form this meekness will take for Darcourt. The same problem is evident in Darcourt's idea of " 'God's Saving Grace.' " He equates it with " 'sheer, bald-headed Luck' " and declares that " 'the way He sprinkles it around is beyond human comprehension' " (101); this may well be so, since we do not discern much direct evidence of God's grace in *The Rebel Angels*. For this we must wait until the subsequent two Cornish novels, though even *What's Bred in the Bone* — where " 'Luck' " is very crucial — never decisively indicates whether the forces to whom luck is attributed are agents of divine grace.

Davies fares moderately better in incorporating another of Darcourt's theological notions into *The Rebel Angels*. In conversation with Clem Hollier, the priest anticipates Davies's address to the Trinity College *Salterrae*, asserting: " 'God's a rum old joker, Clem, and we must never forget it' " (101). This sentiment is reflected in the story — in the brief statement averring that "The Rum Old Joker had been a bit rowdy with [the metabolisms of] Ozy and Peggy" Froats (112), and in the motley assortment of would-be clerics in Darcourt's graduate seminar who constitute a "complicated Jewish joke" on God's part (36).

Near the book's conclusion, Darcourt uses two discordant sets of nomenclature when alluding to God. Peculiar for an Anglican priest, he refers to the deity as "Whatever It Is" (313), a phrase that is akin to Mamusia's terminology for a difficult-to-know superior being and which Davies revives later in *The Lyre of Orpheus*. Immediately after this, however, Darcourt twice refers to "the one God" (314, 315), suggesting his greater certainty on this subject. Inconsistencies we by now accept; what is troubling here is that, once again, we have no sense of Davies's integrating either of these concepts into "The New Aubrey," Darcourt's sections of *The Rebel Angels*.

The Rebel Angels leaves its readers to consider such a variety of ideas about God that they arguably need an interval in which to catch their contemplative breaths. Also, Darcourt's unassimilated descriptions of Him present a number of aesthetic-theological loose-ends which Davies will address when he resumes the priest's story in *The Lyre of Orpheus*. These are probably the reasons for the author's pausing (relatively speaking) in his exploration of the deity during the trilogy's middle novel, *What's Bred in the Bone*. Here Darcourt, again echoing Davies (*One Half* 244), refers to God as a " 'psychological fact' " (19). Aunt Mary Ben, indicating that He is this and much more, interprets her scalping by a great horned owl not as a "freak accident," but as "God's way of defining her role in life" (52). In addition, there are several short and fairly predictable descriptions of the divine among the orthodox professions of faith expounded to Francis Cornish by this same staunchly Roman Catholic aunt (246–47) and the equally steadfast Presbyterian, Victoria Cameron (165–66) — Cornish, the central character, ultimately pays little heed to either (455). These few instances, all reasonably well integrated into the story, constitute the relatively brief consideration given to God's nature in this lengthy book.

What is absent in this regard in *What's Bred in the Bone* is present and pursued with redoubled vigour in *The Lyre of Orpheus*. Here the examination of the deity is adeptly incorporated into the story, although this is not immediately apparent since the one notable exception involves the novel's first depiction of the divine. Maria's description of the Gnostic theory about the Seven Laughters of a merry God (178–80) does in a very general sense echo the references to God as "a Rum Old Joker" in both this book (cf. Maria's explanation for the circumstances surrounding her pregnancy [247]) and *The Rebel Angels*. However, specific manifestations of these Seven Laughters prove largely elusive. This is especially unfortunate since the entire passage is so delightful and raises such intriguing possibilities. The reader, finally, can only conjecture how such an accomplished comic writer, particularly one as fascinated by religion as Davies, might have depicted those basic elements of a world established by a jovial creator. Light, the firmament, mind, generation, fate, time, and the soul, as products of God's laughter — and in some cases his tendency towards waggishness — all offer tremendous opportunities for clarification through specific fictional elaboration. With the possible exception of generation, Davies forgoes these.

Conversely, he now exploits and develops Simon Darcourt's unelaborated theories about the divine from *The Rebel Angels*. For instance, although no one ever directly expresses it in *The Lyre of Orpheus*, the priest's concept of humility before God (*Rebel* 56) is elucidated through both dialogue and the unfolding of plot. When Darcourt attempts to place Maria's infidelity and resulting pregnancy within a larger context, he informs her distraught husband, Arthur, that

> "God may want you for something more important than begetting children. God has lots of sexual journeymen who can attend to that. So you'd better ask God what he wants of you. . . . If you don't ask God . . . God will certainly tell you, and in no unmistakable terms, and if you don't heed, you'll be so miserable your present grief will look like a child's tantrum." (*Lyre* 231)

Expanding on this advice, Darcourt offers yet another of those loosely circumscribed notions of the deity prevalent in Davies's work. In *The Rebel Angels*, Darcourt simultaneously alluded to "the one God" (314, 315) and "Whatever It Is" (313). Now, in conversation with Arthur, he explains these seemingly discordant terms by equating them both with a force like that posited by Davies in the 1976 Larkin-Stuart lectures, "a power of good . . . external to man, and working through him as an agency — a God, in fact, infinitely greater than man can conceive" (*One Half* 264):

> ". . . God. That's only a shorthand term anyhow. Call it Fate or Destiny or Kismet or the Life Force or the It or any damned name you like but don't pretend it doesn't exist! And don't pretend that Whatever-You-Call-It doesn't live out a portion — a tiny portion — of its purpose through you, and that your pretensions to live your own life by the dictates of your intelligence are just so much nonsense, flattering to fools." (*Lyre* 231)

Humility before God thus entails graciously accepting and amenably responding to those promptings of a superior force, ill defined as they and It may sometimes be. As an illustration of this, Darcourt suggests that Maria is likely to acquiesce in the role set out for her, so that with or without Arthur's approval she will raise the child sired by Geraint Powell " 'because that's the job Whatever-It-Is has given her and she knows that there is no denying those orders' " (233). Maria's ensuing conduct confirms Darcourt's hypothesis. Arthur soon plumps for the humility option and emulates the central figure of *Arthur of Britain, or The Magnanimous Cuckold*, an opera which destiny would appear to have placed in his path. Not only does he accept his cuckoldry with magnanimity, but also, instead of a " 'sexual journeyman,' " he becomes a great patron of the arts — which in view of his position with the Cornish Foundation would seem to be another of those jobs that " 'Whatever-You-Call-It' " had been nudging him towards.

Another of Darcourt's theological notions, offered but left unelaborated in *The Rebel Angels*, is reintroduced as he continues his *tête-à-tête* with Arthur in *The Lyre of Orpheus*. After equating God with fate, he encourages his friend to " 'make peace with your grief and take a long, thoughtful look at your luck' " (232). Because, in his consideration of God as destiny, he has shown that good fortune is not a randomly operating phenomenon, Darcourt's statement reiterates the congruence of " 'Luck' " and " 'God's Saving Grace' " he suggested briefly in the earlier novel (*Rebel* 101). Once this context is established, the "luck" that Arthur experiences in being cuckolded slowly becomes evident. His marriage benefits because he and Maria have together confronted and weathered a major crisis; his character is enriched because he accepts his situation magnanimously; and, sterile himself, he is given a son, Arthur David Nikolas. All of these square with the biblical idea of divine *charis* or "grace," which among its variety of meanings conveys a sense of "benefit," "favour," "gift," "joy," and "liberality" (Strong 77).

Davies suggests these qualities of grace in Darcourt's own life when the priest is discovering both himself and Francis Cornish through his research for Cornish's biography. As he searches for germane material in the university archives, he hums an appropriate prayer of entreaty:

> Guide me, O Thou great Jehovah,
> Pilgrim through this barren land;
> I am weak, but Thou art mighty;
> Hold me with Thy powerful hand;
> Bread of Heaven,
> Feed me till I want no more. (255)

Immediately, he discovers the crucial "Sun Pictures," and thus begins solving the mystery posed by Cornish's *Marriage at Cana* painting. The intervention of God's grace? Fate at work? Davies's third-person narrator (not his central character) is given the final word on this occasion — and he is even more uncertain than Darcourt. In place of Darcourt's assertions concerning Arthur's circumstances, the narrator asks a series of questions: "A great prayer, and because it came from the depths . . . of the mind, it was answered. Oh, surely not answered? Are prayers ever answered? Can the thoroughly modern mind admit such nonsense?" (255). These questions, at most strongly suggestive, return us to the familiar pattern of uncertainty about the nature of God.

So, too, does Darcourt's final statement on the deity. As we have seen, Darcourt has previously circumscribed "It" as " 'Fate or Destiny or Kismet or the Life Force,' " while at the same time emphasizing that even this is tentative by employing the terms " 'Whatever-You-Call-It' " (231) and " 'Whatever-It-Is' " (233). In a later conversation with Mamusia, while not negating his earlier general definition, Darcourt leaves us with our by now accustomed awareness of the difficulties associated with knowing the divine. Here he cites a passage from the Gnostic Gospel of Thomas: " 'The Kingdom of the Father is spread upon the earth and men do not see it. . . . That's what mystery is' " (284).

The other character who discusses God at some length is Geraint Powell. When rueing his tryst with Maria, he explains that " 'the flesh' " has long been his downfall and provides a theological justification for his transgression: " 'You see, Sim, God tempts us. Oh yes, He does. Don't let us pretend otherwise. Why do we pray not to be led into temptation? . . . [W]e are put to the test' " (269–70). This assertion is just the tip of a concealed Jungian iceberg, since it uses the same key words employed and discussed in an important passage in Jung's "Answer to Job."

The passage in turn echoes Jung's larger theory of God as encompassing both good and evil, a position with which Davies is familiar (*One Half* 245). Jung uses several precedents to support his assumption. The unknown author of the "so-called Clementine Homilies, a collection of Gnostic-Christian writings dating from about A.D. 150. . . . understands good and evil as the right and left hand of God . . ." (*Collected* 9.2: 99). In "the early Jewish-Christian Church . . . according to the testimony of Epiphanius, we find the Ebionite notion that God had two sons, an elder one, Satan, and a younger one, Christ" (9.2: 103).[1] The canonical Bible also provides much

---

1 This is echoed briefly by Padre Blazon in *Fifth Business* (249), Tancred Saraceni in *What's Bred in the Bone* (395), and Satan himself in one of Davies's ghost stories (*High Spirits* 57).

useful documentation: "We have plenty of evidence in the Old Testament that Yahweh is moral and immoral at the same time. . . . He is unjust and unreliable. . . . Certainly the God of the Old Testament is good and evil" (18: 1593).[1] As for the deity present in the New Testament, Christ

> cannot help inserting the cautious petition — and warning — into the Lord's Prayer: "Lead us not into temptation, but deliver us from evil." God is asked not to entice us outright into doing evil, but rather to deliver us from it. . . . The incongruity of it is so colossal that if this petition were not in the Lord's Prayer one would have to call it sheer blasphemy, because it really will not do to ascribe such contradictory behaviour to the God of Love and Summum Bonum. (11: 651)

To justify Christ's plea, Jung invokes the Book of Revelation: "There Yahweh again delivers himself up to an unheard-of fury of destruction against the human race, of whom a mere hundred and forty-four thousand specimens appear to survive" (11: 652). Further proof is evident in God's behaviour towards Christ himself: "Certainly if God the Father were nothing else than a loving Father, Christ's cruel sacrificial death would be thoroughly superfluous. I would not allow my son to be slaughtered in order to be reconciled to my disobedient children" (18: 1593).

While these examples indicate the extent to which Jung posits a God who is both good and evil, they also show by contrast how little this aspect of God emerges in the fiction of Robertson Davies, even though Powell's statement in *The Lyre of Orpheus* does raise the issue. Notwithstanding the author's assertion to Margaret Penman that "if you're going to have a really satisfactory notion of God, you must include evil in it because evil is a part of the universe as we know it" (*Conversations* 154), his novels generally validate his fondness for a comment made by Albert Einstein: " 'God is subtle, but he is not malicious' " (*Enthusiasms* 258). The God whom Davies associates with "benevolent, though often minatory, forces in human

---

1 To substantiate this contention, I suggest the Book of Job (as Jung himself so often does) or Isaiah 45.7, to which, surprisingly, neither Jung nor Davies ever actually refers: "I form the light, and create darkness: I make peace, and create evil: I the Lord do all these things."

destiny" is the deity that presides over the worlds of his fiction (*Conversations* 257).

To be sure, this benevolence is often roughly bestowed and the minatory forces do at times loom large, but Davies's novels never convey Gloucester's sentiment from *King Lear*: "As flies to wanton boys, are we to th' Gods; / They kill us for their sport" (IV.i.36–37). Eisengrim's "Justice" or Mamusia's "Balance" are much more prevalent in Davies's work than the arbitrary, irascible biblical God examined by Jung. Davies's religious vision is, finally, very reassuring, since throughout his fiction rewards and punishments are given to those who deserve them. Eisengrim, David Staunton, Ramsay, Monica Gall, Arthur, Maria, Schnak, and Darcourt secure the former; the likes of Willard the Wizard, Bevill Higgin, Boy Staunton, Urky McVarish, and even Parlabane inexorably invite the latter. Evil is present in the novels, but it is associated with the Devil, and though never eradicated, it is ultimately overcome, or neutralized, or turned to good purposes, as I will show in my later discussion of this topic. Even the supposed temptation by God, about which Powell complained, is finally benevolent because of its consequences: Arthur David Nikolas Cornish.

Powell's later conversation with Schnak indicates that he, too, has distanced himself from his earlier complaint about God's malice. Schnak, recovering from a suicide attempt, has also been tempted — by despair. Rather than repeating his lines about enticement, in this case towards self-annihilation, Powell responds to the girl's expressed hatred of God by saying: " 'Good for you! You don't say, "There is no God," like a fool; you say you hate Him. But Schnak — you won't like this, but you have to know — God doesn't hate you. He's made you special' " (416).

Reiterating the sentiment that Darcourt previously directed to Arthur, Powell urges her to " 'give God His chance. Of course He'll take it anyway, but it's easier for you if you don't kick and scream' " (416). Powell then follows the now time-honoured pattern of combining a degree of uncertainty with a loose circumscription in his final remarks about God, which in this case form his response to Schnak's question, " 'How can anybody live God?' ":

> "By living as well as they can with themselves. It doesn't always look very well to the bystanders. Truth to yourself, I suppose you'd call it. Following your nose. But don't expect me to explain. My dad was the explainer. . . . But he thought God had

one, single, unwinking light for everybody, and that was where he and I fell out." (416)

Davies's next novel, *Murther and Walking Spirits*, aptly described on its dust jacket as "unlike anything else he has written," is unique largely because it substantially chronicles a time prior to our century. This new direction qualifies his exploration of God in previous books, in which he is generally suspicious of those characters who are assumed to have a rigid, orthodox definition of God and try to impose their theology on others. Amasa Dempster, the Baptist preacher in *Fifth Business*, and Schnak's conservative Lutheran parents in *The Lyre of Orpheus* are cases in point. However, in *Murther and Walking Spirits* a preaching contemporary of John Wesley wins our sympathy, even though he embraces such orthodoxy and vigorously proselytizes.

Thomas Gilmartin gains stature through his considerable fortitude and bravery in circumscribing God during an all-night sermon to a band of Welsh ruffians. Even before this he provides a context for his comments with a warning about a very specific biblical God who punishes the wicked: " 'It was God himself who laid the first curse on Cain, the evil-doer and murderer. . . . I am sure upon my soul that you know Cain, for he speaks loud and clear in your filthy songs and your un-Welsh want of hospitality to the stranger among you' " (100). His exhortations on the divine bear fruit, for at dawn the pot boy wishes to sever ties with his associates and accompany the Wesleyan: " 'You have won my heart for Christ, master, and I cannot leave you' " (107). At this point we see that God — to use again the words of Pastor Beamis — is immediately here and now, since He directly tells the preacher what action to take, a notion that would have been ridiculed as too simplistic in the earlier novels:

"God has put it into my mind that the first job is to baptize you. So come here by this stream and get into it as deep as you can. . . . God is prompting me strongly. You are now in Christ's family, well and truly, but I think you had better come into my family, as well." (108–09)

There are several explanations for the sympathetic depiction in this novel of an orthodox circumscriber of the divine. The most important of these is Davies's belief that Thomas Gilmartin is the product of a religious epoch that was profoundly different from our own:

39

Two very big world wars have shaken the popular notions of religion very gravely and I think upon the whole advantageously because religion had reached a point where it needed a substantial rethink. . . . [I]t had become a little bit set in its ways and [required] some new thinking about it and a new application of it to the life that faces us in . . . the world of the atom bomb. . . . (Interview, *Imprint*)

Connor Gilmartin, the twentieth-century narrator of *Murther and Walking Spirits*, echoes Davies's sentiments. He, too, considers his forebear effective in a different and less complex time and place:

I know for the first time how intimately the words of the Bible entered the hearts of the people of Wales, for the Scripture's perpetual symbolism of the hills, the pastures, the flocks and the Good Shepherd were fresh to them as they can never be to dwellers in cities. . . . (108)

Even so, Davies manages the issue of circumscription delicately, as he did in the case of Dean Knapp in *A Mixture of Frailties*. We know for certain — by virtue of his office as Wesleyan minister, by the nature of his prefatory remarks to his homily, and by the boy's specific reaction to his preaching — that Gilmartin is a much more rigid definer (or confiner) of God than are most of Davies's characters. However, what is given with one hand is obscured by the other: we are only *told* that he gave a marathon sermon — never are we offered its precise contents. To illustrate this with a more extreme analogy, it is like Macbeth maintaining our sympathy partially because his misdeeds are performed offstage; there is a certain ameliorating effect, since we are never shown but only told about the villainies.

Moreover, in those early sections of the novel in which it appears, Davies balances the Wesleyan's orthodoxy with a less specific notion of God, associated at approximately the same historical period with Anna Gage. As this other ancestor of the book's narrator flees to Canada through the rugged American wilderness, she discovers that

God had become terrible, but not malignant or unapproachable. The vastness and incalculability of God were apparent to her as she had never dreamed He might be in Trinity Church, or at prayer-time in her New York parlour. And yet, somehow, though she knew herself to be very small in the eye of God, she felt that the eye rested on her, and that it was not an angry eye. (87)

In those portions of the novel set in the twentieth century, there again emerges the familiar uncertainty about God's nature, as presaged by Anna's wilderness experience. Rhodri Gilmartin, like Geraint Powell before him in *The Lyre of Orpheus*, briefly intrigues us with the idea of a God who is both good and evil:

"If Hell is any worse than that first week at the *Courier* I'll be surprised. Not just the cursing and filthy language and the perpetual dirty jokes about women, and the tobacco-chewing and the reek of men who never seemed to wash, but what they used to call in the Chapel the Abjection of Soul, the fear that God had deserted me. That's when I learned that God has two faces. I'd exchanged the Wesleyan chapel for a chapel of the Typographical Union." (241–42)

Yet Rhodri's refusal or inability to follow up this speculation demonstrates a lack of confidence on this point; indeed, the "Hell" at the *Courier* proves most beneficial, since it constitutes his first step in amassing great wealth. Elsewhere, he lacks this notion of a bipartite deity, and clearly expresses his uncertainty when asking whether his successful career has been "evidence of God's goodness? Or luck?" (240). Here he lacks even Simon Darcourt's flaccid assurance of God's nature: whereas the cleric had at least been able to equate God's grace with " 'bald-headed Luck' " (*Rebel* 101), Rhodri either cannot or will not — it is not clear which — do so.

Connor Gilmartin is *Murther and Walking Spirits*'s most obvious example of the extent to which a twentieth-century character can depart from the theological certitude of a Thomas Gilmartin. "Gil's" probing conversations with his newspaper's religious editor indicate just how uncertain he is about the nature of the deity. Most telling, however, is that even the expansion of his metaphysical boundaries into the afterlife provides no commensurate clarification on this point. After he has died, Connor is shown films of autobiographical significance — by God one assumes, though he is not sure of this. Underscoring his bewilderment is his uncertainty about which pronoun is appropriate for describing the phenomenon: "the film-makers, whoever they may be" (47); "Whatever power was showing me this film" (59); "the film-maker, whoever he is" (79).

41

Connor's father, Brochwell Gilmartin, offers another description of God, perhaps the novel's most fascinating. Like Davies, he recognizes that the old religious formulae no longer apply in a century in which periods of peace alternate with internecine world wars, fought on a scale previously unparalleled. Asking whether Christianity is "edging close to senility" (278), this soldier contemplates a different, heterodox theology to explain the widespread destruction he observes and helps to create:

> The Manichees had an idea that was by no means absurd. Theirs was a world that lived under the heaven of the Warring Brothers, Ormuzd and Ahriman, or call it God and Satan, if that pleases you better. The brothers were of wavering but almost equal power, and they slugged it out for the domination of our world. Sometimes Ormuzd the Light One seemed to have the advantage, but never for long, because Ahriman the Dark One would gain a fresh hold, and all the splendours of Light were endangered and some were extinguished. (279)

For Brochwell, who is crouching inside a tomb to shelter from a German artillery barrage, this is much more appropriate than the optimistic certainties provided by Christianity, which "rested firmly on the idea that the Right must always triumph, and . . . knew beyond any doubt what Right was" (279). Ironically, while this Manichean idea of the Gods may be relevant to the larger world in which this infantryman fights — the world of war, Auschwitz, and the Soviet gulag — it is not very pertinent, as I suggested in my discussion of *The Lyre of Orpheus*, to the immediate, specific world of Davies's fiction. Indeed, even here, in a rough sort of way, "Right" generally does triumph, as we see typified by Brochwell who leaves his tomb and the army to prosper after the war concludes.

Brochwell himself soon steps back from his Manichean supposition, thinking it too absolute, too definite:

> Am I a Manichee. . . . Thank God I don't have to answer that question. I take refuge in what I believe to be the Shakespearean world-outlook: credulity about everything, tempered by scepticism about everything. Credulity and Scepticism, my Warring Brothers. (280)

This pair of warring brothers points to the *conjunctio oppositorum* underlying the uncertainty about, and exploration of, the deity's

42

nature, from Humphrey Cobbler's comical speculation concerning the Ancient of Days, through Dunstan Ramsay's quest for God through his study of saints, to Brochwell Gilmartin's cogitation about Ormuzd and Ahriman. Credulity is the *sine qua non* for this, since an initial belief in the existence of some type of superior transcendent power is predicated on it. Yet by itself credulity produces only a smug, God-confining, religious complacency associated with some of Davies's less attractive characters. Conversely, theological scepticism alone, while rarer, eschews these restraining notions of God and prompts exploration, though ultimately at the cost of producing such epistemological pessimism that suicide — as we see with John Parlabane — is a real and logical possibility. Bring the two into play and a more salubrious middle ground emerges. Credulity provides the initial impetus, the metaphysical toehold which permits the search for God and eventually allows a loose circumscription. Equally important, it constitutes the tempering element which harnesses and focuses the requisite dynamism created by scepticism. Therefore, impetus and controlled energy, both of which are required to explore the deity, are the end result of the crucial exchange between these two "Warring Brothers." This interplay, as we have seen, sustains and is sustained throughout Davies's fiction.

THREE

The Devils of Robertson Davies

The true realist is he who believes in both God and the Devil, and is prepared to attempt, with humility, to sort out some corner of the extraordinary tangle of their works which is our world. (*A Voice from the Attic* 327)

Robertson Davies's fascination with the Devil appears even in his earliest writings. Various Hallowe'ens through the 1940s and 1950s occasioned newspaper articles by Davies examining the interrelated phenomena associated with the festival. Although these often explore witches, because Davies applies Lord Coke's characterization of a witch as " 'a person who hath conference of the Devil,' " the Devil is himself either directly considered or implicit in the general discussion. For instance, a 1942 column, "The Night of the Witches," investigates the genesis of our present-day image of the Devil, relating how he was derived from a previously worshipped god who, displaced by a newer deity, is now regarded as "wicked." Thus, the importance of animals in former, more primitive religions accounts for our current notions of Satan as possessing horns and hoofs. Davies's 1945 offering loosely presages his later Jungian contention that belief in a God who represents the benevolent forces in the world predicates, by psychological necessity, credence in an equally palpable force of evil:

if we are adjured to have faith in the tenets of religion can we prevent our faith from spreading over into less hallowed regions? The great ages of witchcraft, be it noted, were also great ages of religious fervour. Faith, like everything else, has two sides. ("Familiar Spirits")

44

This interest in Hallowe'en provides much of the momentum in Davies's second novel, *Leaven of Malice*, in which the festival is punctuated by a dynamic combination of high jinks, malice, and fear, and presents the opportunity for him to offer the Salterton trilogy's only comments about the Devil. His character, Dean Jevon Knapp, investigating a Hallowe'en commotion at St. Nicholas's Cathedral, hesitates momentarily on the steps of the church, fearful about the origin of the music that is reverberating within. The reasons for his trepidation echo those sentiments expressed in that 31 October 1945 newspaper column:

> He was a devout man, and while devotion undoubtedly brings its spiritual rewards it brings its spiritual terrors too. This was All Hallow's Eve, and if he truly believed in All Saints on the morrow, why should he not believe in the Powers of Darkness tonight? He had never been the sort of Christian who wants to have things all his own way — to preach the love of God and to deny the existence of the Devil. (54)

The Dean, first of many characters to hold this belief, is finally able to enter the building: "if he had to meet the Devil in the line of duty, he would do so like a man. He muttered a prayer, unlocked the door and tiptoed into the vast shadows of the church" (54) where he discovers his organist presiding over an impromptu fête.

Davies's concern with the Devil also appears in his 1950s endeavours in other genres. He opened the decade with the play *At My Heart's Core*, whose main character, the silken-tongued tempter Edmund Cantwell, is very appropriately described by W.J. Keith as "a Byronic figure complete with a whiff of Satan" (*Canadian Literature* 186). At the close of the decade, Davies composed another Hallowe'en newspaper article, in which he asserted that, "sceptical though I am, I cannot think that all the people who believed, and believe, in witches, were utterly wrong, and certainly Hallowe'en is no night to run around shouting that the devil is dead" ("Believe Science Why not Witches?").

The increasing number of comments Davies offers on this topic in the ensuing years bespeaks an intensification of his fascination. Among these are fairly consistent descriptions of an evil force, which, unlike the creature of legend, is probably sans hoofs and horns. In the 1976 Larkin-Stuart lectures, Davies argues that the Devil is

45

a power of evil external to man, and working through him as an agency . . . vastly more terrible than even the uttermost terrors of human evil. . . . Any assertion we may make that the forces we call, for brevity and convenience, God and the Devil are forces contained in ourselves, and without external being, is open to . . . doubt. (*One Half* 264)

Similarly, making somewhat more prescriptive Jung's statement that "If you regard the principle of evil as a reality you can just as well call it the devil" (*Collected* 10: 879), Davies asserted to Terence Green that a term like " 'the Devil' " is necessary as a means of identifying wickedness (*Conversations* 222); as such, "It's just shorthand for a power which is hostile to the good order of the world and to the happiness of man" (*Conversations* 228).

In this same vein he subsequently told Michael Hulse that

the Devil is just a metaphor for negative forces that are at work in human destiny. . . . [Y]ou know, the Devil's almost banished in modern theology. But I think that the Devil is having a high old time laughing at just exactly that. I speak of him, you see, as "he", but I really mean a very large force that intrudes itself into human life at almost every point and which creates the most frightful havoc. To be tempted by the Devil does not necessarily mean that a sulphurous demon appears to you and asks you to sign something in your blood; but he may offer you a job, or . . . a girl, or . . . some kind of apparent benefit which is really your destruction. (*Conversations* 257)

He also informed Margaret Penman that the Devil's work is obvious in phenomena "like the wards full of dreadfully malformed children" (*Conversations* 154).

Because he sees tangible evidence for the existence of the Devil "in certain sections of daily life" (Interview, *Harpur's*), Davies takes strong exception to those churches that either ignore or dismiss this potent force of evil; in so doing, he promulgates Jung's warning — and orthodox Christianity's — that "the less he is recognized the more dangerous he is" (*Collected* 9.2: 141):

I do not believe very much in the God of somebody who hasn't a first-class Devil as well. We have all seen during the past fifty years what happens to God when you try to pretend there is no

Devil; God develops rheumatoid arthritis and senile dementia and rumours of his death are heard everywhere, including some of the very advanced church groups. . . . And as the invitations are being issued to God's funeral, the Devil is laughing so hard that he can hardly cope with his extraordinary flow of business. (*One Half* 208)

Davies clarifies these comments when, affirming that "Under the Freudian flag, the Devil has gained a good deal of ground" (245), he censures Freudians for their general debunking of metaphysical religious tenets:

Extraordinary horrors and indecencies are now regarded, not as simply evil, but as a consequence of some inequity in society, or in nature, for which we are all, in very vague terms, thought to be responsible, and against which, therefore, we should not seek redress. The supposed death of God has loaded us all with a new kind of guilt. . . . We are all, somehow, thought to be responsible for the robber. His personal responsibility has almost vanished. Any notion that the homicidal robber may be the instrument of a force of Evil which is rather more than his personal psychological disturbance is rarely discussed, and the anti-God party does not want it to be discussed. (*One Half* 244–45)

Diabolical ground has been gained precisely because the supposedly anthropocentric world of "half-baked Freudian morality" (245) has not rid us of evil but has rather oppressed humanity with "the burden of guilt and fear that might suitably be considered as the Devil's realm" (246).

While criticizing those who dismiss all notions of a transcendent agency of wickedness and, instead, would reduce evil to the level of mankind, Davies is careful not to overlook our culpability for some of the world's ills. He urges an acknowledgement of the Devil's counterpart, the force of evil that exists inside each one of us, and argues that accepting our suppressed but innate potential for evil *ipso facto* diminishes that inner devil's realm of fear and guilt. That this — at first in nonmetaphorical form — has been a longstanding concern for Davies is apparent from his earlier newspaper writings: a 1953 book review praises *The Well Adjusted Personality* because its author, Phillip Polatin, urges us to "show a little tender regard for our failings and shortcomings or we shall come to grief." Davies concludes with a sentiment that will become increasingly familiar to his readers: "as many people sacrifice their happiness to impossible yearnings for perfection as destroy their lives by self-indulgence" ("Of the Human Predicament" 20).

By the 1970s Davies was adeptly wielding the notion of an inner devil to warn individuals against the danger of suppressing their flaws:

> I think it is absolutely necessary for a man to recognize and accept the evil in himself. If he does that he is in a position to make the evil work in a different way; the charges of psychological energy involved can be re-directed in not necessarily good paths, but at least in understood paths.
>
> When you behave badly, at least then you're sufficiently far ahead to know what you're doing and to count the cost. . . .
>
> The devil seems to me to be not the commonplace symbol of evil but the symbol of unconsciousness, of unknowing, of acting without knowledge of what you're intending to do. It's from that that I think the great evils spring. The devil is the unexamined side of life; it's unexamined but it's certainly not powerless. (*Conversations* 137–38)

Jung makes a similar case for self-awareness in *Psychology and Religion*:

> If an inferiority is conscious, one always has a chance to correct it. Furthermore, it is constantly in contact with other interests, so that it is steadily subjected to modifications. But if it is repressed and isolated from consciousness, it never gets corrected. It is, moreover, liable to burst forth in a moment of unawareness. (93)

We also find in Jung the probable origin of Davies's concept of the internal devil, for in "The Psychology of the Unconscious" Jung affirms the devil as "a variant of the 'shadow' archetype, i.e., of the dangerous aspect of the unrecognized dark half of the personality" (*Collected* 7: 152). It is in this sense that Davies discusses his communication with his inner devil as a form of continuous self-examination which effects a coming to terms with his previously unaccepted imperfections, his own evil: "I talk to my personal devil and he is remarkably interesting company." When asked if this devil responds, Davies retorts, "Oh ho! Never stops. The devil is a very social being" (Interview, *Magic*).

The Deptford trilogy of the 1970s considers devils of both types: transcendent wickedness and this personal, internal counterpart. At the beginning of *Fifth Business*, the Ramsay household sees an external malevolent agency at work in the unknown stone-thrower's disastrous striking of Mary Dempster. Fiona Ramsay concludes that " 'Whoever it was, the Devil guided his hand,' " while her son Dunstan, the stone's intended target, accepts this and credits further diabolical participation: "Yes, and the Devil shifted his mark" (25). Although Amasa Dempster, Deptford's Baptist minister, shares this certainty about an external evil power, he earns our censure for his essentially Devil-confining attitude — this in the face of his wife's increasing simple-mindedness and his son's close brush with death as a result of that thrown stone. The minister, as far as Davies shows us, associates Satan exclusively with Dunstan Ramsay's magic tricks and tales of saints, both of which open up a world of splendour for Paul as, indeed, for the novel's reader. Dempster claims these things have "brought corruption into the innocent world of childhood": Ramsay "had been the agent — unknowingly, he hoped — by means of which the Evil One had trailed his black slime across a pure life" (41). Playing cards seem to be particularly high on the preacher's index of wickedness, for he identifies them as "the Devil's picture-book" (42).

As if to underscore the superficiality of Dempster's assumptions, Davies sets the ensuing chapter in Deptford's gravel pit, where the reader is exposed to genuine corruption in the depravity of the tramps who inhabit it. This quarry has clear diabolical associations for Ramsay, who relates how his Presbyterian minister, Andrew Bowyer, compares it with the biblical valley of outcasts outside Jerusalem, whose fires may have initiated the idea of a burning hell:

He liked to make his hearers jump, now and then, and he said that our gravel pit was much the same sort of place as Gehenna. My elders thought this far-fetched, but I saw no reason then why hell should not have, so to speak, visible branch establishments throughout the earth, and I have visited quite a few of them since. (46)

The prevalent drunkenness, rape, and sodomy identified with the pit, and the ruin brought upon the Dempster family by Mary's conduct there, all give some credibility to Bowyer's comparison. Clearly it is a venue for those negative forces at work in human destiny, which Davies associates with the Devil in his interview with Michael Hulse (*Conversations* 257).

The adult Ramsay not only credits those places where an external malevolent presence is palpable, but he also comes, rather reluctantly, to acknowledge the existence of his own inner devil. Paradoxically, his exploration of the saints — men and women usually venerated for the stories of their pre-eminent virtue — anticipates this. The Bollandist Padre Blazon emphasizes that a parallel trade in tales about the failings of the saints has evolved precisely because most of us, in spite of our best efforts, have not managed to eliminate or even consistently control our wicked tendencies:

> "The saint triumphs over sin. Yes, but most of us cannot do that, and because we love the saint and want him to be more like ourselves, we attribute some imperfection to him. . . . Thomas Aquinas was monstrously fat; St Jerome had a terrible temper. This gives comfort to fat men, and cross men. . . . If they, these holy ones who have lived so greatly but who still carry their shadows with them, can approach God, well then, there is hope for the worst of us." (172–73)

Liesl relates the significance of this to Ramsay's own life, emphasizing her meaning through the metaphor of the personal devil. Urging her gloomy, severe, now middle-aged friend to come to terms with his humanity, " 'to make a real life' " (227), she affirms that

> "every man has a devil, and a man of unusual quality, like yourself, Ramsay, has an unusual devil. You must get to know your personal devil. You must even get to know his father, the Old Devil. . . . Why don't you shake hands with your devil, Ramsay, and change this foolish life of yours? Why don't you, just for once, do something inexplicable, irrational, at the devil's bidding, and just for the hell of it?" (226)

Tangibly embracing Liesl's precepts — albeit after some fierce initial opposition — he " 'shake[s] hands with [his] devil' " by going to bed with her and enjoys its immediate benefits: "never have I known such deep delight or such an aftermath of healing tenderness" (227).

Ramsay subsequently relates his experience with Liesl in familiar terms to Padre Blazon: " 'The Devil proved to be a very good fellow. He suggested that a little compromise would not hurt me. He even suggested that an acquaintance with Him might improve my character.' " The Jesuit agrees:

I find no fault with that. The Devil knows corners of us all of which Christ Himself is ignorant. Indeed, I am sure Christ learned a great deal that was salutary about Himself when He met the Devil in the wilderness. Of course, that was a meeting of brothers; people forget too readily that Satan is Christ's elder brother and has certain advantages in argument that pertain to a senior." (249)

Blazon recognizes the importance of Ramsay's tenacious resistance to Liesl before his "compromise" with her: " 'You met the Devil as an equal, not cringing or frightened or begging for a trashy favour. That is the heroic life, Ramezay. You are fit to be the Devil's friend, without any fear of losing yourself to Him!' " (250).

Determining the specific meaning of Davies's metaphors here — from Liesl's statement, to Ramsay's description of his tussle and ensuing *rapprochement* with her, to Blazon's reaction to both of these — seems rather like putting a butterfly on the wheel. However, it does permit a clearer perception of what Davies and his characters mean when they speak of the Devil. At least two commentators have indicated justifiable uneasiness at their findings. David Dooley lists the "audacious propositions" in the novel: that to conquer in the inner struggle does not mean overcoming the Devil's promptings but acting upon them; that the Devil is wise and should be listened to; that the Devil is Christ's older brother. Dooley, who attributes the last of these to the Jungian concept of a dualist God, objects particularly that a Catholic priest posits it (121). The seeming insouciance with which the author portrays his character going to bed with the Devil likewise troubles Dennis Duffy (16).

As if anticipating concerns of this nature, soon after the publication of *Fifth Business* Davies attempted to clarify some of the confusion created by his use of metaphor:

When Dunstan Ramsay in the book sleeps with the devil he is accepting the evil in himself, which up until then he had been fighting vigorously because that is the way he had been trained.

51

After he has found out that the devil is not really as black as he's painted he's a much better man. (qtd. in Sypnowich)

This is entirely congruous with the general Jungian view of the debilitating effect of totally repressing our wicked tendencies, and it is consistent with Davies's stated belief in recognizing and accepting our imperfections, our innate evil, for the greater good of our psychological health. By the time of his sexual encounter with Liesl, Dunstan Ramsay has for years been suppressing major unpleasant elements of his personality, but after he "sleeps with the devil" he becomes a truly "much better man" because a more honest one; only now is the candid self-evaluation that inspires *Fifth Business* possible. Ramsay's autobiographical acknowledgement of his strains of cruelty, coldness, spite, blind prejudice, and greed is vital by the standards of Davies and Jung, since it diminishes his fear and guilt and, hence, some of his devil's blackness.

But what are we to make of Liesl's concomitant urging that Ramsay go beyond recognizing his innate evil and " 'do something . . . at the devil's bidding, and just for the hell of it' " (226) — the lower-case *d* indicating the inner devil. Little wonder that Dennis Duffy chafes at this idea, fearing that to make it a general rule, while perhaps tolerable in the instance of Dunstan Ramsay in a safe stable country like Canada, might be disastrous in the case of a Hitler who harbours a very pernicious devil and operates in a volatile environment (16). Accepting one's capacity for wickedness and willingly acting on its promptings are two significantly different moral issues. Because Davies never adequately explores or even clearly recognizes the distinction in *Fifth Business*, Duffy's objection (and the first of Dooley's three) is legitimate.

When Padre Blazon speaks of the Devil, because he uses an upper-case *D* and juxtaposes him with Christ, the immediate sense he conveys is that of a transcendent power of malevolence. Yet because he also relates him to Ramsay's encounter with Liesl, which symbolizes intimacy with one's personal devil, the Jesuit seems to be deliberately conflating the external and internal manifestations of evil. Nonetheless, his advice to Ramsay echoes that given by Liesl — who does overtly discriminate between the two — as he, too, asserts metaphorically the necessity of knowing the evil in the world and in ourselves. Because Christ exists without sin, He is less knowledgeable about it than Satan (cf. Jung, *Collected* 18: 1620, 1645; cf. also Appendix 1). This counters Dooley's second objection, that concerning the Devil's wisdom, as does Blazon's recognition of an essential perimeter in the process of achieving one's dark insight: he praises Ramsay for acquainting himself with the Devil without "'losing himself'" to him.

Finally, regarding Blazon's assertion that Christ and Satan are brothers,[1] here the Bollandist is probably less illustrating Jung's dualism, as Dooley supposes, than echoing Davies's more general recognition that good and evil are closely linked: "I think of evil as the twin of good" (qtd. in Sypnowich). Without one we cannot have the other, as Davies's statement about religion needing both a God and a "first-class Devil" makes clear (*One Half* 208).[2]

Having staked out his metaphysical terrain in *Fifth Business*, Davies uses the two subsequent novels of the Deptford trilogy to explore, qualify, and clarify the diabolical questions he has raised. *The Manticore* addresses, albeit in a nonmetaphorical manner, the problems involved in Liesl's exhortations to know one's personal devil and respond periodically to his "'bidding.'" While Davies continues to emphasize the need for constant self-recognition and our recurring inability to prevent our imperfections from expressing themselves as deeds, he now uses two narrative techniques to distance himself from Liesl's attendant counsel that we should deliberately will such actions into existence.

The first of these distancing techniques is his associating several contrary precepts with a very attractive, reliable character. Stating that "about purity, he got down to brass tacks better than anybody I have ever known" (135), David Staunton presents Father Gervase Knopwood as a credible moralist. He describes the essence of Knopwood's ethical principles as follows: "He didn't expect you to chalk up a hundred per cent score, but he expected you to try, and if you sinned, he expected you to know what you had done and why it was sin. If you knew that, you were better armed next time" (135). Here one is not exhorted to act on the devil's prompting — indeed, the converse is true because using a convincing paradox, Knopwood expects his wards to strive to achieve a perfect "score" while

---

1 Davies also emphasizes this when Satan himself appears in *High Spirits* (54, 57, 59).

2 As for Satan being Christ's elder brother, perhaps Blazon is referring to the chronological unfolding of the Bible, in which Satan first appears in the book of Job while prophecy about the Messiah, and indeed the actual arrival of Christ, occur later.

remaining fully conscious that this is impossible.[1] Concomitant with this distancing through precept, Davies draws back by depicting the repugnant behaviour of certain characters: in a premeditated act, David, Bill Unsworth, and two accomplices savagely demolish the interior of a cottage, senselessly defiling the memorabilia of the unknown family that owns the dwelling. David, fully aware that they are deliberately responding to impulses of evil (154), stresses that there is no motive for their crime other than this capitulation to the promptings of wickedness.

The adult David, long repenting his actions at the cottage, remains acutely conscious of evil. Describing the face of a depraved murderer in terms of the power that is both inherent in and external to man, David emphasizes the correlation between the personal devil and " 'his father, the Old Devil,' " metaphorically proposed by Liesl in *Fifth Business* (226) and implicit in Blazon's later discussion with Ramsay. Jimmy Veale, David's former client now on death row, had "the look of one who has laid himself open to a force that is inimical to man, and whose power to loose that force upon the world is limited only by his imagination, his opportunities, and his daring" (*Manticore* 227–28).

These comments preface David's depiction of his own entanglement with wickedness, in which he uses the very words previously employed by Blazon to characterize Dunstan Ramsay's successful encounter with the devil: " 'That is the heroic life' " (*Fifth* 250). However, more so than either Liesl or the Jesuit, David articulates the moral danger involved in an association with the Devil:

> I was always aware that I stood very near to the power of evil when I undertook the cases that brought me the greatest part of my reputation. I was a highly skilled, highly paid, and cunning mercenary in a fight which was as old as man and greater than man. I have consciously played the Devil's Advocate and I must say I have enjoyed it. I like the struggle, and I had better admit that I like the moral danger. I am like a man who has built his

---

1 Lest this appear facile, the Catholic rite of confession is arguably informed by a similar paradox. Upon leaving the confessional, the penitent must recite the Act of Contrition, promising "to sin no more" and even "to avoid the near occasions of sin" (Lovasik 32). Were it possible to achieve this, the confessional would clearly become superfluous.

house on the lip of a volcano. Until the volcano claims me I live, in a sense, heroically. (228)

Even though David underscores the peril of his propinquity to evil, he retains an element of nonchalance about the danger. This is probably why Patricia Monk senses a certain glibness in David's statement (134). It is not enough to advance beyond Liesl's position simply by speaking of the hazard — this is merely a cerebral exercise. In keeping with the novel's general sentiments, to appreciate fully the jeopardy one must proceed further and actually *feel* the risk that is associated with life at the volcano's lip.

Another important issue briefly and somewhat enigmatically raised by *Fifth Business* and then explored in *The Manticore* involves the applicability of the Jungian concept of the "shadow" to the notion of the personal devil. In the earlier novel, Padre Blazon creates some confusion on this point by seeming to indicate, though never conclusively, that there exists a one-to-one correspondence between the two. In discussing our motivation for attending to the imperfections of saints, he argues: " 'If they, these holy ones who have lived so greatly but who still carry their shadows with them, can approach God, well then, there is hope for the worst of us' " (173). Blazon places "shadow" in apposition with "unredeemed nature," then ambiguously remarks that his " 'manifested itself quite late in life' " (176). David's *anamnesis* with Johanna von Haller in *The Manticore* resolves this confusion by confirming that the shadow is not exclusively evil — indeed, referring to his own shadow as "Staunton-as-Son-of-a-Bitch," David even speaks of redeeming its "good qualities" (87). Dr. von Haller recognizes both elements, stating that "He is not such a terrible fellow if you know him. He is not lovable; he is quite ugly," and she discourages David from working to banish him (87).

As one might expect with a novel as overtly Jungian as *The Manticore*, Jung's writings confirm the sentiments expressed here. However, unlike Padre Blazon, nowhere does Jung draw an exact correlation between our personal devil and the shadow. As I mentioned earlier, Jung identifies the devil as "a *variant* of the 'shadow' archetype" (*Collected* 7: 152; emphasis added). Elsewhere he corroborates this by recognising the archetype's beneficial characteristics: the shadow "does not consist only of morally reprehensible tendencies, but also displays a number of good qualities, such as normal instincts, appropriate reactions, realistic insights, creative

55

impulses, etc." (9.2: 423). The shadow therefore encompasses more than just our personal devil, although it would seem to contain him as well.

The exploration of the diabolical concepts posited in *Fifth Business* continues in *World of Wonders* to the extent that, "By making his characters . . . preoccupied with the devil, Davies gives the devil equal time, so to speak . . ." (Monk 172). This is germane for what is arguably Davies's darkest novel. Yet, whereas *The Manticore* largely investigates the inner devil, *World of Wonders* concentrates mainly on examining his external counterpart, a process that realizes its dynamic through the opposition between Magnus Eisengrim's personal experiences and Dunstan Ramsay's more detached, cerebral probings. Davies establishes this contrast early in the book. When Eisengrim asks Ramsay if he believes in the Devil, he responds: " 'In an extremely sophisticated way, which would take several hours to explain, I do.' " The magician is immediately dissatisfied and retorts, " 'when the Devil is walking beside you, as he was walking beside me . . . it doesn't take a lot of argument to make him seem real.' " Unwilling to concede the last word to his friend, Ramsay replies: " 'I won't insult you by saying you're a simple man, but you're certainly a man of strong feeling, and your feelings take concrete shapes' " (39).

Dismissive as this supposition may at first appear, its unequivocal confirmation that Eisengrim has felt the Devil's presence enhances Eisengrim's credibility, particularly given the context established in the previous novel. While David Staunton's pronouncement in *The Manticore* about the moral danger of life on the volcano's lip may contain an element of glibness because he has never actually experienced this, Eisengrim's statements about the power of evil suffer no such shortcoming. Recalling when the paedophile magician, Willard the Wizard, first fondled him at the Deptford fair, Eisengrim states that the Devil was palpably involved in the process, " 'prompting me, and pushing me on to what looked then, and for years after, like my own destruction' " (40). Further, he believes his own responding " 'smile of complicity' " made him " 'an accomplice in what followed' " (40); this, in turn, initiated his seven-year descent into hell (17).

Somewhat surprisingly given his strong sentiments, Eisengrim has little further to say on the topic, apart from an ambiguous assertion that one of the Devil's " 'most endearing qualities' " is that he is not above jokes (40). Eisengrim never precisely describes the " 'concrete shapes' " (to use Ramsay's words) his feelings about the Devil take, leaving us instead with a notion akin to Davies's general sense of "a power which is hostile to the good order of the world and to the happiness of man" (*Conversations* 228). There are probably several reasons for this lack of specificity. Possibly Eisengrim is satisfied that he has experienced the Devil and thus feels no necessity to speak of him in more than general terms — a sentiment that has its parallel in Davies's own occasional refusal to define God, remaining "content that God should encompass me" (*One Half* 243). A more likely answer, however, given the magician's compulsion to talk in this novel, is Davies's realization that a direct encounter with the metaphysically transcendent is distinguished by a certain "ineffability" and "noetic quality," to use two of William James's terms. The experience both "defies expression, [since] no adequate report of its contents can be given in words," and is a state "of insight into depths of truth unplumbed by the discursive intellect" (*Varieties* 292–93). Consequently, to attempt much more than a general description might have risked trivializing an episode Davies considered profoundly significant. Exploration of the Devil's specific attributes, while initiated by the strong but general assertions of Eisengrim, is thereafter pursued by the more detached, intellectual Dunstan Ramsay.

From the outset Ramsay cautions against the pitfalls and difficulties involved in the attempt to circumscribe the Devil, rejecting as metaphysically invalid "the notion that although the Devil is a very clever fellow, he is no match for some ninny who is merely good" in a "Mom and apple pie" sense of the word (41). He also notes the problems scholars have experienced in the endeavour: "Theologians have not been so successful in their definitions of the Devil as they have been in their definitions of God" (41), a *caveat* that proves particularly pertinent since Ramsay's own investigation of the topic is marked by a mixture of insight, ambiguity, and superficiality. After his warning, and after a timely reminder of his theological credentials through his recitation from memory of the Westminster Confession's definition of God, Ramsay begins his exploration proper. He starts with the dictum that the Devil "is something decidedly more subtle than just God's opposite" (42) — yet the promise of this potentially fascinating assertion is never realized. Since he doesn't explain how the Devil is something more than the opposite of the philosophically complex God he has just described at length, Ramsay's pronouncement rings more facile than profound.

Once we grudgingly make the leap of faith necessitated by Ramsay's unsubstantiated statement, we see that his ensuing speculations take different forms: they become either more tentative and thus, paradoxically, more plausible, or they are better articulated and therefore also more credible. Ramsay reiterates Davies's belief in a transcendent, upper-case *D* Devil, arguing that since human choice is involved in sin, the Devil cannot be equivalent to sin, although he finds it "very useful" (42). We already know from his reference to hell's "visible branch establishments" in *Fifth Business* (46) that Ramsay believes in evil as a powerful external presence in the world. But about the Devil's relationship to evil he is less certain than his friend Eisengrim, presenting his observations in the form of conjecture rather than conclusion:

> What about evil, then? Is the Devil the origin and ruler of that great realm of manifestly dreadful and appalling things which are not, so far as we can determine, anybody's fault or the consequences of any sin? Of the cancer wards, and the wards for children born misshapen and mindless? . . . Was Eisengrim, whose intuitions and directness of observation in all things concerning himself I had come to respect, right in saying the Devil stood beside him when Willard the Wizard solicited him to an action which, under the circumstances, I should certainly have to call evil? Both God and the Devil wish to intervene in the world, and the Devil chooses his moments shrewdly. (42–43)

Subsequently, Ramsay encounters difficulty when he leaves off conjecturing and again includes a largely unexplained, absolute assertion within his speculation:

> ". . . the Devil is a setter of prices, and a usurer, as well. You buy from him at an agreed price, but the payments are all on time, and the interest is charged on the whole of the principal, right up to the last payment, however much of the principal you think you have paid off in the meantime." (57)

Although he rounds out this confident pronouncement with a more tentative suspicion that the Devil may have invented numbers and possibly time, " 'with all the subtle terrors that Time comprises,' " the damage has been done. When he deems himself a " 'diabologian,' " it all proves too much for Eisengrim, the one character in the novel who has had more than a passing acquaintance with a diabolical presence: " 'Do you think you can study evil without living

58

it? How are you going to discover the attributes of the Devil without getting close to him? Are you the man for that? Don't bother your old grey head, Dunny' " (57).

Seeming somewhat chastened, Ramsay enters the next discussion with a less pontificating, more speculative approach. He follows up on one of Eisengrim's earlier suppositions that the Devil is not above jokes, " 'wondering if humour isn't one of the most brilliant inventions of the Devil' " — this, because humour allows us to dissemble those horrors that might otherwise lead to important, salutary discoveries. Liesl counters, arguing that " 'Humour is quite as often the pointer to truth as it is a cloud over truth' " (85). However, her otherwise credible dissenting view is compromised here by her frivolous invention of a story from the Talmud to support her point.

Roland Ingestree, a not very credible speaker in much of the novel, responds to these comments with his own observations about evil and humour: " 'the Devil, when he is represented in literature, is full of excellent jokes, and we can't resist him because he and his jokes make so much sense' " (86). He seals his statement with a jocular toast to the Devil, and, as if to underscore her frivolity on this topic, Liesl is the only character who joins him. Ramsay, having stumbled in the past, stands justifiably decisive in his reaction to this display, and his response upholds the prevailing values of the Deptford trilogy: " 'I wish you hadn't done that. I quite agree that the Devil is a great joker, but I don't think it is particularly jolly to be the butt of one of his jokes. You have called his attention to you in what I must call a frivolous way . . .' " (86). Davies himself echoed this sentiment when interviewed shortly after the publication of *World of Wonders*:

you don't think the Devil's very funny when you look at some of the things with which you'd associate him, like the wards full of dreadfully malformed children and so on and so forth. You'd have to have a very refined sense of humor to consider that funny. (*Conversations* 154)

Notwithstanding Ramsay's timely declaration in this instance, the attempt in *World of Wonders* to flesh out the skeletal form of the Devil is distinguished by the contrast between a character whose personal experience in this regard has been so intense that he will not or, more likely, cannot describe him, and another, erudite char-

59

acter who lacks this experience but is willing, sometimes too willing, to offer his impressions. When these take the form of ringing declarations, they generally ring hollow; conversely, when advanced tentatively, as speculation or questions, they seem more engaging and, indeed, more plausible. As in his discussions of God, Davies seems to be indicating here that personal experience, exploration, and even a tentative, loose circumscription of the Devil are all possible — anything more than this becomes problematic, perhaps frivolous.

Although the overwhelming focus of *World of Wonders*, at least with regard to diabolical forces, is the investigation of the external Devil, his personal, internal counterpart is not entirely neglected. Just as Davies introduced us to this concept early in the trilogy through Padre Blazon's remarks about the imperfections of the saints, here he similarly concludes discussion of it. Ramsay, a more credible speaker when explaining his area of expertise, interprets the iconography associated with certain saints: " 'the dragons represent not simply evil in the world but their personal evil, as well. Of course, being saints, they are said to have killed their dragons, but we know that dragons are not killed; at best they are tamed, and kept on the chain' " (140).[1]

Ramsay proceeds to extend the concept of the interrelationship between good and evil. In *Fifth Business*, Blazon argues that Satan and Christ are brothers. Correspondingly, Davies has asserted that he does "not believe very much in the God of somebody who hasn't a first-class Devil as well" (*One Half* 208) and, more generally, that he thinks "of evil as the twin of good" (qtd. in Sypnowich). Now, in *World of Wonders*, Ramsay applies this interrelationship, indeed interdependence, between the two to the level of the individual: " 'I am strongly of the opinion that St George and St Catherine did not kill those dragons, for then they would have been wholly good, and inhuman, and useless and probably great sources of mischief, as one-sided people always are' " (140–41). In other words, to be

---

1 This notion is evident in much more dramatic fashion in Davies's "Refuge of Insulted Saints." Here, when Saint Catherine of Alexandria visits Massey College, her dragon accompanies her. She assures a fearful Davies that it is " 'a pet, a symbol of all that is evil in my nature, which I have utterly subdued.' " The Master of Massey remains sceptical, observing that "the dragon did not look as subdued as I should have liked, and we had high words" (*High Spirits* 69–70).

fully human and effective in a world permeated by both good and evil, not only must one acknowledge one's personal, inner devil, but, just as important, one must have a personal, inner devil to acknowledge. This surely underscores the message conveyed by the interplay between Ramsay and Eisengrim in their discussions about the external Devil: only through personal experience with evil can one effectively understand the nature of this powerful, pervasive force. In view of Eisengrim's travails, *World of Wonders* seems to suggest that if we are very lucky we gain this necessary understanding largely from recognizing our own innate wickedness rather than by confronting its external counterpart.

Following his exploration of the two sorts of devils in the Deptford trilogy, Davies can assume in succeeding books that his reader is familiar with these concepts. He consequently turns his attention to other concerns. This is not to suggest, however, that mention of the devils is entirely absent from the Cornish novels, for Davies includes brief references to them throughout the trilogy as a means of confirming and reemphasizing his metaphysics. In *The Rebel Angels*, Simon Darcourt suspects that John Parlabane, a character described unequivocally as evil, may be working in the Devil's service (119). Upholding Eisengrim's belief in a palpable external force of wickedness, Ludlow, the professor of law, exclaims at the Warden's table: " 'I've never seen God, but twice I've caught a glimpse of the Devil in court, once in the dock, and once on the Bench' " (184).

Throwing such statements into relief, the trilogy also offers a character who does not take the Devil as seriously as he should. *What's Bred in the Bone*'s Tancred Saraceni asserts that " 'Christ would have had no time for a man like me. Have you noticed how, in the Gospels, He keeps so resolutely clear of anybody who might be suspected of having any brains' " (395). We might excuse the painter for disregarding the story of young Jesus in the temple (Luke 2.41ff.); however, more difficult to accept is his breezy, unelaborated declaration that as an artist he must — by default it seems — work under the Devil's wing. Knowing what we do of Magnus Eisengrim's apprenticeship to his art, nonchalance on this point seems extremely superficial, particularly given the suffering Eisengrim associates with those periods during which he considers himself most influenced by the Devil. But at other times, especially in relation to his stint with Sir John Tresize's theatre company, the entire notion of labouring exclusively under diabolical patronage seems misplaced.

Davies also reaffirms the existence of the other, personal devil in the Cornish trilogy, as evident in his description of Darcourt's reflections on Arthur's bout with the mumps:

> Christian charity required that Darcourt should be properly regretful, but the Old Harry, never totally subdued in him, made him smile as he thought that Arthur's balls were going to swell to the size of grapefruit. . . . (*Lyre* 10)

Later, when explaining the tarot cards to Gunilla Dahl-Soot and Darcourt, Mamusia confides: " 'There is too much of the devil in our good Father for him to be the Hermit' " (282).

Through the character of William McOmish, *Murther and Walking Spirits* continues to draw on the metaphysical distinctions explicated in the Deptford trilogy, as this builder's story constitutes something of a cautionary tale about the perils of misunderstanding the nature of the personal devil and, thus, underestimating the danger he poses. In his autobiographical monologue, McOmish tells his son-in-law:

> "I am an Old Devil, now, and when I was young I was a Young Devil, which is a totally different thing. I wouldn't give a York shilling for any feller that hadn't some devil in him. I've always had plenty of devil, and I came by it honestly." (167)

McOmish's discussion of his ancestors' hardships in the New World makes clearer the meaning of his last sentence. Of the group of Scottish crofters who came to British North America as the first Selkirk settlers, only those " 'who had the devil in them' " survived the harsh initial winter at Baldoon (169), and on a subsequent, arduous trek to better land, " 'the ones with the Devil in them made it, and my Devils made it to not far from here' " (170). McOmish employs the same terminology to describe his first glimpse of his future wife, Virginia:

> "Oh, there was vanity, even among Wesleyan Methodists, let me tell you! You can't quell vanity, because the Devil won't have it, that's why. I heard [girls] laughing, and I didn't show myself among the bushes, and I peeked. The Devil, you see. . . [S]he was dabbing her mouth with [a ribbon], to make her lips a pretty pink! The Devil! And I thought that's the one for me, the girl with the Devil in her!" (172–73)

An immediate problem with the nomenclature is apparent to the reader of the previous two trilogies. The typography indicates that, unlike most of Davies's other characters, McOmish is not always consistent in his use of the upper-case *D* to denote what is obviously the external Devil, and the lower-case *d* to indicate his personal, inner counterpart. Through this Davies signifies the master builder's larger, more debilitating confusion about the two types of devils. While McOmish correctly posits a transcendent power of malice that is able to counteract the best laid plans of men — yes, even determined Methodists — he mistakes the meaning of the inner devil, and appears to leach out his evil by presenting him as the personification of more positive qualities. These would comprise the energy, persistence, and will to survive in the instance of McOmish's pioneering ancestors, and the independence from an austere religion's edict against facial make-up in his wife's case. As for McOmish, who characterizes himself as a " 'Young Devil,' " he equates his inner devil with his resourcefulness and self-assurance (173).

McOmish's disregard for personal wickedness leads to tragedy, and I use the word advisedly in the classical sense of a falling down from a high position. He originally thinks that he has married merely an independent woman, but soon discovers, instead, that his spouse is physically and emotionally frigid and that her sole arousal takes the form of directing vituperation at him and her neighbours. With respect to his own unacknowledged inner evil, McOmish scores highly on the deadly sins of pride and ire (189); consequently, his family lives in fear of his violence (178), he has become addicted to morphine to sustain his efforts in his demanding job, and he is suffering financial catastrophe. Finally, with his declaration that he is now " 'an Old Devil' " — no longer " 'a Young Devil' " (167) — he comes to articulate some recognition of the evil within himself, and the narrator subsequently confirms this by equating the term "Old Devil" with McOmish as wild-eyed morphine addict (185). However, McOmish's acknowledgement has come too late to save him from ruin.

As in classical tragedy, where the inner devil only partially effects the character's downfall, Davies indicates that "the Great Devil, Old Horny himself, who is the Contrary Destiny of so many proud folk" (189), also plays a role here. This external force originally helped McOmish take the ominous first step in courting his shrewish wife (172); it later works through the hypocritical elders of the builder's own congregation. Having driven him to the verge of disaster by their insistence that he reduce his fee for church construction, the elders refuse, in their capacity as town bankers, to extend him the credit he requires to escape his financial morass (189–90). Eventually, brought low by both devils, William McOmish is taken away to an institution for the poor and mentally unstable (217–18).

Throughout his writings, Davies urges the acknowledgement of both external and innate evil. This advocacy reaches a crescendo of sorts in *Murther and Walking Spirits*, his most unambiguous, forceful presentation of the consequences suffered through failing to recognize our devils, both without and within.

FOUR

The Ambiguity of Good and Evil

Lest my title appear to undermine in any way the contents of the previous chapter, let me reiterate that Davies is decisive and unambiguous about the existence of evil even in his very earliest writing, and uncompromisingly critical of those who would minimize or deny its presence:

> There are a great many people who will not believe in the reality of evil. It is a theological doctrine — the doctrine of the *privatio bone* [sic] — which insists that there is no evil, there is merely an absence of good, or a diminishing of good; that the world is essentially good because God is good, and that if something appears that is evil it is a temporary falling away. Now I think, and a very great many other people think too, that this is the most manifest nonsense, and that things appear in life and have appeared in history, ever since we had any records of the doings of mankind, which are directly evil, contrary to the good of either one person or perhaps a hundred thousand people or several million people, and that they are to be explained only by the existence of an element in life which is definitely evil, and which is the enemy of what we regard as best and most hopeful. (*Conversations* 221)

Here and elsewhere Davies presents the Holocaust as "a very, very potent example" of evil (cf. also Campau). His criticism of the doctrine of *privatio boni*, associated with St. Augustine and Thomas Aquinas, echoes that of Jung (*Collected* 9.2: 80–96), who likewise uses the example of the concentration camps to support his argument.

However, not content with this unequivocal acknowledgement that evil exists, Davies evolves his argument one significant stage

65

further and insists on the absolute *necessity* of its existence: "If you have a power which is totally and wholly good, I think that it posits also a power which is wholly and totally evil, or there is no balance; everything is jerked in one direction (*Conversations* 222). This view corresponds with — indeed, probably derives from — Jung's ontological tenet that

> as psychological experience shows, "good" and "evil" are opposite poles of a moral judgment which, as such, originates in man. A judgment can be made about a thing only if its opposite is equally real and possible. The opposite of a seeming evil can only be a seeming good, and an evil that lacks substance can only be contrasted with a good that is equally non-substantial. . . . If, therefore, evil is said to be a mere privation of good, the opposition of good and evil is denied outright. How can one speak of "good" at all if there is no "evil"? (*Collected* 11: 247)

This tenet underlies several important assertions Davies offers in both his fiction and nonfiction. For instance, soon after the publication of *Murther and Walking Spirits*, which depicts wickedness as manifested in civil strife, world war, domestic violence, deceit, and, of course, murder, he affirms:

> I think that one of the curious things about our age is our almost neurotic emphasis on the necessity for both national and international peace and cooperation, and how that is partnered by very violent, single acts of destruction — shootings, killings, mass murders — as though people couldn't bear the intensity of the push towards total peace, which is, I think an unnatural state for mankind. ("Canada")

Davies's sentiment squares with Dunstan Ramsay's observation in *World of Wonders*: "how constant this evil is! Let mankind laboriously suppress leprosy, and tuberculosis rages: when tuberculosis is chained, cancer rushes to take its place. One might almost conclude that such evils were necessities of our collective life" (42–43).

Because evil is both present and essential in the world and in ourselves, Davies takes issue with basic Christian belief: "Christianity's focus is entirely on the achievement of perfection and I don't think that is either a possibility or indeed, perhaps, desirable, because perfection is inhuman" ("Conversations"). That this reflects a longstanding concern for Davies is evident from *King Phoenix*, an early play that offers much the same perspective in rudimentary form.[1] When asked if she might come to love her seemingly perfect fiancé, Princess Helena responds:

> I might, if he ever showed any fire. Leolin is a man of the greatest goodwill; he loves all mankind, and, as I am part of mankind, he loves me. . . . I think if he ever hurt me, or did anything violent and unexpected, I might love him as much as I respect him. (*Hunting* 125)

Moreover, Davies's understanding of evil as a *sine qua non* in life has its logical correlative in his statements about his craft. For example, in the Larkin-Stuart lectures he argues that

> Evil [is] a requirement — indeed, a necessity — for a plot that will hold our attention and provoke our concern. Without Evil there is no tension, and without tension there is no drama. One of the things that makes the usual descriptions of Heaven so repulsive is that it is shown as a place utterly wanting in tension. (*One Half* 199)

These assertions provide the philosophical underpinning for the much noted, pervasive depiction of wickedness in Davies's fiction and also justify, or at least explain, the vigour of his portrayals of such characters as John Parlabane, Boy Staunton, Willard the Wizard, William McOmish, and Giles Revelstoke. However, while unequivocally affirming and portraying the inexorable presence of evil, Davies correspondingly emphasizes the tremendous practical difficulty in distinguishing it from good:

> I'm interested in the duality and the ambiguity of evil and good because so often what seems to be evil may eventually produce some good thing and vice versa. . . . It's all a terrible ambiguity of good and evil and that's what fascinates me: trying to find some kind of thread through this maze. ("Canada")

---

1 The date of this play is subject to dispute: Patricia Morley attributes its creation to "the late forties" (26), yet Gordon Roper offers a date of 1953 ("Davies Log" 7).

Davies voices this notion in his 1956 play, *General Confession*, whose central character, Casanova de Seingault, holds that "in this imperfect life good comes out of evil quite as often as evil comes out of good" (*Hunting* 269). In Davies's fiction this view is best articulated by Dunstan Ramsay, when he exclaims in *World of Wonders* that God and the Devil " 'both speak so compellingly it's tricky work to know who's talking' " (316). Similarly, Magnus Eisengrim observes:

> "We can't know the quality or the results of our actions except in the most limited way. All we can do is to try to be as sure as we can of what we are doing so far as it relates to ourselves. In fact, not to flail about and be the deluded victims of our passions. If you're going to do something that looks evil, don't smear it with icing and pretend it's good; just bloody well do it and keep your eyes peeled. That's all." (239–40)

This belief in the ambiguity of good and evil is, at least in part, an extrapolation from the Heraclitean notion of *enantiodromia*, with which Davies is abundantly familiar since Jung characterized it as "the most marvellous of all psychological laws." Heraclitus's observation "that sooner or later everything runs into its opposite" (*Collected* 7: 111) not only explains the general structure of Davies's novels, but also illuminates the range of literary treatments of the problematic interrelation of good and evil. In medieval literature the notion of *felix culpa*, evident in the following poem, insists that man's fall was ultimately beneficial since it necessitated the incarnation of Christ as Redeemer and brought with it numerous associated acts of grace:

> Adam lay ibounden,
>   Bounden in a bond;
> Four thousand winter
>   Thoght he not too long;
> And all was for an appil,
>   An appil that he tok,
> As clerkès finden
>   Wreten in here book.
> Ne hadde the appil takè ben,
>   The appil takè ben,
> Ne haddè never our lady

A ben hevenè quene.
Blessèd be the time
   That appil takè was.
Therefore we moun singen
   "*Deo gracias.*" (Chambers 102)

In the Renaissance, Shakespeare acknowledged both faces of the ambiguity. Timon of Athens, a man ruined by his own generosity, is described by his former steward in the following terms:

Poor honest lord, brought low by his own heart,
Undone by goodness; strange, unusual blood,
When man's worst sin is he does too much good!
(IV.ii.37–39)

Conversely, immediately prior to the battle of Agincourt, Henry V observes the French camp and concludes:

There is some soul of goodness in things evil,
Would men observingly distil it out;
For our bad neighbour makes us early stirrers,
Which is both healthful and good husbandry:
Besides, they are our outward consciences,
And preachers to us all; admonishing
That we should dress us fairly for our end.
Thus may we gather honey from the weed,
And make a moral of the devil himself.
(*Henry V* IV.i.4–12)

John Milton also recognized the eliciting of good from evil. In *Paradise Lost*, a wary Beelzebub fears this possibility:

But what if he our Conqueror . . .
Have left us this our spirit and strength entire
Strongly to suffer and support our pains,
That we may so suffice his vengeful ire
Or do him mightier service as his thralls. . . .
(I: 143, 146–49)

Satan, acknowledging this, retorts:

69

If then his providence
Out of our evil seek to bring forth good,
Our labour must be to pervert that end,
And out of good still to find means of evil. . . . (162–65)

Subsequently, however, Milton unambiguously indicates that wickedness operates only at the forbearance of good and, as Beelzebub suspects, is being allowed to persist solely in the interest of producing an even greater benefit:

So stretched out huge in length the Arch-Fiend lay,
Chained on the burning lake; nor ever thence
Had risen or heaved his head but that the will
And high permission of all-ruling Heaven
Left him at large to his own dark designs,
That with reiterated crimes he might
Heap on himself damnation, while he sought
Evil to others, and enraged might see
How all his malice served but to bring forth
Infinite goodness, grace, and mercy. . . . (209–18)

Towards the poem's conclusion, after the archangel Michael has pledged Christ's salvation of mankind, Adam celebrates this *modus operandi* of the powers of benevolence:

"O goodness infinite, goodness immense,
That all this good of evil shall produce,
And evil turn to good, more wonderful
Than that by which creation first brought forth
Light out of darkness!" (XII. 469–73)

Meaningful as these precedents are in providing a general literary context for my discussion, significant differences distinguish them from Davies's approach. Unlike Shakespeare's plays, the structures of each of Davies's novels is informed by his belief in the *enantiodromian* ambiguity of good and evil. Although Shakespeare's drama presents this sentiment — without the Heraclitean nomenclature — it is not nearly as influenced by it.[1] Likewise, Davies differs from

---

1 In their analyses of the structure of Shakespeare's comedies — surely those of his plays most similar to Davies's novels — neither Nevo (8) nor Frye (*Natural Perspective* 73) mentions this phenomenon.

Milton, for the first five lines of *Paradise Lost* promise that in the battle between good and evil, good will triumph; this fundamentally reflects the Puritan poet's Christian assurance about the future. While good does emerge as a rather bruised victor in Davies's novels, this achievement is by no means to be presumed at the beginning of most of them. In fact, his books exhibit none of Milton's initial epistemological confidence, not even about what constitutes good and evil, so one must be much more tentative when attempting to determine the moral qualities or consequences of an action in Davies's fiction.

In view of these uncertainties, I must acknowledge that exploring the concept of good and evil in Davies's art is something like wrestling a metaphysical shark. I shall designate certain actions as demonstrating one or the other ethical attribute, while tacitly conceding the absence of an easily accessible touchstone that permits this with any degree of finality. Like Davies himself, I must participate in the schizophrenic exercise of exploring what I regard as a particular evil, without total certainty that it is, in fact, evil. I can be reasonably sure only that in this process I am moulded by the same general culture as the author, an indication that I share with him at least a common standard — imperfect as it may be — about what seems to be good or what seems to be wicked. In regard to this Jung aptly asserts:

> To see through a concrete situation to the bottom is God's affair alone. We may perhaps form an opinion about it but we do not know whether it is finally valid. At most we can say cautiously: judged by such and such a standard such and such a thing is good or evil. Something that appears evil to one nation may be regarded as good to another nation. (*Collected* 10: 862)

That good and evil are difficult to determine because what at first looks like one either leads to, or eventually appears to be, the other is an idea that informs Davies's first novel. The wickedness examined here is certainly very minor compared with that explored in his subsequent fiction; nonetheless, *Tempest-Tost* marks a significant beginning, since it presents in rudimentary fashion a pattern that persists and intensifies in those future works. This book exposes and satirizes small-town pettiness and pretension as Davies depicts how Mrs. Roscoe Forrester encourages and organizes a production of *The Tempest*. Social rather than artistic considerations primarily influence her decision to stage the play and prompt her ensuing suggestions for the apportioning of roles. However, base as the motives of some of those assisting with the production may be, the book clearly indicates that their efforts ensure both that Salterton will see *The Tempest* and that the capable Val Rich, whom Mrs. Forrester herself has recruited, will direct its performances.

The other important story concurrently unfolding in the novel chronicles the tribulations of Hector Mackilwraith, a middle-aged mathematics teacher. Although this account is also shaped by moral ambiguity, Davies here no longer focuses on philistinism and the eventual performance of a play, but instead considers potential self-annihilation and personal redemption. The inversion in this case occurs in both directions, for that which we originally assumed to be good is finally seen as pernicious, and vice versa. Mackilwraith deifies mathematics, reason, common sense, and planning (87) — all touted as supreme virtues in our technological society. These, apparently, have guided him well for much of his life, yet we eventually behold their deleterious side since his excessive and virtually exclusive reliance on them almost destroys him: disconcerted by circumstances in which his erstwhile gods prove to be ineffective, he tries to kill himself.

However, at this point of crisis Davies begins to manoeuvre us in the opposite direction, and that which we had hitherto assumed to be undesirable comes to bear good fruit. While most of us, conventionally religious or not, share reservations " 'gainst self slaughter" — and this would have been particularly so in 1951, the year of the novel's original publication — Davies emphasizes the unexpected benefits accruing from the attempted suicide. Mackilwraith's act facilitates Val Rich's discovery of his debilitating infatuation for Griselda Webster, a girl less than one half his age. Once aware of this, Val effects a private meeting between the two which at last permits him to see "that she was not much more than a child" (283). Even more important is what the bid for self-annihilation signifies for his life as a whole. Characterizing the suicide as a "sacrifice" (269), Mackilwraith undertook it — albeit misguidedly — as a means of impressing Griselda with his love for her and therefore with her own true worth; this, in turn, would encourage her to reject the worthless Roger Tasset. Such a sacrifice signifies an important change for a man who has hitherto lived egocentrically, deriving pleasure, as his Christian name, Hector, would suggest, largely from bullying students. The terms Davies uses to describe Mackilwraith soon after the failed suicide convey a strong sense of its salutary consequences: "happily" (282); "blissfully at rest" (283); "too happy" (283); and "for the first time in weeks, he laughed" (284). The reader thus completes *Tempest-Tost* feeling that as a result of Mackilwraith's conduct, life hereafter will be much more agreeable for him and his acquaintances.

This same pattern of ambiguity informs *Leaven of Malice*; here, however, Davies sharpens the focus of his exploration of evil. This time, philistinism and a deluded attempt at suicide, both ranking fairly low on the diabolical scale, give way to an act deliberately intended to inflict suffering on others. The immediate result of Bevill Higgin's malicious engagement notice in *The Bellman* is commensurate with his general expectations: it exacerbates long-running intergenerational tensions in the Vambrace and Bridgetower households, destroys Solly Bridgetower's hopes of marriage with Griselda Webster, throws Gloster Ridley's *Bellman* into turmoil, and heightens animosities within Dean Knapp's cathedral community.

Ironically, as Elspeth Buitenhuis observes, "An act of malice may, in the end, bring good to those it intended to harm, as Bevill Higgin learns" (76). Recognizing this, Dean Knapp asserts that while malice " 'may cause the greatest misery and distress in many unexpected quarters[,] I have even known it to have quite unforeseen good results' " (267). The vindictive newspaper announcement generates a crisis in Gloster Ridley's life which finally allows him to make peace with his memory of a disastrous marriage. Further, its repercussions send into eclipse those in St. Nicholas's Cathedral imbued with a spirit of enmity and enhance the standing of the talented cathedral organist, Humphrey Cobbler, who has been the object of much unjust animosity. Most important, it effects the engagement of Solly Bridgetower and Pearl (Veronica) Vambrace, the two characters it originally targeted, thus, we hope, liberating them from their overbearing parents.

In *A Mixture of Frailties*, what has now become an established pattern continues. As in *Leaven of Malice*, here Davies "ups the ante" from the previous novel, heightening that which constitutes the evil action that will eventually bear good fruit, for, although he still explores malice in this novel, he intensifies its wickedness. This time a mother directs it toward her child, and it even reaches beyond the grave, for the conditions of Louisa Bridgetower's will dictate that her son and his wife will enjoy the benefits of her sizeable fortune only if they produce a male offspring. Until then, while watching the substantial interest compounded by her holdings finance the education of a local artist, they are condemned to inhabit and maintain her large home on a scanty allowance. Humphrey Cobbler rightly describes the will as " 'a grisly practical joke' " (20). His wife, Molly, fears that its terms are " 'laying the Dead Hand on the living' " (22) and believes it will " 'dry up the organs of increase' " in Solly and Veronica (23), who will strain and labour to produce a suitable child.

Mrs. Bridgetower's deleterious last testament very nearly accomplishes what she apparently desired, since for Solly and Veronica the four years after her death are a lengthy period of infertility, even impotence, interrupted only by the stillborn birth of a Bridgetower son. Tainting their lives and souring their marriage, the " 'Dead Hand' " even seems to haunt the house (271–73). However, the will ultimately yields unintended good. During her life Mrs. Bridgetower could hardly have been characterized as a champion of the arts — Humphrey Cobbler, who could be, declares that " 'she symbolized all the forces that have been standing on my neck ever since I was old enough to have a mind of my own' " (25). Yet some of the money she had sought to deny her childless son educates a young singer into considerable artistic competence and the rest finances the production of an innovative opera. As Solly remarks: " 'My Mother cared too much about having her own way; result — a remarkable artist gets her start . . . [and] an extraordinary opera gets its first production. Neither of them things Mother would have foreseen or desired, to be truthful' " (367).

Nor, perhaps, would she have predicted the crisis in her daughter-in-law's life that four years of oppression by the " 'Dead Hand' " finally provoke. While in labour for the second time, the previously rather meek Veronica decisively asserts her independence by successfully wrestling Mrs. Bridgetower's malevolent ghost, or what Veronica thinks is her ghost — the book is equivocal on this point — to protect the life of her soon-to-be-born son. What the novel leaves unambiguous is that this exorcizes the household and her marriage of her mother-in-law's pernicious influence in a way that Mrs. Bridgetower's mere death never could. Ironically, the will provides the very emancipation it had sought to deny.

The Deptford novels exhibit a greater subtlety and complexity in Davies's treatment of good and evil than we have seen in the three Salterton books. No longer does he develop, explore, and qualify the ambiguity associated with a specific deed only in the work in which that act occurs; instead, he pursues the uncertainty throughout the trilogy. This greater scope continually forces us to change and rechange our assessment of an action's ultimate moral qualities, as the instance of the stone in Boy Staunton's snowball so clearly demonstrates. The motivation underlying Boy's behaviour is by now well known to us, since this is, after all, the third consecutive novel in which an act of malice supplies the inciting force. What is unfamiliar is the length of the ethical labyrinth through which Davies leads us in our attempt to determine the final value of that stone.

Assessing the quality of its immediate consequences hardly seems a labyrinthine undertaking, for the woman it hits partially loses her sanity and the baby boy it impels her to deliver prematurely almost dies. Yet, soon after this begins a trilogy-long muddying of waters. Mrs. Dempster and her son Paul acquire special interest for Dunstan Ramsay, the snowball's intended target, for their fate fills him with guilt and inspires him to good works for their benefit. In return, Paul becomes a junior companion in magic for the otherwise solitary Ramsay, while Mary Dempster's inner peace, seemingly gained after the snowball's impact made her "simple," provides a salutary contrast to the stridency of Ramsay's mother.

As the novel proceeds, the snowball's effects multiply with impeccable causality. The now "simple" Mrs. Dempster, to the chagrin of her husband and the town as a whole, is discovered copulating with a tramp in the local gravel pit. This, in turn, initiates numerous reverberations. For the reader, *Fifth Business* presents a dilemma, since we uncomfortably discover that our morality is closer to that of Deptford's citizens than we might have wished. We are probably more gentle in our censure, but our disapproval of Mrs. Dempster's behaviour remains, and ensuing events seem to substantiate our judgment. Her action swiftly and apparently disastrously diminishes her family: she has to be tied up; her husband loses his pastorship at the Baptist church; and young Paul is mercilessly tormented by his vindictive peers, among whom Boy Staunton is the most vituperative. Further, Dunstan Ramsay's continued association with the now ostracized Mary Dempster provokes such conflict with his mother, Fiona, that in 1915 he flees to join the army under-aged. Experiencing the dangers of trench warfare, Ramsay is wounded and very nearly dies in combat; he is fortunate only to lose a leg and receive extensive scarring.

Yet the repercussions of that snowball continue increasingly and inexorably to reveal themselves. Unlike Fiona Ramsay, who never relinquishes her steadfast conviction that "Mrs Dempster had transgressed in a realm where there could be no shades of right and wrong" (49), we are presently forced to reconsider our initial appraisal of her conduct in the gravel pit. We learn that her fornication there so miraculously reformed Joel Surgeoner, the depraved tramp who enjoyed her favours, that Dunstan Ramsay comes to regard it as a saintly act. Indeed, so transformed does the morality of her deed become, that in *The Manticore* Ramsay regrets being unable to emulate it when his best friend's distraught wife offers him the same opportunity under different circumstances: "In spite of one very great example I had in my life I couldn't rise to love as an act of charity. The failure was mine, and a bitter one" (262).

Even prior to his discovery of Surgeoner's redemption, Ramsay was awed by Mrs. Dempster's inner peace and her apparent ability to recall his brother Willie from the dead. Subsequently, he experiences a profound vision of her as he lingers near death during a battle — a battle in which he would not have participated but for his desire to escape his mother's outrage at Mrs. Dempster's "filthy behaviour and adultery" (*Fifth* 49). Ramsay's experiences of Mrs. Dempster — her internal tranquility and invocation of Willie, the wartime vision, the miracle with the tramp — generate an interest in hagiography that comes to constitute the central purpose of his life. This vocation suffuses his otherwise mundane existence as a high-school teacher with splendour and propels and sustains him on a crucial inner voyage of self-discovery.

However, the most unlikely beneficiary of Mary Dempster's unorthodox conduct is her son Paul. Davies pursues at length the complexities of his life story and again forces readers to consider ethical aspects of a particular act. Initially Paul proves an able student who quickly masters the card and coin tricks that young Ramsay teaches him but is himself too clumsy to perform. In his adult incarnation as Magnus Eisengrim, Paul reveals that this comradeship was vitally important to him, since it constituted the only goodwill he encountered in a community that had become almost uniformly hostile to his family (*World* 34). Yet when his father, the Baptist parson, discovers the boys' interest in sleights of hand, his condemnation is severe. Regarding cards as anathema — "the Devil's picture-book" (42) — Amasa Dempster accuses Ramsay of being "the agent — unknowingly, he hoped — by means of which the Evil One had trailed his black slime across a pure life" (*Fifth* 41). Consequently, he banishes Ramsay from his household.

Unless we are strict Baptists — and this in itself says something about the relativity of good and evil — most readers will censure the preacher's attitude towards cards and his consequent attempt to exile the friend who has performed many acts of kindness in his home. The excessive rhetoric assigned to Dempster in this situation would seem to indicate that this is Davies's own attitude, but as we shall soon see, Davies will not only qualify this position but also subsequently qualify the qualification. In an attempt to ensure that Paul never succumbs to the "bad instincts" exhibited by his mother, Dempster, as well as banning cards, determines that the boy should memorize the Psalms as a bulwark against evil (*World* 24). To the reader, advocating intimacy with the Psalms seems immediately much more reasonable than proscribing the cards, for even if not conventionally religious we recognize the morality explicated in the Bible as generally worth learning. Also, by the standards of the Deptford trilogy, the Bible is one of the key literary and mythological documents of our civilization and, as such, yields important information about ourselves.

Ironically, in addition to the original disgrace brought on the family by Mrs. Dempster, both the Psalms and the card techniques are crucial factors in ten-year-old Paul's " 'descen[t] into hell' " (*World* 17), a phrase he uses to describe his seven years as the victim of sodomy. For a time, then, the reader is forced to the uncomfortable conclusion that Amasa Dempster may be accurate about the cards but mistaken about the Psalms. Indeed, the first in the relentless chain of events that occurs on the day of Paul's descent is his father's instruction that he commit Psalm 79 to memory. Far from bolstering the boy's faith as his father expects, one of the verses immediately reminds Paul of the general position to which his family has fallen within the community: " '*We are become a reproach to our neighbours, a scorn and derision to them that are round about us*' " (*World* 24). The psalm compels him to imagine the impending consequences of Mary Dempster's deed: when the school year begins in less than a week, he will again be exposed to the taunts of his peers calling his mother a " 'hoor' " (24). Further reading only heightens his sense of imminent misery:

"Onward I went with Psalm 79. *O remember not against us former iniquities: let thy tender mercies speedily prevent us: for we are brought very low.* But as soon as I put my nose into the schoolyard they would remember former iniquities against me. God's tender mercies had never reached the Deptford schoolyard. And I was unquestionably brought very low, for all that desolation would begin again next Tuesday." (25)

Desperate, the young boy craves a " 'delicious release' " (25) and consequently steals some money from his parents to view the exhibits at the local fair.

It is at this point that Paul's experiences with magic and the Bible merge ruinously. Once at the fair, and obviously still fascinated by the card tricks Ramsay had taught him, Paul is enthralled by Willard the Wizard, " 'who was doing wonders with decks of cards' " (27). Although his earlier reading about Robert-Houdin should logically lead him to describe Willard in terms of this supreme magician, Paul employs the language recently learned from the Psalms: " 'I longed with my whole soul to know what Willard knew. As the hart pants after the water brooks, even so my blasphemous soul panted after the Wizard' " (28). Paul then shifts from this altered rendering of Psalm 42.1, in which "Wizard" has been substituted for "God," to a description of his feelings using the apocalyptic terms of the New Testament:

> "For me the Book of Revelation came alive: here was an angel come down from heaven, having great power, and the earth was lightened with his glory; if only I could be like him, surely there would be no more sorrow, nor crying, nor any more pain, and all former things — my dark home, my mad, disgraceful mother, the torment of school — would pass away." (29–30; cf. Revelation 18.1; 21.4).

Because his biblical training has led him to expect and search for a saviour, Paul is susceptible to the overtures of the magician he perceives in these terms. As Jurgen Lind, an associate of the adult Paul, perceptively remarks, " 'The Bible obsession must somehow have supported the obsession with the conjurer. Not even a great revelation wipes out a childhood's indoctrination; the two must have come together in some way' " (30). Thus begins the sodomizing of the unfortunate boy by Willard, who seduces and then kidnaps him at the fair.

At this point we may suspect that Davies is finally allowing us to stand on moral *terra firma*. Pederasty seems an unambiguously evil act, and in terms of the intensification of evil as Davies's career as a novelist progresses, the wickedness in *World of Wonders* appears darker than that of any of the five earlier books. However, while Davies would obviously not endorse sexually abusing a child, his protean moral sense forces us to conclude that this does eventually yield some good in Paul's life. Only through his distressing experiences with Willard does the boy gain the skills that will transform him into the adult Magnus Eisengrim, consummate sorcerer and illusionist. Once again, we are retroactively compelled to reconsider our attitudes towards those things that originally brought Paul under the magician's influence. Since his contact with Willard eventually yields positive results, we are, finally, returned to our initial impression that Amasa Dempster was mistaken about the merit of the cards but correct about the Psalms.

This reappraisal correspondingly forces yet another assessment of the moral qualities of that first causal domino that has set all the subsequent dominoes falling in Paul's life. Paul himself best articulates this when, much later as Magnus Eisengrim, he recognizes the debt he owes to Boy Staunton, the thrower of the snowball:

"If he hadn't hit my mother on the head with that snowball — having hidden a rock in it, which was dirty play — I might now be what my father was: a Baptist parson in a small town. I have had my ups and downs, and the downs were very far down indeed, but I am now a celebrity in a limited way, and I am a master of a craft, which is a better thing by far. . . . I get my living by doing what I most enjoy, and that is rare indeed. Who gave me my start? Boy Staunton!" (*World* 301)

Eisengrim's statement points us indirectly and retrospectively to one other benefit produced by the seemingly unequivocally evil act of throwing that snowball: perhaps most ironic of all is the consequence of Staunton's action for his own son, David. *The Manticore* is largely a study of Boy's near destruction of his son through what he genuinely believes constitutes good parenting. Only when David takes strong exception to the magician Eisengrim — a figure in part produced by his father's malicious action — does his ensuing psychological breakdown at the Royal Alexandra Theatre impel him to seek the Jungian counselling which in turn remedies the pernicious "good" his father had forced into his boyhood.

The Cornish trilogy marks yet another shift in Davies's treatment of ethical ambiguity. It parallels the Salterton trilogy in that the exploration of iniquity or a sinister act is again confined largely to each individual novel rather than extended over the three books. Also, in the first Cornish novel at least, he continues to adhere to his practice of intensifying the depth of the evil portrayed in each successive work. In *The Rebel Angels*, however, this wickedness has become more dangerous because much more complex and subtle than anything hitherto depicted, marking Davies's increasing confidence and perspicacity in his exploration of the topic.

Here Davies investigates good and evil, less by probing the consequences of a single act than by analyzing a dynamic figure, John Parlabane. Parlabane's long-time associate, Clem Hollier, says of him: " 'Evil isn't what one does, it's something one is that infects everything one does' " (78). Yet such is Parlabane's sophistication that both the reader and Maria Theotoky, one of the book's two narrators, are at first more inclined to dismiss him as an industrious nuisance than to fear him as a force of prodigious wickedness. After all, in the context of a novel that celebrates the academy, Davies portrays Parlabane as a towering, energetic, intellectual presence — qualities that, initially, hardly seem to indicate depravity. Also, the reader may well be expecting an individual of Willard the Wizard's ilk, whose evil Davies blatantly portrayed in his preceding novel. Indeed, we only begin to become cognizant of the serious threat posed by this renegade monk when, approximately a quarter of the way through the book, Hollier warns Maria against him in the following unequivocal terms:

> "Parlabane is an evil man, and evil is infectious, and you mustn't catch the infection. . . . There are evil people; they're not common, but they exist. It takes just as much energy to be evil as it does to be good and few people have energy enough for either course. But he has. There is a destroying demon in him, and he would drag you down, and then jeer at you because you had yielded to him." (77)

The yielding against which Hollier warns is not physical. Bodily violation forms the central evil of *World of Wonders*, but, horrible as the experience is, Paul Dempster recovers from it. Parlabane's attempt to debauch Maria is purely intellectual and psychological, and more dangerous because it affords less hope of recuperation. His vigorous scepticism threatens to taint all that he touches: as Susan Stone-Blackburn puts it, "in his consistent denial of the meaning and worth of anything in life, he is the embodiment of evil" (99). Yet so insidious is his naysaying that only long after Hollier's initial warning does Maria come to articulate the danger it poses:

> in Goethe's play the Devil appears handsomely dressed as a travelling scholar; Parlabane was at the other end of the scale, but in his command of any conversation he had with me, and his ability under all circumstances to make the worse seem the better thing, he was acceptable as Mephistopheles. (200)

> Parlabane was trying to seduce me intellectually, to put me with my back on the floor and leave me gasping and rumpled, and all with words. (201)

Through Parlabane's progressive deterioration, *The Rebel Angels* suggests those depths to which Maria might be dragged if, like him, she comes to believe in nothing. He has already failed as a monk, and before this as a teacher; presently his physical appearance, never pretty, degenerates so that

> he looked like a sinister bum. The suit somebody had given him . . . had never been a fit and now it was a baggy, food-stained mess. The trousers . . . dragged at his heels, the bottoms dirty and frayed. His shirt was always dirty, and it occurred to me that perhaps advanced scepticism made ordinary cleanliness seem a folly. He had a bad smell; not just dirty clothes, but a living, heavy stench. (199)

He becomes increasingly threatening, and Maria fears for her physical safety when, improvident, he continually demands money from her. He sinks into drug dependency, and finally, sceptical about the publication of his novel, he perpetrates a murder and commits suicide in order to generate advance publicity for his book.

As to the moral questions generated by Parlabane's existence, one may now ask: "Where shall ambiguity be found? And where is the place of ambivalence?" In fact, Parlabane's baleful life produces some good. During one of their discussions, he deliberately humiliates Maria about her Gypsy heritage as a means of weakening her resistance to his request that she "lend" him fifty dollars. He concludes their strained conversation with this counsel, tauntingly offered I strongly suspect:

"I think you are trying to suppress [your Gypsy blood] because it is the opposite of what you are trying to be — the modern woman, the learned woman, the creature wholly of this age and this somewhat thin and sour civilization. You are not trying to conceal it; you are trying to tear it out. But you can't, you know. My advice to you, my dear, is to let your [Gypsy] root feed your [academic] crown." (205)

This recommendation and Parlabane's general scepticism about intellectual endeavours eventually force Maria to acknowledge the immoderate emphasis she has been placing on her university career and her coinciding renunciation of her ancestry. Consequently, she not only changes her behaviour, as her quasi-Gypsy wedding to Arthur indicates, but also directs full credit to Parlabane for her new-found sense of balance:

". . . his talk about the need to recognize your root and your crown as of equal importance has made me understand that my Gypsy part is inescapable. It has to be recognized, because if it isn't it will plague me all my life as a canker at the root." (310)

Nor are the beneficial effects of his malignant presence confined only to Maria's " 'root,' " for his malevolence also facilitates the nurture of her " 'crown.' " Parlabane's murder of Urky McVarish effects the recovery of an important manuscript stolen by McVarish, a text Maria will now be able to use as the cornerstone of her future academic research.

Davies's managing of good and evil in *What's Bred in the Bone*, the second of the Cornish books, largely parallels his treatment of this theme in *A Mixture of Frailties* and *World of Wonders*. In all of these novels, what at first appears to be evil proves essential for the creation of superb, soul-nurturing art. The young and somewhat delicate Francis Cornish is forced to enrol in Blairlogie's Carlyle Rural School, where he is relentlessly bullied and beaten. The very terms that Magnus Eisengrim employed to describe his sodomization by Willard now confirm the magnitude of Cornish's persecution by his schoolmates: "Francis, for all purposes sufficient to his age and stage of life, descended into Hell, and stayed there for what seemed to him an eternity" (*What's Bred* 92). When spared being the target of his sadistic peers' cruelty, he suffers by witnessing their savagery towards others:

The game was to catch a frog, stick a straw up its cloaca, and blow it up to enormous size. As the frog swelled, there was a delightful apprehension that it might burst. There was an even more splendid hope that the boy who was blowing might, if enough funny things were said to him, stop blowing for a moment and suck and then — why, he might even die, which would richly crown the fun. (96–97)

Nor is this brutality confined to amphibians. Etched indelibly on Cornish's memory is "the day some boys caught a tomcat and cut off its testicles, and let it loose to rush away, howling and bleeding!" (97).

The cruelty Cornish experiences is not limited to that perpetrated by his sadistic schoolmates, for the depravity of some of the community's adults forces him to confront even greater misery. As Cornish observes him embalming the corpse of F.X. Bouchard, Zadok Hoyle grieves: " 'Poor, poor little soul. We've got to do our best for old F.X., Francis, not that anything can make up for a life like his' " (144). Hoyle explains that during a Masonic initiation ritual some of Blairlogie's lodge members kidnapped the unfortunate dwarf tailor and inflicted on him a humiliating washing:

"They did it quite a few times. Everybody had a grab at him, or pushed the soap in his face, or tried to take the hide off him with the towel. Then they'd make him run up and down the room; they'd flick him with wet towels and sool him on so they could see his little legs go, and his big what's-its-name whack and thrash around. . . . I guess the poor little mortal couldn't stand it any more, and went home and hanged himself. In a pair of braces, I understand." (145)

Cornish's experiences with cruelty and anguish in the community are to some extent mirrored in his domestic life. The picture given him by his Aunt — entitled *Love Locked Out* — is especially significant: it reflects Cornish's own acute suffering because his parents, particularly his mother, largely ignore him (122). At home he is again compelled to face the consequences of human brutality — in the person of his mentally deficient, physically malformed older brother, "the Looner." This unfortunate sibling, the casualty of his grandmother's primitive attempt to induce the termination of her daughter's unwanted pregnancy, is like a gothic character, forced to

83

spend his pathetic life hidden from the world in an attic. Nor does a change in location diminish Cornish's experience of evil, for after he leaves Blairlogie — indeed, leaves the country — he, too, endures misery resulting from an undesired pregnancy. At Oxford, his cousin, who is carrying another man's baby, tricks Cornish into a disastrous marriage then callously deserts him for her lover soon after the child's birth.

Marking a change from his previous novels, however, Davies continually promises that the evils Cornish experiences will finally yield good. This assurance is proffered through "the cosmically omniscient narrator" (Keith, "Robertson Davies" 142), the Daimon Maimas, who, as Cornish's *"Tutelary Spirit, the Indwelling Essence"* (71), claims responsibility for forcing him to encounter much wickedness. Maimas maintains that suffering is the *sine qua non* to ensure that his ward consummate his destiny and become a great artist: *"I learned that when a tutelary spirit like myself is given a life to watch over, pity merely makes a mess of things. Far better to put your man over the hurdles and scrape him through the hedges, and toughen him up."* (71) An early indication of the good that Maimas intends for his charge concerns that aloofness of Cornish's parents, which, although causing the boy much immediate pain, eventually comes to nurture his teenage quest for the Grail, so decisive to his progress as an artist:

It made it possible for him to idealize his parents and love them as distant, glorious figures, quite apart from the everyday world. At school, and at the expensive camps where he spent his summers, he had always with him a folder in which were pictures of his father, looking distinguished, and his mother, looking beautiful, and these were holy ikons that comforted and reassured him when he doubted himself. And as the Grail took command of his inner life, they were associated with it, not directly and foolishly, but as the kind of people who made such splendour possible and perpetuated it in the modern world. (196)

The brilliant art of the adult Francis Cornish provides the ultimate testament to the methods of his Daimon. This is the good into which Cornish — like the alchemists who so fascinate Jung and Davies — has transformed the base elements of his experience, the evils from his past. His first highly renowned painting, *Drollig Hansel*, presents an intensely sympathetic portrait of the persecuted F.X. Bouchard, depicted in the guise of a sixteenth-century dwarf jester. Cornish intends this work as "an *ex voto* almost, a memorial to a man he had never spoken to, and had come to know only after his death" (393). His patron's observations verify the artist's strong compassion towards his subject, the emotion that produces the picture's considerable vigour:

"Poor wretch . . . to be born a dwarf and kept as a Fool." (382)

"[The painting] speaks of the dull, inescapable misery of being a dwarf, of having to make oneself ridiculous in order to be tolerated, of feeling that God has not used you well. If it makes me feel these things so strongly, it is certainly a picture of unusual quality." (383)

The general misery of Cornish's past also spawns his other superb painting, *The Marriage at Cana*, which is of considerable benefit to him because in it he has " 'made up' " his soul (479). Here, too, he depicts F.X. Bouchard, but also prominent as wedding guests are his parents, particularly his mother as "a lady of great but cold beauty" (472). Palpably representing evil is a "rabble of children with twisted, ugly, hungry faces. They are not looking toward the marriage scene, but are concentrated on one of their number who is gouging the eye from a cat with a sharp stone" (472). From his hapless marriage Cornish draws the central image of the painting: he and his treacherous wife, his cousin Ismay Glasson, so similar in appearance as bride and groom, symbolize the male and female halves of his soul, whose crucial union Cornish renders in the picture (476).

Even "the Looner," pathetic victim of prenatal brutality, exists as a force for good in his younger brother's life. Maimas states that

> *for Francis the Looner was a lifelong reminder of the inadmissible primitive in the most cultivated life, a lifelong adjuration to pity, a sign that disorder and abjection stand less than a hair's breadth away from every human creature. A continual counsel to make the best of whatever fortune had given him. . . . [T]he Looner did not live in vain.* (249)

As such, he, too, is given an important place in Cornish's painting: "high on the left above the heads of the bridal pair" (471).[1]

---

1 The specific details of the transmutation of evil into good in this novel are fascinating because external sources prove that Davies himself accomplished

Augmenting those painful personal experiences that furnish Cornish with raw material for his paintings is evil of another sort, evil that propels his craft to maturity and to a palpable, though peculiar, prominence. His artistic drillmaster, Tancred Saraceni, flamboyantly associates himself with the Devil, proclaiming that Christ would have little use for a man of his, Saraceni's, genius (395). Notwithstanding the absolutist nature of this statement (cf. my discussion p. 61 above), *What's Bred in the Bone* illustrates that Saraceni both possesses potent evil and wields it dexterously. Fraud, forgery, and deception characterize his world, and he vanquishes the Third Reich with its own weapons: duplicity and betrayal. When another counterfeiter unwittingly threatens the success of his nebulous operation in Germany, Saraceni ruthlessly orders the destruction of his career and later greets with cold indifference the news that this has precipitated the man's suicide (426–27). He promotes hate as pedagogically productive (400); thus, it is appropriate that his pupil compares him to Mephistopheles (407).[1] The novel intimates that Saraceni has the "Evil Eye"; indeed, his malignant glance seems to generate a nasty fall and broken hip for one of his enemies. Acting as chorus, the Daimon Maimas asserts: "*Nobody becomes as great a man as Saraceni without extraordinary spiritual energy, and it isn't all benevolent*" (480). Yet, however tainted this energy may be from a moral standpoint, it yields impressive aesthetic results. An extraordinary painter-restorer in his own right, Saraceni bullies into fruition Cornish's artistic promise. Not only does his nebulous forging-enterprise nurture his apprentice's talent, it also ensures prominence for the young man's work: ironically, only because the world believes — thanks to Saraceni's duplicity — that Cornish's paintings are

---

precisely what Francis Cornish achieves. He, too, has fashioned a formidable work of art, in part by exploiting his boyhood encounters with wickedness in Renfrew. The cruelty he confronted at school (*Conversations* 215, 246) is effectively rendered in *What's Bred in the Bone*, both during Francis Cornish's Blairlogie youth and later in his brilliant pictures. Similarly, Davies has memorialized the dwarf tailor, whom Renfrew's Masons so persecuted that he was driven to suicide (Peterman 4). The diminutive F.X. Bouchard is such a vital presence in the book, in terms of both his pathetic story and his effect on the central character's life and art, that Davies's presentation of him might surely be seen as his own "*ex voto*" to a victim of unwarranted brutality.

1 In this same diabolical vein, Davies, I believe, exploits the legendary confrontation between the Devil and a bottle-throwing Martin Luther. Here, the unscrupulous Saraceni becomes the target of Francis Cornish's ink vial (404).

products of an earlier era are they accorded the attention and, indeed, the acclaim they warrant.

The exploration of the ambiguity of good and evil in *The Lyre of Orpheus* to a great extent focuses on cuckolding, which in literature (as in life) is less often associated with evil than with ridicule. Davies, however, largely fastens onto its gravity, since in his work he identifies lust as a sin (cf., for example, "Fiction and Seven Deadly Sins" and *Rebel* 44). Whenever marital infidelity appears in his writing, he seldom neglects to examine the misery it spawns. Thus we witness Amasa Dempster in *Fifth Business* and Francis Cornish in *What's Bred in the Bone* both suffering, and even David Staunton in *The Manticore*, who is anguished at the mere suggestion that Dunstan Ramsay had cuckolded his father (and consequently that he is, perhaps, not Boy Staunton's son). Similarly, *The Lyre of Orpheus* features the pain of both Arthur Cornish, the aggrieved husband, and Geraint Powell, the offender, rather than any splendour, daring, or humour associated with the act of adultery.

Yet here again evil engenders good. Like his namesake from the legend that shapes this novel, Arthur is ennobled by being cuckolded, for he chooses to respond with magnanimity and correspondingly enriches the lives of his friends and spouse. Furthermore, gratitude that he will no longer be without progeny — a predicament to which his own sterility would otherwise have condemned him — comes to supplant his initial anguish. The now familiar motif of evil being important for the creation of art also gently asserts itself here: though nothing is ever directly stated in this regard, Davies intimates that the new opera, *Arthur of Britain, or the Magnanimous Cuckold*, is better because of the direct involvement in a real-life cuckolding by several of the show's principal figures.

The theme of marital infidelity opens Davies's next book, *Murther and Walking Spirits*, in which the "murther" promised in the title is perpetrated against the narrator, Connor Gilmartin, when he surprises his wife in bed with her irascible lover. Homicide is clearly reprehensible *per se*, and the novel unequivocally maintains this stance, but, consistent with the numerous precedents we have examined, Davies soon presents some salubrious repercussions. The reader by now realizes that Davies, motivated by a leavening combination of philosophical playfulness and sincere commitment to his metaphysical beliefs, consistently depicts actions of ever-increasing wickedness and then takes upon himself the challenge of providing them with some salutary results. In this instance, while the newly deceased cuckold is justifiably embittered at having been prematurely deprived of his life, his death inaugurates a transcendent journey of self-discovery that was previously inaccessible. Because this takes the form of an investigation of the vicissitudes of Gilmartin's ancestors, Davies provides himself here with yet further opportunities of examining the twistings and turnings of good and evil into one another.

First, he depicts how the American War of Independence throws the life of United Empire Loyalist Anna Gage into initial disarray. Yet the death of her British officer husband, and the confiscation of her sizeable land and financial holdings, are the origin of much benefit. Only after she has been forced to flee her comfortable urban domicile and journey to Canada in a consciously Bunyanesque manner — through what for her is a fearsome, foreboding wilderness — is she vouchsafed a profound experience of the deity:

> this was for Anna a time of incalculable spiritual growth. . . . God had become terrible, but not malignant or unapproachable. The vastness and incalculability of God were apparent to her as she had never dreamed He might be in Trinity Church, or at prayer-time in her New York parlour. (87)

Nor does the evil that she originally suffers yield solely spiritual rewards. Unlike Bunyan's Christian, her newly discovered vigour enables her to transcend the adjuration from Matthew's gospel (6.24) and serve both Mammon and God, for after depicting her travails, Davies establishes her as the matriarch of an affluent family in Canada.

The interplay between religion and money provides the context for Davies's subsequent exploration of the ambiguity of good and evil, when he turns his attention to a parallel, Welsh branch of Connor Gilmartin's genealogy. As we follow these British Gilmartins through several generations, we observe as their waxing and waning financial fortunes become intertwined with varying degrees of attachment to Methodism. Davies portrays this religion at its finest in the first Wesleyan Gilmartin, an almost larger-than-life figure who out-blathers, out-faces, and generally outlasts, a band of malevolent mountain ruffians in order to preach the gospel to them. In the process, Thomas Gilmartin rescues their pot-boy for God, christens him (appropriately Wesley), and adopts him as his son.

However, moral ambiguity presently asserts itself, since as the

Gilmartin generations succeed one another, this good produces its opposite:

Finely educated as he was, it is unlikely that John Wesley paid any attention to that curmudgeonly Greek sage Heraclitus who was the first, so far as we know, to point out the psychological fact that anything, if pursued beyond a reasonable point, turns into its opposite. But John Wesley saw too much of life to escape the fact, and in a moment of terrible prophetic knowledge said: "Godliness begets Industry; Industry begets Wealth; Wealth begets Ungodliness." And I now see this law at work in the family of Old Wesley Gilmartin. . . . (118)

The wealth garnered by Thomas's heirs through their successes in the cloth trade, the food-services industry, and later in various sartorial enterprises, is at least partially responsible for the gambling, alcohol abuse, and sexual profligacy in some of these descendants.

Ironically, however, it is not this particular sort of evil fruit born of good that finally throws the family into a state of near-destitution. Davies further emphasizes the Heraclitean concept of *enantiodromia* by showing that what appear to be two exemplary acts of Christian charity ultimately ruin the Gilmartins and force them to depart insolvent from Wales. When Samuel Gilmartin, because of a "life-long principle that a man must never turn his back on a friend" (131), sponsors a bank loan for a dishonest fellow Deacon at the chapel, his friend's business is saved but Samuel is thrown into grave financial turmoil. Acting as something of a chorus to this development, the book's narrator aptly cries, "Oh, Heraclitus" (131). The grievous consequences of this initial beneficent act are soon compounded by the results of another, since Walter, Samuel's devout son, is forced by his dying mother to abandon an assured, lucrative career in the civil service in order to return and help his father in their faltering tailoring shop. Although this honouring of father and mother is unquestionably a fine act in terms of conventional morality, it spells disaster from a practical standpoint because it places the young man in an occupation at which he is singularly inept. The business finally fails, and Walter, bankrupt, is forced to emigrate from Wales in the hope of better prospects in Canada. Much later his son Rhodri, possessed with Davies's sense of the Heraclitean in life, incisively summarizes the causes of the family's penury: "A little

89

intelligent hypocrisy might have saved the Pater. Too good. Excess in virtue can be ruinous" (240).[1]

Rhodri is the character who witnesses both faces of good and evil's ambiguity, as his father-in-law's story runs counter to his father's. William McOmish embodies Davies's oft-stated and depicted belief that evil can frequently facilitate the production of great art, since McOmish's accomplishments as a master builder are to a large extent the result of his immense pride — "first among the Deadly Sins" (189) — which is, in turn, sustained by a morphine addiction that makes him the terror of his family. Like the charity of the Welsh Gilmartins, McOmish's vices eventually carry him over the brink of financial ruin, but not before they effect the construction of many superb buildings, the most magnificent of which is the handsome Methodist church whose splendour the novel describes in such detail.

Davies's fictional treatment of the ambiguity of good and evil finds a sort of parallel, though on a slightly different plane, in his personal statements about himself. On one hand, in a 1979 interview with Peter Gzowski, Davies affirmed: "I think, you know, that people tend to have a sort of dominating attitude of mind. And certainly mine is comic rather than tragic" (*Conversations* 186).[2] Similarly, in conversation with Michael Hulse, he stated quite simply: "I am essentially of an optimistic nature, and I think that pessimism, at the moment, is a sort of literary and artistic and philosophic mannerism . . ." (*Conversations* 256).

Elsewhere, however, Davies expounds a dualism that would seem to qualify, if not contradict, these assertions. In the Larkin-Stuart lectures, he defines dualism as "the continual opposition of Good and Evil, the war in heaven between God and the Devil, with the implication that at some time one of the opposed forces will emerge as undoubted victor — but without saying which it may be" (*One Half* 263). Jung thoroughly examines the character of evil offering praise for the Gnostics and arguing that "it is no exaggeration to assume that in this world good and evil more or less balance each other, like day and night, and that this is the reason why the victory

---

1 Similarly, William James argues that "appeals to sympathy or justice, are folly when we are dealing with human crocodiles and boa-constrictors. The saint may simply give the universe into the hands of the enemy by his trustfulness" (276).

2 "My pull is toward comedy" ("Art" 32).

of the good is always a special act of grace" (*Collected* 11: 253). This "balance" is implicit in Davies's statements cited at the beginning of this chapter; in addition, he offers explicit evidence of his uncertainty about the final outcome in the battle between the two forces:

> because we recognize evil, and confront it as wisely as we may, we do not necessarily succumb to it. When we watch two men wrestling, they seem almost to be in a lovers' embrace, but we know that at last one will fall. Our hope is that Evil may fall at last. (*One Half* 269)[1]

Yet, in spite of his professed uncertainty, my structural examination of Davies's fiction demonstrates that his novels ultimately present a much more assured, optimistic worldview, reflecting what he says about himself to Peter Gzowski and Michael Hulse. In other words, Davies the artist expounds a different vision from Davies the supposed dualist. Clearly, both accept the ambiguity of good and evil. Both also acknowledge the often deleterious effects of wickedness: Mrs. Dempster loses her sanity; her husband is ruined by the rock in the snowball; Paul spends several years in "hell"; Parlabane commits murder; F.X. Bouchard is driven to suicide by the cruel inhabitants of Blairlogie. Nevertheless, in almost all of his novels Davies's strong tendency is to provide a plot structure by focusing on the good elicited from evil acts, so that what in the beginning seems unequivocally negative will eventually be identified — albeit after the suffering of intense pain — as the midwife to a salubrious, often life-enhancing good. The one anomaly is his evenhandedness in *Murther and Walking Spirits,* where good does sometimes produce outright evil — where bankruptcy has few redeeming qualities and a murder victim is never entirely compensated for his untimely death. However, although more in keeping with Davies's rhetoric of dualism, this book stands as an exception, throwing into relief the otherwise dominant structural rule that good is to be elicited from evil. In a manifestation of T.S. Eliot's observation that "the more perfect the artist, the more completely separate in him will be the man who suffers and the mind which creates" (479), Davies's comic sensibility in his fiction subdues his declared dualism.

---

1 See also Davies's earlier comments on his dualism (*One Half* 208).

F I V E

"Walking on One Leg":
On Christianity's Neglect
of the Feminine

In addition to faulting the Augustinian-Thomistic doctrine of evil as the *privatio boni* and the concomitant insistence that humans must strive for perfection, Davies simultaneously impugns Christianity's neglect of women:

> my complaint about Christianity is the fact that it does not come to grips with certain basic problems. One is sexuality and the other is evil. Christian teaching on both those points, it seems to me, is inadequate. ("Conversations")

Subsequently, he maintains that "Unless Christianity can reconcile itself to women as it has not done up to now, I don't see how it can continue to maintain its hold over thoughtful people" ("Art" 30). However, whereas Davies's professed dualism concerning good and evil is ultimately overwhelmed in his fiction by his comic vision, his call for a sweeping transformation of Christianity's attitude towards feminine values is significantly substantiated in his novels.

The statements cited above, from 1975 and 1986 interviews respectively, are not only timely assertions within the context of current feminist debate, but also confirmation of Davies's position on an issue that had increasingly engaged him over the preceding decades. His 1949 review of *The White Goddess* by Robert Graves attests to the longevity of his interest; characterizing this work as "the strangest and most fascinating book that I have ever read," and identifying it as "likely to be a book of permanent value," Davies writes:

> Who, pray, is the White Goddess? She is, [Graves] says, the original Triple Deity who was worshipped throughout the whole

of Europe long before the gods of Olympus were dreamed of; she was the goddess whose worship was dominant in that immensely distant past when civilization was not patriarchal, but matriarchal. . . . Christianity, he says, contains not one single original element except the personality of Jesus himself; all else is Judaic, or Olympian, or perversion of the original worship of the White Goddess, who was given a somewhat inferior place in Christian worship as the Virgin Mary. But Christianity is essentially a religion which exalts the male above the female, and that is directly contrary to the rule of the Goddess. ("From the Critic's Notebook")

Two years after this review of Graves's book, Davies's first novel, *Tempest-Tost*, very briefly acknowledged Christianity's masculine character when the Anglican cathedral's organist, Humphrey Cobbler, jocosely observes: " 'You can't have women in Church choirs; they sour the Communion wine, or something' " (188). In 1958, this was echoed more seriously in *A Mixture of Frailties* with respect to Monica Gall's role at the final Bridgetower sermon in the cathedral: "She was not to walk with the choir in procession: no women — apparently it was another Anglican caprice. 'You're to be clearly heard but not clearly seen,' Cobbler had said . . ." (371–72).

Yet this is not an isolated reference to the masculinity of the Anglican rite, for the late Mrs. Bridgetower's instructions concerning her funeral constitute another, more important manifestation of this theme in *A Mixture of Frailties*:

She had attended many funerals in her time, and had been unfavourably impressed by the fact that what the Prayer Book had to say about death seemed to apply chiefly to men. A feminist of a dignified sort all her life, she felt that the funeral service lacked the feminine touch, and she had arranged for this to be supplied at her own burial. She had specified that a certain piece of music be sung, and that it be sung by a female voice. She admired, she said in her last letter to her son, the fine choir of men and boys which Mr. Cobbler had made so great an adornment of St. Nicholas', but at her funeral she wanted a woman to sing. . . . (3)

While both Cobbler and the cathedral's Dean question her choice of *My Task*, "E.L. Ashford's lovely setting of Maude Louise Ray's dear and inspiring poem" (3), Mrs. Bridgetower's initial premise remains unchallenged. This proves significant since her recognition that feminine elements need to be injected into the masculine ceremony eventually produces the novel's central story. Only through her insistence that a woman sing at her funeral are the embryonic talents of Monica Gall brought to the attention of the Bridgetower Trust's executors. In turn, this ultimately results in funding for the young woman's musical apprenticeship in Europe.

Just as Mrs. Bridgetower attempts in her way to compensate for the masculinity of religion, so, too, does Davies when he focuses, albeit briefly, on the figure of a female saint, arguably one of the few feminine elements conceded by Christianity. Confused and anguished by her travails in England, Monica Gall is sent to the continent for recuperation and further artistic and social instruction. While in Paris, still bewildered by the demands of her new experiences abroad, she tours the city in an attempt to attain some resolution of her difficulties or at least bring order to her turmoil. She first visits the Panthéon, the temple to Reason, where she is repelled by "the grey, courteous unfriendliness of its barren stones" and is forced to depart after only five minutes, since "everywhere the bleak, naked horror of enthroned Reason was ghastly palpable" (247). Fleeing this chilly reception, she enters the church of Saint Étienne du Mont, which instead nurtures the emotions — "Here was feeling, and feeling was reality." Almost immediately Gall senses her new environment's therapeutic qualities: "She was warmed and soothed by the dark splendour, and some of the pain in her head — the fullness and muddle — began to go away" (247).

The climax of her visit to the church is her experience at the grave of Saint Geneviève, the patroness of Paris, where an emphasis on the emotions becomes strongly congruent with the figure of this female saint. Two occurrences here reinforce the dichotomy already established between reason, associated with the Panthéon, and emotion, prompted by the church generally: Gall's observation of a woman tearfully praying at Geneviève's crypt and the sacristan's intelligence that the tomb had been originally housed in the Panthéon, burned when that building was rededicated to reason, and afterwards brought to Saint Étienne in the form of ashes and relics, " 'when all that foolishness was over' " (248). Consequently, although Gall's Thirteener background precludes the consideration of saints, Geneviève's remains enhance the beneficial emotional response the church has already elicited from her. This prompts a passionate appeal:

with a sense of awe and wonder that she had never known, Monica went to the tomb and, when no one was near, knelt and stretched her hand through the grille.

"Help me," she prayed, touching the smooth stone, "I can't think; I can't clarify; I don't know what I want. Help me to do what is right — *no*! Help me — Help me — ." (248)

Gall's experience in the church appears to have several consequences. Later that afternoon, "she seemed in splendid spirits" (248), and upon her return to London, she discovers that the composer, Giles Revelstoke, has prepared Coleridge's "Kubla Khan" for her to perform. This represents a potentially modest advance both in her relationship with Revelstoke and in her musical apprenticeship, so at the news of this good fortune, Gall wonders: "Oh, Saint Geneviève, was this your doing?" (249).

Yet, while the episode with Saint Geneviève is one of the book's memorable moments, its significance in *A Mixture of Frailties* should not be overemphasized, particularly in light of its more significant parallels in Davies's later writings. This incident is not nearly as paramount, for example, as Dunstan Ramsay's battlefield vision (Radford, "Apprentice" 17), or Simon Darcourt's sudden infatuation with Maria Theotoky, both of which are not only intense but also pivotal moments in their respective novels. What *is* notable about the scene at the tomb, however, and indeed about the unorthodox funeral arrangements of Louisa Bridgetower, is that these mark an increase in Davies's concern with the issue of gender and religion, from his one brief reference in *Tempest-Tost* to his complete silence in *Leaven of Malice*. As such, these two episodes from *A Mixture of Frailties* are precursors of much that is to come.

A brief digression here will illuminate the background and extent of Davies's expanding concern with the place of the feminine in Christianity. The Old Testament personifies Wisdom (the Hebrew *chokmah* or *hokhmah*; *sophia* in Greek) in feminine terms; so, for instance, Proverbs states: "Wisdom crieth without; she uttereth her voice in the streets" (1.20) and "She is more precious than rubies" (3.15).[1] It also presents her as a largely benevolent force: "Forsake her not, and she shall preserve thee: love her, and she shall keep

---

[1] Even in the New Testament Christ states, "But wisdom is justified of her children" (Matthew 11.19).

thee. . . . Exalt her, and she shall promote thee: she shall bring thee to honour, when thou dost embrace her" (4.6, 8). The apocryphal (for Protestants and Jews) Book of Wisdom describes her as "beneficent" and "humane" (7.23) and "a kindly spirit" (1.6). Portrayed as a creative principle — "The Lord by wisdom hath founded the earth" (Proverbs 3.19); "wisdom [is] the fashioner of all things" (Wisdom 7.22) — she is very ancient:

The Lord possessed me [wisdom] in the beginning of his way, before his works of old. I was set up from everlasting, from the beginning, or ever the earth was. When there were no depths, I was brought forth; when there were no fountains abounding with water. (Proverbs 8.22–24)

Wisdom is constantly with God, pleasing him: "I was daily his delight, rejoicing always before him" (Proverbs 8.30); "She glorifies her noble birth by living with God, and the Lord of all loves her" (Wisdom 8.3).

This Old Testament female entity is an important survivor after "Prophets and priests in Judaea did all they could to represent Yahveh as exclusively male and to delete all traces of the primeval matriarchy" (Quispel, "Gnosticism" 568). Jung argues that in our Christocentric, New-Testament world the feminine element embodied in this figure persists — notwithstanding the predominantly masculine orientation of Christianity — in the person of the Blessed Virgin (*Collected* 18: 1552; 11: 625), and he underscores Mary's importance by asserting that her exclusion from the traditional Trinity renders it incomplete:

The third element . . . the connecting link between "Father" and "Son," is spirit and not a human figure. The masculine father-son relationship is thus lifted out of the natural order (which includes mothers and daughters) and translated to a sphere from which the feminine element is excluded: . . . in Christianity the Theotokos[1] stands outside the Trinity. (11: 197)

Jung also chronicles early attempts to remedy this: "Medieval iconology . . . evolved a quaternity symbol in its representations of the

---

1 i.e., "the one who gave birth to God" (Wilken 373).

coronation of the Virgin and surreptitiously put it in place of the Trinity" (11: 251). Consequently, he applauds the 1950 papal pronouncement concerning the Assumption of Mary:

> ... the Pope has recently announced the dogma of the *Assumptio Mariae*, very much to the astonishment of all rationalists. Mary as the bride is united with the son in the heavenly bridal-chamber, and, as Sophia, with the Godhead. (11: 743)

> ... among the many articles published in the Catholic and Protestant press on the declaration of the dogma, there was not one, so far as I could see, which laid anything like the proper emphasis on what was undoubtedly the most powerful motive: namely, the popular movement and the psychological need behind it. Essentially, the writers of the articles were satisfied with learned considerations, dogmatic and historical, which have no bearing on the living religious process. But anyone who has followed with attention the visions of Mary which have been increasing in number over the last few decades, and has taken their psychological significance into account, might have known what was brewing. The fact, especially, that it was largely children who had the visions might have given pause for thought, for in such cases the collective unconscious is always at work. Incidentally, the Pope himself is rumoured to have had several visions of the Mother of God on the occasion of the declaration. One could have known for a long time that there was a deep longing in the masses for an intercessor and mediatrix who would at last take her place alongside the Holy Trinity and be received as the "Queen of Heaven and Bride at the heavenly court." For more than a thousand years it had been taken for granted that the Mother of God dwelt there, and we know from the Old Testament that Sophia was with God before the creation. (11: 748)

In 1959, the year after both the publication of *A Mixture of Frailties* and his decisive acceptance of Jung's tenets (Peterman 116), Davies reviewed Jung's *Answer to Job*, the work that contains the psychologist's most complete discussion of the need for feminine elements in Christianity. Davies asserts that Jung considers

> the declaration by the late Pope Pius XII of the Dogma of the Assumption of the Virgin Mary, in 1950, ... to be the most

important religious event since the Reformation. "It leaves Protestantism with the odium of being nothing but a man's religion, which allows no metaphysical representation of a woman", says he [11: 753]. . . . I, a Protestant by education and long tradition, find his argument amply convincing. ("Answer to Job")

Yet in his final book, his 1961 autobiography *Memories, Dreams, Reflections,* Jung qualifies his previous encomiums for the recently enhanced status of Mary by identifying it as only a "partial recognition" of the feminine principle (202). In an interview with Tom Harpur over a decade later, himself still troubled by the general exclusion of female elements from much of Christian belief, Davies expands the sentiments he expressed in his review of *Answer to Job*:

> The trouble with Christianity is that it's too Hebraically based with its single Father God and its masculine Saviour. We've got to get rid of that fearful masculine insistence if we're going to have a religion which is a workable, comforting and dear one to humanity at large.
>
> We've got to stop pounding away at the Logos idea (word, reason) and do some serious thinking about the Eros principle; i.e. the principle of love and relationship as women know it, instead of a frosty, disembodied love of God which seems so often to exercise itself in such horrifying ways. (*Conversations* 138–39)

To the paucity of metaphysical representation of women, Davies offers his answer in the Deptford trilogy — mainly *Fifth Business*, but with corroborating information provided in both *The Manticore* and *World of Wonders.* Mary Dempster is the creative offspring born of the synthesis of Davies's own interest in hagiology — evidenced in the already-cited Saint Geneviève episode — and the emphasis on the Blessed Virgin that he discovered in Jung's writings. As such, Mrs. Dempster is the quintessential incarnation of the "Jungian idea," which Davies outlined in his interview with Tom Harpur and subsequently augmented in conversation with Bronwyn Drainie:

> a man's brain works on a kind of logos line, [so] that law and order and rule and logic and precedent are enormously important to him, and the women are more inclined to function on

the eros principle which means that they would consider every case as a particular case and that, on the whole, they are less rigid and conformist in their attitude toward the important things of life. (*Conversations* 180)

Elsewhere, he puts it more succinctly: "Man understands Law, but . . . Woman understands Mercy" (*One Half* 41).

As the embodiment of the eros principle, Mary Dempster elicits considerable, often hostile, attention from the logos-oriented community in which she lives. In Deptford, where even the relative cleanliness of privies constitutes a type of social hierarchy (*Fifth* 18), she transgresses because her house is decidedly untidy; yet her mildness and ingenuous affection establish her parsonage as an oasis in which Dunstan Ramsay finds respite from the often chilly Presbyterian ethos of his own home — indeed, he regards his friendship with Mrs. Dempster as "the tap-root that fed my life" (53). The town largely ignores her considerable solicitude for her son Paul, noting merely that the boy is unkempt and his clothing needs mending (40). Her charity, particularly before it comes to be manifest in giving useless gifts, may be considered exemplary by biblical standards — "Mrs. Dempster gave away everything" (28) — but instead, this increasingly effects her social quarantine in a thrifty town comprised of "the descendants of hard-bitten pioneers" (25). Her isolation extends even to her own home, for in *World of Wonders* Paul attests that, unlike her logos-motivated husband who endorses the old Hebraic rules prescribing harsh discipline for children, she eschews those actions that eventually contribute to the boy's departure:

"My father was no brute, and I think he hated beating me, but he knew his duty. 'He that spareth his rod hateth his son; but he that loveth him chasteneth him betimes'; this was part of the prayer that always preceded a beating and he laid the rod on hard, while my mother wept or — this was very much worse, and indeed quite horrible — laughed sadly as if at something my father and I did not and could not know." (47)

In commenting on the qualities of his character, Davies is unequivocal:

"Mrs. Dempster is exactly the kind of woman who would have been considered a saint in an earlier period. . . . But at the time of the novel, her saintly qualities are put down to her simple-mindedness. She also had the disadvantage of living in a small Ontario town where non-conformity can be dealt with viciously." (qtd. in Campau 58)

The culmination of Mary Dempster's anti-logos conduct is her palpably erotic behaviour — in Davies's sense of the term — when she copulates with a vagabond in the gravel pit. Yet, although this offence against rigid "standards of decency" constitutes her social nadir in Deptford (49), for after this her isolation within the community is almost total, we later discover that Mary Dempster's unconventional act has miraculously transformed the tramp, Joel Surgeoner. Originally fleeing his father, who as " 'hard and mean-religious' " is unquestionably a logos sort (134), he had become a dissolute drifter. Only the " 'great mercy of that woman' " wrests him from his depraved existence and returns him to God (135): in contrast to his father, and to the world that shuns him, she speaks amicably, and when he indicates that only sex will " 'put me right,' " she compassionately assents (135). Surgeoner summarizes the transforming moment using evangelical language:

> ". . . it was glory come into my life. It was as if I had gone right down into Hell and through the worst of the fire, and come on a clear, pure pool where I could wash and be clean. . . . Our Lord. . . . worked through that woman, and she is a blessed saint, for what she did for me — I mean it as I say it — was a miracle." (135–36)

Davies thus cogently establishes his views about eros, mercy, and the concomitant eschewing of social mores, since his character willingly transgresses one of Deptford's most rigid taboos in order to provide solace — indeed, redemption — to a fellow creature.

Having established her eros credentials, so to speak, Mary Dempster increasingly comes to comprise the raw material that Dunstan Ramsay will translate from the mundane to the metaphysical, symbolic realm. Soon after her encounter with the tramp, the boy observes that she disregards her wretched state within the community and exists in oblivious comfort, living by "a light that arose from within; I could not comprehend it, except that it seemed to be somewhat akin to the splendours I found in books, though not in any way bookish" (52–53). To the scandal of his family and the community at large, her star soars for Ramsay when she performs the apparent miracle of raising his brother Willie from the dead — ironically, so that Willie may be preserved to die in war, another "Logos-created problem" (*Conversations* 124).

Later, while himself a combatant, Ramsay is gravely injured, but his extraordinary vision of what he assumes to be the crowned woman of Revelation sustains him. Thus occurs a major confluence of many of Davies's and Jung's concerns with the slighting of the feminine by religion: neglect the female — as Christianity may — and it will nonetheless still surface because of "psychological need" (*Collected* 11: 748). So Ramsay, the erstwhile Presbyterian, joins numerous children and apparently Pope Pius xii himself in having a salutary vision of the Blessed Virgin,[1] although in his case her face has acquired the features of Mary Dempster.

During his subsequent coma, "the little Madonna appeared and looked at [him] with friendly concern" (78); Ramsay proposes this as a probable cause for his eventual recovery (79). That he recognizes the possibility of these visitations originating from an inner prompting — as does Jung when he equates visions of the Virgin Mary with the collective unconscious (11: 748) — is evident when Ramsay twice rejects his nurse's conventional religious interpretation of them (82, 92). Many years later, the Bollandist Padre Blazon vindicates Ramsay's steadfastness on this point, advising him: " 'If she appeared to save you on the battlefield, as you say, it has just as much to do with you as it has with her — much more probably.' " Echoing Jung's emphasis on the psychological over the dogmatic import of Mary (11: 748), Blazon maintains that " 'you must find your answer in psychological truth, not in objective truth' " (177).

The three miracles that Ramsay attributes to Mrs. Dempster inaugurate his lifelong study of saints, an endeavour that concurrently involves a search for the feminine in religion. His exploration is both initiated by a woman, the "saintly" Mrs. Dempster, and conducted as a general quest for a woman: "The little Madonna was a bee in my bonnet; I wanted to see her again, and . . . I kept hoping to find her" (123). The one saint-seeking journey he describes in any detail is the pursuit of a canonized maiden, Uncumber or Wilgefortis.

---

1 The Blessed Virgin is, in fact, associated with the crowned woman of Revelation in Roman Catholic doctrine and art (Kealy 167); the iconography for the two is very similar (Radford, "Great Mother" 68).

Even Ramsay's seemingly flippant characterization of his general inquiry indicates a quest for the feminine: "I ... began to *whore* after rare and difficult saints" (124, emphasis added).

Later, when Ramsay slightly shifts his focus to analyse the psychological nature of faith — part of his ongoing effort "to carry the work of William James a step further" (161) — his concerns with the feminine remain in the fore. Visiting the shrine of the Virgin of Guadalupe to gather material for his book, Ramsay sees its portrait of Mary — apparently bestowed on a sixteenth-century peasant whom she visited — which has become the object of numerous pilgrimages. The eros principle is palpably evident here:

> The picture was not my chief concern. . . . My eyes were on the kneeling petitioners, whose faces had the beauty virtually every face reveals in the presence of the goddess of mercy,[1] the Holy Mother, the figure of divine compassion. Very different, these, from the squinnying, lip-biting, calculating faces of the art lovers one sees looking at Madonnas in galleries. (199)

Subsequently, Davies sustains the novel's emphasis on faith and the feminine when Ramsay and Padre Blazon discuss Mrs. Dempster and the soon-to-be canonized Bertilla Boscardin. Both women provided mercy to hospital patients during World War I, in spite of being "fool saints" lacking that worldly prudence that Father Regan, Deptford's priest, claims is essential for true sainthood (138–39). Each enjoys the sort of transcendent comprehension prescribed by Saint Paul — "If any man among you seemeth to be wise in this world, let him become a fool, that he may be wise" (1 Corinthians 3.18) — and which Blazon characterizes as " 'that special perception that St Bonaventura spoke of as beyond the power of even the wisest scholar' " (248). The novel reaffirms this when Ramsay finally finds his statue of the little Madonna. In a final, succinct summary of the eros qualities of a metaphysical female figure, Ramsay writes:

> was it truly the face of Mary Dempster? No, it was not, though the hair was very like; Mary Dempster, whose face my mother

---

1 This is a strange term to employ in the context of a monotheistic religion. It is perhaps Davies echoing Jung's use of the term *goddess* when, for example, the psychologist celebrates what he sees as the inclusion of Mary as an equal in the Trinity (*Collected* 11: 252).

had described as being like a pan of milk, had never been so beautiful in feature, but the expression was undeniably hers — an expression of mercy and love, tempered with perception and penetration. (251)

Between A Mixture of Frailties and Fifth Business, Davies's exploration of the need for feminine elements in religion exhibits not only the quantitative shift examined above, but also a significant change in focus. The message he promotes in the former novel is that a female presence needs to be infused into, or reemphasized by, Christianity in order to meet the requirements of its women members: thus, Mrs. Bridgetower receives a less masculine funeral service and Monica Gall discovers a helpful female saint. By the time he wrote Fifth Business, Davies's reasoning had become more complex: since he had by then been immersed in Jungian thought for over a decade, he shows that for men also the presence of female attributes is essential in the doctrine and symbolism of religion. What he compellingly illuminates in this first novel of the trilogy, he gives theoretical underpinning in the second. David Staunton's Jungian anamnesis in The Manticore clearly illustrates that because all men have an anima — " 'the feminine part of your nature' " (165) — they are to some extent psychologically androgynous; accordingly, their feminine component has to be recognized and nurtured (165–66). Any religion that fails to do this is by implication, then, deficient in meeting the fundamental psychological needs of its male as well as its female adherents.

Although Davies alters his focus on the issue of gender and faith when he moves from the Salterton to the Deptford trilogy, it remains largely unchanged in the subsequent Cornish books. However, while his emphasis is essentially the same, his tone in the first of these novels differs. Because the often severe Dunstan Ramsay has now given way as narrator to the merrier Simon Darcourt and Maria Theotoky, The Rebel Angels is, on the whole, a more mirthful, frolicsome book; as a corollary of this, Davies here maintains a more playful attitude toward the feminine in religion. While no less committed, having already established his beliefs Davies can now render them more blithely without the fear of compromising his fundamental message.

One indication of this change is his main female character's conspicuously peculiar name. While "Mary Dempster" can — given its possessor's actions — invoke comparison with the Blessed Virgin, it remains believable in its own right; in contrast, the symbolism of "Maria Magdalena Theotoky" appears outrageously overt. Davies clearly intends this, since he immediately exploits the name's transparency. Before we are ten pages into the story, John Parlabane has twice emphasized its unusual quality. He first remarks: " 'what a contrast! Theotoky — with the accent firmly on the first "o" — linked with the name of the sinner out of whom Our Lord cast seven devils. . . . That name — Theotoky — means the bringer of God, doesn't it?' " (5–6). Not one to let the matter drop, the waggish Parlabane underscores this four pages later: " 'With your beautiful name — Maria, the Motherhood of God — you must be filled with understanding and forgiveness' " (10). Davies soon enhances the redolent transcendence of the name. We discover that Maria is, appropriately, enrolled in the New-Testament Greek seminar of Simon Darcourt, vice-warden of Ploughwright College, who describes her in these terms: "She was beyond doubt a great beauty, though it was beauty of a kind not everybody would notice, or like, and which I suspected did not appeal greatly to her contemporaries. A calm, transfixing face, of the kind one sees in an ikon, or a mosaic portrait . . ." (17).

As a further means of providing humour in the novel, Davies fuses this too obvious symbolism with his belief that men yearn for a feminine presence in religion. Through a clever reversal of biblical metaphysics, the flesh is made word: Darcourt, an Anglican priest, falls hopelessly in love with Maria Theotoky because for him this conspicuously named, iconic-featured graduate student becomes a universal expression of those female qualities largely absent in Christian cosmology. In what may be a comic equivalent of Dunstan Ramsay's battlefield metamorphosis of the Blessed Virgin, he transforms Maria into "Sophia":

I had decided that Maria was a revelation, and such a revelation that I hardly dare to set it down even for my own eyes. . . . [The Gnostic] notion of Sophia seized upon my mind because it suited some ideas that I had tentatively and fearfully developed of my own accord.

I like women, and the lack of a feminine presence in Christianity has long troubled me. . . . [T]he elaborate edifice of doctrine we call [Christ's] church offers no woman in authority — only a Trinity made up, to put it profanely, of two men and a bird — and even the belated amends offered to Mary by the

Church of Rome does not undo the mischief. The Gnostics did better than that; they offered their followers Sophia. (235)

Darcourt's infatuation with Sophia is to some extent an elaboration of what now proves to be a prototypal episode in an earlier Davies story. In "When Satan Goes Home for Christmas," the author himself converses with the Devil in Massey College — the model from which Darcourt's Ploughwright is fashioned in *The Rebel Angels*. They speak near the chapel's seventeenth-century Russian reredos, and Davies describes his response when his diabolical interlocutor asks him what he desires:

> my eyes . . . were fixed on the reredos. At the extreme of the third row of pictures is one that very few people recognize. It is a symbol so extraordinary, so deep in significance and broad in application that even Professor Marshall McLuhan has not been able to explode it. It is the Santa Sophia, the Ultimate Wisdom.[1] (*High Spirits* 61)

This saint of Massey College fame is the "legendary mother of the virgin martyrs Faith, Hope and Charity. . . . [Her] story seems to have come from the East and is thought to be an allegorical explanation of the cult of the Divine Wisdom, from whom proceed faith, hope and charity" (*Book of Saints* 518). It is strictly the Eastern genesis of this Christianized symbol that engages the besotted, middle-aged Darcourt in his obsession with Sophia. She is the Gnostic development of the Old Testament figure which the priest initially discovered through his study of the canonical and apocryphal Bible:

> Sophia, the feminine personification of God's Wisdom. . . . Sophia, through whom God became conscious of himself. Sophia, by whose agency the universe was brought to completion, a partner in Creation. Sophia — in my eyes at least — through whom the chill glory of the patriarchal God becomes the embracing splendour of a completed World Soul. (*Rebel* 235–36)

---

1 This figure does exist in the Massey chapel in a row of pictures largely devoted to Mary. The icon resembles the Virgin with child: both mother and baby have haloes, and gold lines extending towards the perimeter of the defining circle illuminate the picture.

Yet Sophia's "embracing splendour" proves to be much more than this. Just as Mary Dempster's merciful copulation with the tramp in Deptford's gravel pit contributes to her being linked to the Blessed Virgin, so is Maria's being "had" by Clem Hollier on his rickety old office couch partially the basis of Darcourt's transformation of her into Sophia. The apocryphal book of Wisdom, one of the biblical texts that forms the centre of Darcourt's academic endeavours (235), presents a Sophia who is the object of the sort of physical yearning we normally associate with the Song of Solomon: "I loved her and sought her from my youth; I desired to take her for my bride, and became enamored of her beauty" (Wisdom 8.2). However, it is the Gnostic apotheosis of this that utterly enraptures Darcourt — "this is where my scholarly madness shows" (236) — and he envisions Maria as the

"fallen Sophia" who put on mortal flesh and sank at last to being a whore in a brothel in Tyre, from which she was rescued by the Gnostic Simon Magus.[1] I myself think of that as the Passion of Sophia, for did she not assume flesh and suffer a shameful fate for the redemption of mankind? It was this that led the Gnostics to hail her both as Wisdom and also as the *anima mundi*, the World Soul, who demands redemption and, in order to achieve it, arouses desire. Well, was not Maria's name Theotoky — the Motherhood of God? . . . [This] was to me a sign, an assurance that my Maria was, perhaps for me alone, a messenger of special grace and redemption. (236)

Further, Darcourt suggests that he needs Maria for "the completion of [his] soul" (235), which also pertains to the Gnostic Sophia, for according to the modern *gnosis* begun by Jakob Boehme,

In addition to Christ . . . [is] the feminine Sophia, a goddess (the Holy Spirit?) and bride to the wise man. To become like Adam before the birth of Eve from his side, man must unite with his inner Sophia and become androgynous. (Quispel, "Sophia" 417)

Finally, completing the synthesis of Maria with his need for a feminine element in his faith, Darcourt concludes:

---

1 See Jonas for further elaboration of Darcourt's information (104–09).

For me Maria was wholeness, the glory and gift of God and also the dark earth as well, so foreign to the conventional Christian mind. The Persians believed that when a man dies he meets his soul in the form of a beautiful woman who is also infinitely old and wise, and this was what seemed to have happened to me, living though I undoubtedly was.

It is a terrible thing for an intellectual when he encounters an idea as a reality, and that was what I had done. (236)

Ultimately, after he undergoes a number of comically depicted travails — best typified, perhaps, by his ambitious attempt to diet — Darcourt's metaphysical disorientation is remedied: he returns Sophia to the symbolic realm, relinquishes Maria to be married to Arthur Cornish, and, no longer peevishly compelled by a supramundane infatuation to make slender his "pudgy body" (251), again merrily patronizes his larder. One can only assume, however, that the priest's objection to the scarcity of female elements in Christianity continues unabated.

Most of the ideas concerning the feminine in religion explored in *What's Bred in the Bone* will not seem new. However, like no other Davies novel, this story cogently unites the tripartite examination of the specifics of man's psychological constitution, his ensuing emotional yearning, and his resultant appeal to metaphysical symbolism. As such, the book provides Davies's most inclusive summary of the essential interrelationship between feminine qualities and religious belief.

In his youth, Francis Cornish unwittingly acknowledges the female present in all men by secretly dressing as a woman. He is, in the words of his omniscient — and hermaphrodite — Daimon Maimas, *"looking for The Girl, the girl deep in himself, the feminine ideal that has some sort of existence in every man of any substance. . . . Francis . . . yearn[s] to know the feminine side of his own nature, in order that he might be a complete and spiritually whole man"* (148–49). The external correlative of this inner search is the boy's longing for his mother, a seldom-present, and so frequently idealized, figure in his life. As such, Davies is simply reworking those interrelationships he explicated in *The Manticore*; his new departure in *What's Bred in the Bone* is to link these associated phenomena directly with specific religious symbolism.

To the dismay of Cornish's Catholic Aunt, Mary-Ben — and consistent with Jung's and Davies's characterization of Protestantism

107

as having "the odium of being nothing but a *man's religion* which allows no metaphysical representation of a woman" (*Collected* 11: 753; "Answer to Job") — the young boy's Anglican parents tell him nothing about the Virgin Mary: "As for the Holy Mother, friend and guardian of children, Francis had never heard of her" (90). However, when his parents send him to reside in St. Kilda, the house of his Catholic grandparents, his aunt determines to remedy this deficiency through the sheer force of constant iteration. The rosary plays an initial and significant part in her strategy, and even before Cornish has made the journey to his new domicile, Mary-Ben surreptitiously introduces it to him:

"It's called a rosary, dear, because it's a rose-garden of prayer. It's the garden of Jesus' dear Mother, and when we say our prayers with it, we are very near Her, and we may even see Her sweet face. But this is our secret, dear. Don't say anything to Daddy." (80)

Once her nephew is safely ensconced in St. Kilda's under her tutelage, Mary-Ben begins her proselytizing work in earnest, giving Cornish a rosary of his own (98) and daily saying it "at its full length, with Francis, who [soon] knew it by heart" (119). She augments this with "many a wondrous story about the mercy of God's Mother, as she had seen it evinced in the visible world" (98).

Epitomizing Davies's beliefs, Cornish embraces the metaphysical figure of the Blessed Virgin when, bullied at school and ignored by his mother, he needs a female, eros figure. For instance, it is "during the trouble of the black eye" that he receives his rosary, and at this time his Aunt also counsels that "you could always go to Her . . . when you were troubled" (98). When Mary-Ben further underscores the importance of Mary through religious art, Davies concurrently emphasizes the relationship between this symbol and Cornish's yearning for the feminine:

one day Francis found a large oleograph of Mary hanging in his room; it was a reproduction of a Murillo, and, contrary to what might have been expected, he liked it very much. Its soft beauty reminded him of his own mother, whom he saw so rarely, and he listened with interest as Aunt explained how tender and kind the Mother of God was, and how watchful of the fate of little boys. . . . Francis had never heard of anybody's mother at St. Alban's [Anglican Church], when he went there with his parents.

But he was open to stories about someone who pitied those who were in distress, and increasingly he was in distress. (91–92)

Subsequently, when Cornish again suffers, both emotionally and bodily (117–19), Mary-Ben offers him metaphysical expressions of those feminine qualities he so desires. Among the portraits that she shows him is one of the Virgin of Consolation: "see the poor soul who has lost her baby, comforted by the Holy Mother ... this [is a] truly sacred picture that assures us of the Virgin's mercy" (121). Similarly, the other religious painting she provides for his bedroom is entitled *St. Veronica's Napkin,* "because you know, dear, that when Our Lord stumbled and fell on the terrible walk to Calvary, St. Veronica wiped His dear Face with her napkin ... and lo! His Image was imprinted on it forever" (122).

Indeed, Mary-Ben so feminizes the Christianity she introduces to her nephew that its masculine-logos elements are rather eclipsed at times. While not sharing Dr. J.A. Jerome's open hostility to Jesus — " 'Far better the Blessed Mother than that Son of hers. I never knew a boy yet that I'd trust who really took to that searching, seeking fella' " (92) — she sometimes appears to neglect Him in favour of Mary. When she does consider Christ, she envisions a male equivalent of his merciful mother, a sympathetic figure whose wounds are opened by the "naughty" actions of his earthly children (97). Nowhere in her religious instruction does she remark, for instance, the Jesus who dealt so sternly with the vendors and money-changers at the temple (John 2.14–16), or who cursed the unproductive fig tree (Mark 11.13–14, 21). Discussion of His severe, irascible Father is also noticeably absent from Mary-Ben's lessons. Given its emphasis on the qualities of eros, the religion Mary-Ben teaches to young Cornish is aptly described as "the sweet Catholicism of Mary-Ben rather than that of the rigorous Church Fathers" (431).

The eminence Mary-Ben's religious metaphysics accords to feminine qualities endures into her nephew's post-Catholic adult years. In addition to Mary, the more conventionally erotic figure of Venus in the Bronzino painting *Allegory of Time* becomes central to his life. The explanation of the painting by Cornish's mentor in art, Tancred Saraceni, again addresses the relationship between an individual's general psychological configuration and the symbolism he or she values. Saraceni asserts: " 'What is a picture of the Madonna ... but a picture of a Mother and her Son.' " To his student's ensuing qualifications, " 'A Holy Mother and the Son of God,' " he retorts:

"In the worlds of myth and art all mothers are holy because that is what we feel in the depths of our hearts. No, not the heart. . . . During the Renaissance they would have said, the liver. In the gut, in fact. Worship of the Mother, real or mythical, comes from the gut. . . . [O]ne of the unspoken foundation stones of our mighty Faith . . . [is] the love affair between Mother and Son, and according to the Scriptures no other woman ever challenged her place of supremacy. But in these Madonnas [i.e., pictures] there is nothing overtly erotic. There is in Bronzino. . . ." (313–14)[1]

In a different, more Jungian fashion, Ruth Nibsmith emphasizes this same importance of the feminine principle in one's psychological makeup. When she discloses Cornish's horoscope, she contends that his peculiar astrological alignment of planets is

"a giver of spiritual power, and takes you deep into the underworld, the dream world, what Goethe called the realm of the Mothers. There's a fad now for calling them the Archetypes, because it sounds so learned and scientific. But the Mothers is truer to what they really are. The Mothers are the creators, the matrixes of all human experience." (370)

Jung terms this underworld "the unconscious," and maintains that a woman, the anima figure, personifies it in men (*Psychology* 35, 91). More specifically, as F.L. Radford notes, "the underworld of the unconscious . . . is symbolized in Jungian terms as the Mother ("Great Mother" 69). Of paramount importance for *What's Bred in the Bone*, both Ruth Nibsmith and the Lesser Zadkiel, the book's narrator, declare that art originates in this realm of the Mothers (*What's Bred* 370, 501).

---

1 In his joint emphasis on the Madonna and Venus, Cornish — like Dunstan Ramsay with Mary Dempster, and Simon Darcourt with Maria-Sophia — combines the sexual and the maternal in his metaphysics of the feminine. Thus Davies depicts in his own work a concept he had acknowledged many years earlier in that of Robert Graves. In his review of *The White Goddess*, Davies notes that Graves identifies two manifestations of the goddess: the Maiden or Beloved and the Mother. Dr. Johanna von Haller, the Jungian analyst in *The Manticore*, describes the anima to David Staunton in very similar terms. However, the hag or layer out of dead, the third major incarnation of the figure described by Graves — and von Haller (*Manticore* 165–66) — is notably and inexplicably absent as a symbol of any importance in Davies's fiction.

The culmination of the novel's recurring scrutiny of psychological configuration and its relationship to the central character's personal yearning is Cornish's masterpiece, *The Marriage at Cana*, a painting in which — as one might by now logically expect — a metaphysical feminine figure plays a central role. Prior to praising his former pupil for having " 'made up your soul in that picture' " (479), Saraceni explains that

"this is plainly a depiction, given a Christian gloss, of what was called The Chymical Wedding. The alchemical uniting of the elements of the soul, that is to say. Look at it: the Bride and Groom look like brother and sister because they are the male and female elements of a single soul, which it was one of the higher aims of alchemy to unite. . . . That such a unity is brought about by the intervention of the highest and purest element in the soul — which is, of course, what Christ has long been . . . — is plain enough. Here we see Christ as a beneficent power at the Wedding. But in this picture it is the Holy Mother — what unorthodox but not heretical thinkers sometimes call Mother Nature — who blesses the Marriage of the Soul, the achievement of spiritual union." (476)

And well she might, given the preeminent position of the mother in the underworld of the psyche, that domain whence these elements of the soul arise. The subsequent description of Cornish's picture provided in *The Lyre of Orpheus*, the final novel of the trilogy, again underscores the importance of this feminine symbol:

there was the woman who stood beside the bridal couple, the only figure in the pictured [sic] graced with a halo. The Mother of God? Yes, for the convention in which the picture was cast demanded that. But more probably the Mighty Mother of All. . . . [T]he mother of everybody and everything. . . . Her grave beauty was universal and her smile was of a serenity that rose beyond earthly considerations. (322)

Additionally affirming the recurrent stress placed on the feminine in the novel, Davies depicts the final and perhaps ultimate moment in Cornish's life in the following terms:

he dropped deeper into the gulf that was enclosing him.
     Where was this? Unknown, yet familiar, more the true abode of his spirit than he had ever known before; a place never visited,

but from which intimations had come that were the most precious gifts of his life.

It must be — it was — the Realm of the Mothers. How lucky he was, at the last, to taste this transporting wine! (*What's Bred* 523)

At this juncture Davies leaves his readers only with this brief, enticing description of the state of existence after a man's death — hinting at its possible feminine component.

Clearly this matter interests Davies, for examination of the afterlife forms the central focus of his next novel, *Murther and Walking Spirits*. While *What's Bred in the Bone* essentially concludes with the demise of its main character, this latest book commences with it, and then chronicles the subsequent experiences of the deceased Connor Gilmartin. The dead Gilmartin determines to make some sense of his predicament, so he considers an earlier discussion about the afterlife with his friend Hugh McWearie, an ex-Presbyterian minister, who as religion editor for the *Colonial Advocate* is the novel's theologian and philosopher. After exploring questions of reincarnation and the experiences of the temporarily dead who return to tell of their adventures, McWearie explains the Tibetan notion of the Eight Wrathful Ones:

"Rather like walking naked through a very long car-wash. Darkness, terrifying noise, and all the while you are slapped, spanked, squirted on from above and below and mauled and insulted until at last you emerge into the light, cleansed and humbled and ready for rebirth in whatever form you now merit." (24)

Presently, McWearie juxtaposes this frightening Far Eastern idea of the hereafter with his view of Gilmartin's more probable, benign fate:

"I doubt if it would be the same for you as for a Tibetan monk. You're a Celt, like myself. If there is a waiting-period for us after we peg out, I rather hope it will include some encounters with Arawn,[1] or Brigit, or Arianrhod, or Gwen of the Three Breasts. . . . I'd rather take my chances with a goddess than with the

---

1 Perhaps because of his enthusiasm to illustrate metaphysical manifestations of the feminine, McWearie oversteps himself. In fact, Arawn is male, the king of the underworld (Bonnefoy 261; Senior 29).

Eight Wrathful Ones. What reason have we to suppose that Ultimate Reality isn't feminine?" (24)

At Gilmartin's retort that " 'We were both brought up with a prejudice in favour of a masculine God,' " McWearie reaches the peroration of his explication: " 'That's one of the reasons why I hung up my gown and fled from the pulpit. These male Gods — damn them — all lawgivers and judges. All eternally right. . . . No, no, my lad; it is the Eternal Feminine that leads us aloft, as Goethe very finely said at the end of his eighty years' " (24).

These statements reiterate Davies's by now inevitable concern about the need for a female presence in the metaphysical realm. However, because McWearie's particular grievance is predicated on the abrupt eclipse of the traditional Celtic regard for the feminine, it introduces a very specific corollary to the recurring general theme. A Celt himself, Davies has lamented that an established Christian civilization in which women enjoyed a high status was forcibly supplanted — using religion as a justification — by a more severe society that tended to downgrade them. In "The Table Talk of Robertson Davies," he outlines the considerable rights women held under old Celtic law, and observes that "as soon as they came under the dominance of Roman law and the Catholic church, women had an awful time" (*Enthusiasms* 310). Davies recognizes this cultural dislocation in *What's Bred in the Bone* through Francis Cornish's remembrance of

> the saints of the ancient Celtic Church [who] had proclaimed Christ's gospel in a truly Celtic voice, long before the dark-skinned missionaries of Augustine had come from Rome with their Mediterranean Catholicism, to preach and impose belief with all the fanaticism of their kind. (213)

Of particular importance is that this original church comfortably assimilated much of the pagan mythology that preceded it (Cavendish 396; Roy 184–85). For instance, the Celtic Christians simply adopted as a prominent saint at least one of the goddesses McWearie identifies:

> There seems to be little real doubt that the widespread and popular cult of the pagan goddess Brigit was replaced in Christian times by the cult of the saint, doubtless identical with the goddess in more than name. The worship of this Christian Brigit,

with her curative and fertility associations, was as widespread and persistent as would be expected in the light of the earlier cult [which had venerated the goddess for the same attributes]. (Cavendish 346)

Contrast this harmonious, evolutionary religious amalgamation with Davies's view of Roman Christianity in *Murther and Walking Spirits*. In accordance with his previous assertions, he depicts Christianity violently and relentlessly displacing its pagan predecessor. As Brochwell Gilmartin contemplates the halting progress of civilization, exemplified by the recently bombed Monte Cassino near which he sits, he is piqued by the destructive behaviour the founder of the monastery had exhibited many centuries earlier:

> When Benedict — not then a saint but an energetic zealot — decided to found his monastery, he chose the place on Monte Cassino because it was the site of a temple of Apollo that had survived into the sixth century of our Christian Era. Benedict's first act was to smash the image of the god and destroy his altar. (276)

Elsewhere Davies underscores the psychological ramifications of this sort of abrupt cultural displacement, characterizing the divorce from one's roots as "spiritual suicide" (*Enthusiasms* 311). In addressing a specific contemporary instance of this, he argues:

> I think that the attempt to incorporate Eastern religious practices into the Western world is enormously suspect, because I don't think we're temperamentally and psychologically well-suited for it.
> Meditation is a good Hebrew and Christian practice, so why do you have to sit around with your legs tied up in knots saying: "O mani padme hum," which nobody understands, in order to promote spirituality? If you want to meditate no one's stopping you, but do it in a manner which is historically yours instead of kidding yourself you're an Indian. (*Conversations* 140; cf. also Jung, *Collected* 9.2: 271)

McWearie expresses essentially the same sentiments in *Murther and Walking Spirits*, concluding that " 'You can't neglect the demands of geography and race in determining what people can seriously believe' " (23).

How potentially disastrous, then, is Benedict's attempt to extirpate the foundations underlying generations of spiritual belief in order to substitute an alien faith. And, paradoxically, how — at least partially — futile; for here Davies's concern with the harm unleashed by the abrupt destruction of an indigenous religion dovetails with his — and Jung's — conviction that, suppressed as they might be, psychologically valid tenets endure. In spite of Benedict's fanatical rigour, *Murther and Walking Spirits* questions his success in totally expunging the established principles of the paganism he sought to replace. Psychological right — the focus of so much of Davies's fiction — ultimately counters a narrow and dangerous theological might:

Things are never so clear-cut as even a great sage like Benedict believes them to be. Did not his sister, later known to the pious as Saint Scholastica, set up her nunnery five miles away, and meet with her brother once a year to discuss holy matters? Hindered as it was by the difficult five-mile journey, the feminine spirit still asserted itself at Monte Cassino, and one wonders whether Apollo, wherever he was, did not smile that it was so. Even Benedict could not drive femininity out of the realm of the gods, though he might banish it five miles away from his House of God.

The light of the spirit, as Apollo knew then, and probably still knows, was not the privilege of a single sex, and Benedict and his followers had to pay a heavy price because that idea never occurred to them. Nevertheless they travelled far, walking as they did, on one leg. (277)

The compensatory psychological prosthesis to redress this amputation is, of course, much in evidence in Davies's fiction. From Saint Geneviève and the feminized funeral rite in *A Mixture of Frailties*, through the female saints and Virgin Mary in *Fifth Business*, and the figure of Theotokos-Sophia in *Rebel Angels*, to the Venus-Mary dichotomy in *What's Bred in the Bone*, and finally to the assertions of Hugh McWearie in *Murther and Walking Spirits*, Davies provides what is often deficient or underemphasized in Christianity. His work stands as a tangible expression of his conviction that the feminine simply will not be ignored in religion.

Davies's novels also anticipate the future course of human belief, demonstrating the fruition of what he has elsewhere stated in the strongest possible terms:

I think that the bringing of the feminine principle, feminine values and insights into greater prominence in Christianity will be the greatest revolution in the faith in the last 1,000 years. (*Conversations* 138)

I think that we're due for a new religious revelation. It will build on what we have, Christianity, and a lot of it will be concerned with women and women's place in society. . . . ("Conversations")

In an interview with Tom Harpur, he makes his most polemical prediction concerning the imminent direction of metaphysical religious symbolism. Not arguing simply for greater recognition of the feminine and then exemplifying this through a discussion of the Blessed Virgin, Sophia, and female saints, Davies here sets his sights higher. Expanding upon a view he had articulated in his earliest days as a newspaperman — "Gods are, after all, symbols of the ideals and aspirations of those who worship them . . ." ("New Gods for Old") — he contends:

The Jewish and Christian religions have been hard on women. When you read how Orthodox Judaism looked at women you realize what a gigantic revolution was ushered in by Jesus. Now the church needs another one. People talk about the coming of Messiah; how do they know Messiah isn't going to be a woman? It's a fair deal! (*Conversations* 139)

In addition to McWearie's rough articulation of the same sentiment — " 'What reason have we to suppose that Ultimate Reality isn't feminine?' " (24) — in another very cogent way *Murther and Walking Spirits* provides the logical culmination of Davies's belief in the need for a revolution in religious metaphysics. Previously, *A Mixture of Frailties* argued for a change based on the requirements of a congregation's female members. Complementing this, the Deptford and Cornish trilogies made a similar case but directed it to the needs of males. Davies's assertions, in these cases, were predicated almost entirely on the basis of living well in *this* world. Now, in his latest book, he looks ahead and substantiates the brief hints he offered in *The Rebel Angels* and *What's Bred in the Bone*. In the closing pages of *Murther and Walking Spirits*, the extraordinary novel that explores man's immediate posthumous condition, Davies clearly shows that we must acknowledge the transcendent feminine in order to prepare ourselves for our ultimate encounter in at least the preliminary stages of the next life. What Darcourt strongly suspects — "The Persians believed that when a man dies he meets his soul in the form of a beautiful woman who is also infinitely old and wise, and this was what seemed to have happened to me, living though I undoubtedly was" (*Rebel* 236) — and Francis Cornish briefly experiences in his dying encounter with "the Mothers" before he vanishes from *What's Bred in the Bone* (523), the deceased Connor Gilmartin confronts absolutely in the final pages of *Murther and Walking Spirits*. Here he discovers unequivocally that his immortal soul is in part female:

> [W]ho are *you*? You say I know you. Have I forgotten?
> – *Remember what McWearie said about the woman in the man?*
> – So that's who you are!
> – *None other.*
> – Like in the old morality plays my father used to teach? Are you my Good Deeds? No? Well then, should I call you Lady Soul? Don't laugh. Must I be more up-to-date? Are you my Anima?
> – *Oh, Gil. . . . Just accept what I am. Don't label me. Am I a stranger?*
> – Not now that I see you. A dear companion.
> – *Of course. Always a companion.* (356–57)

Ignoring the feminine as some faiths do would, then, constitute an unbefitting trifling with eternity.

SIX

"Preaching Selfishness": The Search for Self as a Religious Journey

"[T]he religion the world wanted from me didn't work, and it was killing me. Not physically, but spiritually. The world is full of priests who have been killed by religion, and can't, or won't, escape. So I tried scholarship, and that worked pretty well. . . . The funny thing is, the deeper I got into it, the more it began to resemble religion. The real religion, I mean. The intense yielding to what is most significant, but not always most apparent, in life." (*The Lyre of Orpheus* 428–29)

In 1958, the year he decisively embraced the tenets of C.G. Jung, Davies reviewed Jung's book *The Undiscovered Self*, writing:

Our North American feeling that mass good-doing, corporate worship, and concurrence in a body of accepted opinion is "modern" and "efficient" conceals a dread of that loneliness which a soul must encounter when it turns inward toward itself. Where may it not lead? Is there not some danger that the introspective man may find himself divorced, at least in some respects, from the warmth of the crowd? Most certainly there is such a likelihood, but Dr. Jung does not consider it a danger; he thinks it is the greatest hope of mankind. To reform the world, each man must make a beginning with himself. (*Enthusiasms* 175)

Davies underscores his point with a direct quotation from *The Undiscovered Self*:

118

"Ultimately everything depends on the quality of the individual, but the fatally short-sighted habit of our age is to think only in terms of large numbers and mass organizations. . . . I can therefore see it only as a delusion when the Churches try — as they apparently do — to rope the individual into a social organization and reduce him to a condition of diminished responsibility, instead of raising him out of the torpid, mindless mass, and making clear to him that he is the one important factor and that the salvation of the world consists in the salvation of the individual soul." (qtd. in *Enthusiasms* 175; *The Undiscovered Self* 67–69)

Davies does not speak here as a newly won convert from whose eyes the scales have recently fallen; instead, he is confirming what his own writing had expressed with increasing sophistication over the previous decade. Pop, the individualistic central character of Davies's 1948 play, *Overlaid*, warns his daughter Ethel of the consequences of emulating her mother's behaviour:

When she wasn't workin' she was up to some religious didoes at the church. Then come forty-five or fifty she broke down and had to have a spell in the bughouse. Never properly got over it. More and more religion; more and more hell-raisin' at home. Folks say I drove her crazy. It's a lie. Emotional undernourishment is what done it, and it'll do the same for you. (*Overlaid* 7)

In another play, Nicholas Hayward, the protagonist of the 1949 *Fortune my Foe*, complements this: "The only revolutions that make any real difference to the world are revolutions in the hearts of individual men" (73). And in *A Jig for the Gypsy*, written in 1954, Richard Roberts, the only honourable man associated with a nasty election campaign in nineteenth-century Wales, elaborates Hayward's assertion: "We're too much concerned nowadays with helping other people: we don't do enough to help ourselves. If a man wants to be of the greatest possible value to his fellow-creatures let him begin the long, solitary task of perfecting himself. Look within . . . look within" (85).

While these adjurations are not as directly expressed in Davies's two pre-1958 novels, both books serve in part as cautionary tales warning in a rudimentary manner about the consequences of ignoring them. When *Tempest-Tost*'s Hector Mackilwraith reduces the complexities of self-exploration to a series of *pro* and *contra* lists, he debases the sort of "looking within" encouraged by Richard Roberts. Mackilwraith's lack of self-knowledge, particularly concerning the emotional side of his character, renders him a nuisance and a bully, and eventually leads to his suicide attempt. Because this self-inflicted brush with death leaves him unfit to play his assigned role in the opening performance of *The Tempest*, he has diminished even further his "value to his fellow creatures."

In the subsequent novel, *Leaven of Malice*, Gloster Ridley's attempts to insulate himself from guilt through the accumulation of public honours prove, in their own way, to be as superficial as Mackilwraith's lists. When his friend Elspeth Fielding finally suggests introspection as a solution to his turmoil — " 'you must stop torturing yourself. What's the good of winning honours and the good opinion of the world if you can't live on good terms with yourself?' " (233) — she is approximating Nicholas Hayward's prescription for "revolutions in the hearts of individual men." However, Davies continues to confine his examination of this obligatory inward journey largely to the level of verbal precept. What he does portray is the beneficial change in part prompted by his character's new realization that the important answers lie within: "his burden was so much lightened, and confession had so cleansed him, that he was very much changed. . . . [H]is step was light, and he felt free and vigorous" (234). To illustrate the "value to his fellow creatures" of Ridley's transformation, Davies demonstrates its ensuing social consequences. One assumes that Mrs. Fielding's counsel is at least partly responsible for the poise Ridley exhibits in his subsequent meeting with the detractors of his newspaper, where, by maintaining "face," he effectively defends *The Bellman*'s reputation against those who would unjustly impugn it.

As Davies's interest in Jung's psychology intensified in the mid-1950s — a prelude to his full endorsement in 1958 — his attention to introspection became more detailed and pervasive. The search for self that is encouraged but left undepicted in *Leaven of Malice* and *A Jig for the Gypsy* was vigorously chronicled two years later in *General Confession*, a play written in 1956 but never performed (*Hunting* 197). Here, a series of encounters with the two major figures from his past propels the aged Casanova de Seingault through prolonged and painful self-scrutiny. In what Voltaire — who performs the dual role of biographical tour guide and chorus — calls "a unique experience in self-recognition" (*Hunting* 247), Casanova finally perceives these two characters as his Ideal Beloved and Contrary Destiny: he had relentlessly pursued the first and she filled his life with abundant beauty; conversely, the other had opposed him at every turn and always ultimately tainted the splendour he so vigorously sought.

Casanova's acceptance of these figures as aspects of himself is the most important component of his inner journey. Indeed, Davies hoped the three Davises of the Crest Theatre Company would play Casanova's three facets: "the part of Casanova was intended for Donald, that of Cagliostro for Murray, and Barbara was to be Marina; for reasons obvious in the text their family resemblance would have lent an extra dimension to the performances" (*Hunting* 197). Voltaire is "Signor Casanova's wisdom, his better judgement, his philosophy" (246), and the Ideal Beloved, Marina, "his ideal of womanhood. You change like shot silk; you seem to be a dozen women, or three hundred, but you are one" (246). Embracing Cagliostro, his Contrary Destiny, as innate is Casanova's most difficult task (247). Only at the end of his general confession, and after some initial faltering, does he finally achieve a recognition equivalent to Prospero's "this thing of darkness I / Acknowledge mine" (*The Tempest* v.i.275–76):

CASANOVA: What are you? I am the Hero. And you — the Opposition and the Enemy, you said? Does the Hero bear these with him — in his own breast?

CAGLIOSTRO: If he does not carry them there he cannot find them elsewhere. (*Hunting* 261)

CASANOVA: You are my Evil Genius. I have known you in a hundred shapes. I have given you a hundred names. But only now do I see who you are.

CAGLIOSTRO: As truly as Marina, more truly than this temporizing philosopher, I am yourself. (269–70)

Not only does *General Confession* chronicle one example of the "revolutions in the hearts of individual men" urged in various forms in Davies's art since 1949, but in presaging much of Davies's subsequent work, it undertakes this exploration via a roughly Jungian path. Marina and Cagliostro, though never designated specifically as such, correspond to the anima and shadow, both prominent players in "the Comedy Company of the Psyche" of *The Manticore*

(209), Davies's most overtly Jungian novel, published sixteen years later. This time-lapse between *General Confession* and *The Manticore* is significant because it indicates, as in his writings of the early 1950's, that towards the end of the decade Davies's drama was still more obviously Jungian than his fiction. Certainly *A Mixture of Frailties*, like *General Confession* two years before it, implements the psychological wisdom of his previous work: Monica Gall, for instance, following the advice Pop gives Ethel, eschews a confining religion, and her subsequent long, sometimes solitary journey — of the sort Richard Roberts urges — forms the central focus of the book. Yet with the exception of the voice of her dead lover, which speaks to her at the end of the story and may be roughly equivalent to her animus, we never have the sense that Monica's search for self is unfolding along specifically Jungian lines.

However, Davies takes full advantage of what he considers to be the greater possibilities for complexity offered by the novel genre (*Mirror* 7–8) and introduces a theme that will become prominent in his fiction to an extent never evident in his drama. Because *A Mixture of Frailties* inextricably links its protagonist's journey towards self-discovery with the quest for artistic excellence, it constitutes the prototype for such novels as *World of Wonders*, *What's Bred in the Bone*, and *The Lyre of Orpheus*, the title of which, repeated in the epigraph from E.T.A. Hoffmann, alludes to the congruence between art and the inner search: "*The lyre of Orpheus opens the door of the underworld*" (epigraph).

The depiction of artistic endeavour as an avenue to self-discovery in *A Mixture of Frailties* not only presages Davies's future direction as a novelist but also anticipates important nonfictional pronouncements. In a 1961 discussion of *The Tempest* and *A Midsummer Night's Dream*, he states:

These two plays were possible only to a man who had the most uncommon access to the remotest chambers of the Self; to that realm beyond the Ego, at the very heart of being. Here we find the writer who spoke from that vast realm which the depth psychologists and the religious mystics have tried to chart, and which so obstinately resists the approach of anyone but the artist — and only the supreme artist. (*Enthusiasms* 267)

Subsequently, in 1968, he told Gordon Roper that "One of the functions of the artist is the questing inside himself; it is toward self-discovery" (*Conversations* 47); that same year, in a lecture entitled "The Conscience of the Writer," he elaborated this belief:

Now — what is this conscience I have been talking about? It is the writer's inner struggle toward self-knowledge and self-recognition, which he makes manifest through his art. Writers, and artists generally, are notoriously resistant to psycho-analysis, and to put hundreds of thousands of words by both Freud and Jung into a nutshell it is because they are continuously psycho-analysing themselves in their own way, which is through their work, and it is the only way to peace of mind, to integration, open to them. (*One Half* 123)

Here is a translation of one of [Ibsen's] verses, full of meaning and of warning for writers:

To live — is a battle with troll-folk
In the crypts of heart and head;
To write — is a man's self-judgement
As Doom shall judge the dead.

"A man's self-judgement" — that is the conscience of the writer. (124)

After the publication of *The Manticore*, in which the above verse also appears, Davies offered the following response to Margaret Penman's question, "Are you sitting in judgment over yourself as you write?":

I suppose I am. . . . You see a lot of people ask me if I have ever undergone a Jungian analysis because there's one in *The Manticore*. No, but, believe me, writing books is another kind of self-analysis, and you don't blat out everything that you discover in what you write but you have to do a lot of self-investigation before you can write anything at all. (*Conversations* 151)

During this same period, in conjunction with these comments on the value of art to the search for self, Davies delivered two important speeches that continued to stress the significance of this quest. A 1966 lecture polemically entitled "Preaching Selfishness" — and, significantly, delivered to the Ontario Welfare Council — broadens the focus of the comments Davies offered in his 1958 review of *The Undiscovered Self*: whereas in that article he had warned about the danger posed to the inner search by such mass organizations as churches, here he cautions against the lack of balance in a life where too much energy is expended responding to public and professional demands, demands often placed on one in the name of providing assistance to others:

> I am trying to make clear that unless we have something that continually warns us against the pitfalls of allowing the external and public life to devour and diminish the inner and private life, we are in danger of becoming lop-sided. We become professional figures, rather than real people. . . .
> I have said all of this before, to other groups of people. Sometimes they shrug it off; "He is preaching Selfishness," they say. That is true. I am teaching an intelligent regard for the preservation and nourishment of the Self — not the professional self, but the human being who lurks in all of us, and whom we so often neglect and ill-use. . . . We never seem to take time to feed it, clothe it, encourage it, love it, and forgive it. (*One Half* 72–73)

In "What Every Girl Should Know," a 1973 address to the pupils of Bishop Strachan School, Davies places his advice in a religious context, thus offering a practical method of implementing it. He urges these students to "set aside one hour of your life every day for yourself, in which you attempt to understand what you are doing," and warns them about the general demands on their time and the distractions of life:

> It is extremely difficult to claim that hour solely for the task of understanding, questioning, and deciding.
> It used to be somewhat easier, because people used to be religious, or pretended they were. If you went to the chapel, or the church, or a praying-chamber in your own house, and fell on your knees and buried your face in your hands, they [i.e., "all the multifarious army of mankind"] might — not always, but quite often — leave you alone. . . .
> I am not going to advise you to pray, because I am not an expert on that subject. But I do know that it is rather the fashion among many people who do pray to think that it is pretentious

to pray too much for yourself; you are supposed to pray for others, who obviously need Divine assistance more than you do. But when I was a boy at the school down the road, we were taught that prayer has three modes — petition, which is for yourself; intercession, which is for others; and contemplation, which is listening to what is said to *you*. If I might be permitted to advise you on this delicate subject, I would suggest that you skip intercession until you are a little more certain what other people need; stick to petition, in the form of self-examination, and to contemplation, which is waiting for suggestions from the deepest part of you. (*One Half* 51–52)

Davies's increasing insistence on the primacy of the search for self underlies the 1970s Deptford trilogy, in which the central importance of this theme is underscored in two fairly obvious ways. Each of the books is recounted in the first person; no longer are we continually distracted from the inner quest, as in *A Mixture of Frailties* where the story of Monica's personal growth in England is constantly interrupted by the omniscient narrator's change of venue to Salterton and depiction of those administering the Bridgetower Trust. Now we have a novel-long concentration on the searching of the central character, whose consciousness both shapes and sharply focuses the story.[1] Further, every major figure in this trilogy is unmarried, symbolizing the solitary nature of the personal quest. The one exception to this rule proves the point: Boy Staunton has twice been wedded, but he never, in spite of Ramsay's entreaties, undertakes the rigorous introspection pursued by the others.

That the search for self in *Fifth Business* occurs within a Jungian context is apparent from evidence within the book, evidence that is in turn substantiated by *The Manticore*. In the course of his personal quest, Ramsay informs us that he was himself "much concerned with that old fantastical duke of dark corners, C.G. Jung" (182). By this time the novel has already presented various manifestations of what *The Manticore* will identify as the anima, in the form of Ramsay's conceptions of his mother, Mary Dempster, Leola Staunton, Diana Marfleet, and the little Madonna who visits him during his recovery

1 This is true even of *World of Wonders*. Although Dunstan Ramsay is technically the first-person narrator, he is for the most part relating verbatim the story recounted by Magnus Eisengrim, the book's subject.

from battle fatigue and about whom "every scrap of intuition I possessed" rejected a conventional Christian interpretation (92). By the standards of *The Manticore*, Boy Staunton is probably a projection of Ramsay's shadow, exhibiting Ramsay's own rather grasping habits in amassing wealth and his insensitivity towards the pain of others, as we see in his relationships with Leola Staunton, Amasa Dempster, and his parents, whose deaths he long refuses to mourn. Padre Blazon, surely the wise old man in Ramsay's life, directs him to discover the nature of the important archetypal pattern represented by Mary Dempster:

". . . who is she in your personal world? What figure is she in your personal mythology? . . . Lots of men have visions of their mothers in time of danger. Why not you? Why was it this woman? . . . [Y]ou must find your answer in psychological truth, not in objective truth." (177)

Although Liesl broadens this adjuration to apply to Ramsay's life in general — rather than to his anima exclusively — she, too, prods him to undertake the quest: " 'Who are you? Where do you fit into poetry and myth? . . . Are you Fifth Business? You had better find out' " (227).

Accompanying the counsel to embark on the inner search is the Jungian precept that this journey be directed by personal inner resources rather than those of any religious institution. When pressed about the possibility of Mary Dempster's sainthood, the Bollandist Blazon warns Ramsay:

"[W]hy do you worry? What good would it do you if I told you she is indeed a saint? I cannot make saints, nor can the Pope. We can only recognize saints when the plainest evidence shows them to be saintly. If you think her a saint, she is a saint to you. . . . Trust your own judgement" (174).

Since *The Manticore* is so overtly — indeed overwhelmingly — Jungian, identifying its Jungian characteristics here would be redundant. Davies so explicitly nails his psychological colours to the mast in this book that it effectively places his entire oeuvre in a Jungian context; in fact, it has spawned a cottage industry of Jungian interpretations of Davies's work. In this larger sense, the story of David Staunton's *anamnesis* in Zurich not only chronicles his exploration of self, it also illuminates that of his counterparts in Davies's other novels.

Thus, although Jung's name never appears in *World of Wonders*, its readers perceive his guiding hand throughout. For instance, while the book withholds the detailed explication accorded archetypal patterns in *The Manticore*, we discern them nonetheless as Magnus Eisengrim's journey towards self-discovery unfolds. The first of these is the role of Jonah that his fellow circus performers project on him:

> "The idea of the Jonah is strong with show people. A bringer of ill luck can blight a show. Some of the Talent were sure I was a Jonah, which was just a way of focussing their detestation of what I represented, and of Willard, whom they all hated." (92)

After leaving the circus and travelling to Europe with the dying Willard, Eisengrim refuses to administer the fatal overdose of morphine his erstwhile oppressor begs for, preferring instead to keep him alive and watch his pain. Ramsay detects in this another archetype: " 'What is the mythical element in his story? Simply the very old tale of the man who is in search of his soul, and who must struggle with a monster to secure it' " (140). By Davies's standards, even Eisengrim's sojourn with Sir John Tresize's theatrical company shows him participating, albeit vicariously, in mythic patterns. In a lecture entitled "Jung and the Theatre," Davies analyses melodramas of the sort performed by Sir John's troupe, describing at length their archetypal redolence (*One Half* 148–60) and insisting on their psychological merit:

> even at its worst, melodrama continued to draw on that realm where *"everything was seething with life"*, and to transfer as much as possible of that extraordinary psychic vitality to the stage. The plays, so neglectful of the externals of reality, were psychologically convincing because they spoke from these depths to corresponding depths in their audiences. However crude the effect might sometimes be, melodrama did not shrink from that battle with troll-folk, in the crypts of heart and head, which Ibsen said was the essence of life. (*One Half* 159)

His experiences with the circus, Willard, and Sir John's theatre finally oblige Eisengrim to accept his inner wolf, very much as David Staunton is forced to acknowledge the "bear within" in *The Manticore*. Near the end of the book he declares:

"Eisengrim . . . really means the sinister hardness, the cruelty of iron itself. I took the name, and recognized the fact, and thereby got it up out of my depths so that at least I could be aware of it and take a look at it, now and then. I won't say I domesticated the wolf, but I knew where his lair was, and what he might do." (306)

This, too, is quintessentially Jungian, since accepting one's innate evil is obligatory for achieving what the psychologist calls "wholeness" or "totality." Thus, he (and Davies by the time of the Deptford trilogy) would argue that Richard Roberts's desire that man undertake "the long, solitary task of perfecting himself" (*A Jig* 85) is unrealistic, since perfection — in spite of the adjuration in Matthew 5.48 — is impossible for a human race tainted by original sin. Wholeness, not perfection, is the goal of the inner quest (Davies, "A Definitive Jung"). At the conclusion of *World of Wonders*, Eisengrim also eulogizes the Jungian emphasis on personal over institutional experience: " 'Everything has its astonishing, wondrous aspect, if you bring a mind to it that's really your own — a mind that hasn't been smeared and blurred with half-understood muck from schools, or the daily papers, or any other ragbag of reach-me-down notions' " (313).

In *Question Time* Davies offers his strongest artistic statement in the 1970's about the public benefit of individual introspection. Judith Skelton Grant aptly describes this work as "a Jungian play in which Canada's prime minister undergoes an identity crisis that has national implications" ("Robertson Davies" 175). In Davies's words, the central character Peter Macadam must answer the question, "[C]an a man be a leader of his people in the truest and most effective sense if he has devoted his best energies to the external life of statesmanship, and has permitted the feelings and obligations of a fully realized human being to wither away?" (qtd. in Anthony 77). A response is offered early in the play by Macadam himself: "I have no time to wonder about my private happiness. But I sincerely hope it may be said of me that I pushed the public happiness — which is more easily measured — forward a few hard-won inches" (17). *Question Time*, as we might expect, subsequently depicts the naïvety of this answer, with the prime minister's wife most forcefully articulating the play's central message. Elaborating the similar precept given to Gloster Ridley in *Leaven of Malice*, Sarah Macadam admonishes her husband:

Are you so stupid, so besotted with public concerns, that you don't know that everything — everything in the world — comes at last from what you call the personal level? The Prime Minister cannot rise above the level of Peter Macadam, and the party cannot rise above the level of the Prime Minister. (64)

I have outlined at length the perhaps obvious Jungian nature of the search for self in the Deptford trilogy and *Question Time* because it forms the *sine qua non* for recognizing the important theological dimension underlying this inner quest. Jung defines religion as "a subjective relationship to certain metaphysical, extramundane factors" (*The Undiscovered Self* 31) and maintains that the decline of religious life in our century has been catastrophic:

Among all my patients in the second half of life — that is to say, over thirty-five — there has not been one whose problem in the last resort was not that of finding a religious outlook on life. It is safe to say that every one of them fell ill because he had lost what the living religions of every age have given to their followers, and none of them has been really healed who did not regain his religious outlook. This of course has nothing whatever to do with a particular creed or membership of a church. (*Collected* 11: 509)

The Undiscovered Self offers his prescription for achieving this religious outlook:

when the individual is willing to fulfill the demands of rigorous self-examination and self-knowledge. . . . [h]e will have set his hand, as it were, to a declaration of his own human dignity and taken the first step towards the foundations of his consciousness — that is, towards the unconscious, the only accessible source of religious experience. This is certainly not to say that what we call the unconscious is identical with God or is set up in his place. It is the medium from which the religious experience seems to flow. As to what the further cause of such an experience may be, the answer to this lies beyond the range of human knowledge. Knowledge of God is a transcendental problem. (101–02)

And yet Jung argues that we can strive towards, and indeed achieve, partial knowledge of the "image of God" through our personal search for self — the self being "the total personality" (*Collected* 9.2: 9), "the sum total of conscious and unconscious existence" (*Psychology* 100). He also believes that "the spontaneous symbols of the self, or of wholeness, cannot in practice be distinguished from a God-image" (9.2: 73) and premises his assertions on his clinical findings, outlined in an essay appropriately entitled "The Self":

> the quaternity or mandala[1] symbols . . . occur not only in the dreams of modern people who have never heard of them, but are widely disseminated in the historical records of many peoples and many epochs. Their significance as *symbols of unity and totality* is amply confirmed by history as well as by empirical psychology. . . . Wholeness is thus an objective factor that confronts the subject independently of him, like anima or animus; and just as the latter have a higher position in the hierarchy than the shadow, so wholeness lays claim to a position and a value superior to those of the syzygy. . . .[2]
>
> Unity and totality stand at the highest point on the scale of objective values because their symbols can no longer be distinguished from the *imago Dei*. (9.2: 59, 60).

This, in turn, has important theological ramifications. Because "the early Christian spirit" recognized that "[t]he self . . . is a God-image," Clement of Alexandria could maintain: "he who knows himself knows God" (9.2: 42). Confirming his own beliefs, Jung elaborates:

> Since the Holy Ghost is the Third Person of the Trinity and God is present entire in each of the three Persons at any time, the indwelling of the Holy Ghost means nothing less than an approximation of the believer to the status of God's son. One can therefore understand what is meant by the remark "you are gods" [John 10.34]. . . . God, in the shape of the Holy Ghost, puts up his tent in man. . . . (11: 656)

---

1 Sanskrit for "magic circle." For a brief explanation see Jung's *Memories, Dreams, Reflections* (396–97).

2 i.e., the animus and anima; the word means "pair of opposites" (9.2: 99).

Thus, like the Gnostics — of whom many were "nothing other than psychologists" (9.2: 347) — Jung urges the necessity of seeking this divine spark within:

The Self or Christ is present in everybody *a priori*, but as a rule in an *unconscious condition* to begin with. But it is a definite *experience* of later life, when this fact becomes *conscious*. It is not really understood by teaching or suggestion. It is only real when it *happens* and it can only happen when you withdraw your projections from an *outward* historical or metaphysical Christ and thus *wake* up Christ within. . . . An act of *introjection* is needed, i.e. the realization that the Self lives in you and not in an external figure separated and different from yourself. (qtd. in Philp 233)

In a letter to an insufficiently convinced correspondent, Jung emphatically summarizes his contention that the search for self is a religious undertaking:

Individuation is the life in God, as the mandala psychology clearly shows. Have you not read my later books? You can see it in every one of them. The symbols of the Self coincide with those of the Deity. The Self is not the Ego, it symbolizes the totality of Man and he is obviously not whole without God. (qtd. in Philp 225)

That Robertson Davies has long acknowledged the Jungian search for self as a religious quest is obvious from his favourable review of *Journey into Self* written in 1958 by M. Esther Harding, a New York Jungian analyst. This book asserts that the "journey of the soul" travelled by John Bunyan's Christian "is very similar to that undertaken by a patient undergoing a Jungian analysis," and further maintains that the locales through which Christian travels, from the Slough of Despond to the Celestial City, "have counterparts in the succeeding states of mind through which the patient passes during the months of his analysis. So, too, the people whom Christian meets . . . have all equivalents in the aspects of his own character which the man meets who undergoes a thorough Jungian analysis" ("Jung's Theories"). Davies recommends the volume, and concludes his article by first advancing Jung's contention that "without religion in the broad sense of the term, man cannot know peace of mind" and then affirming that "Dr. Harding's book goes far to explain why" ("Jung's Theories").[1]

Davies further demonstrates his belief in the congruence between the search for self and religion in his 1960 review of David Cox's *Jung and Saint Paul*, a work he characterizes as the "most interesting book about religion that has come my way in a long time. . . . a volume of importance to the thoughtful modern Christian" (" 'Jung and Saint Paul' "). Cox, an Anglican clergyman, compares "the Analytical Psychology of C.G. Jung, which has as its goal the Individuated Man, controlled by the Self, and St. Paul's doctrine of the Man Justified by Faith, who lives in Christ." Davies underscores the likeness between the two:

> The psychoanalytic system of C.G. Jung. . . . seeks to probe, expose and dispel the hidden terrors of the mind. But it is also "synthetic": having brought order to the rejected materials of the Unconscious, it seeks to build what remains into a better thing than it was before. The final product of a thorough Jungian analysis is the Individuated Man, controlled not by the Ego but the Self. And — this is important — this Self is an image of God. . . . [T]he Christian who seeks to be Justified by Faith goes through a strikingly similar experience. He must cleanse himself by penitence, and then he must aspire "to be made like unto Christ."

In this article Davies also recognizes the " 'gnostic element' " in Jung's thinking, explaining that the Gnostics believed "only those who had attained 'inner light' could be saved," while the Christian "is obliged to believe that salvation is open to all." Jung, like the Gnostics, takes an elitist stance, since he "does not believe that everybody can be Individuated, or wants to be" (" 'Jung and Saint Paul' "), a position Davies comes to articulate as his own:

> I was once accused by the chaplain of Massey College of being a Gnostic. He was very angry with me indeed. But part of being

---

1 This book so impressed Davies that at the time of his review he consulted Harding about entering analysis with her. She dissuaded him but left a lasting impression, as *The Manticore*'s Dr. Johanna von Haller is partly modelled on Harding (Grant, *Robertson Davies: Man of Myth* 351–52).

Gnostic was using your head if you wanted to achieve salvation or even a tolerable life. This is something which the Christian church tends rather to discourage. Salvation is free for everyone. The greatest idiot and yahoo can be saved, the doctrine goes, because Christ loves him as much as he loves Albert Einstein. I don't think that is true. . . . This sort of opinion has won me the reputation of being an elitist. Behold an elitist. ("Art" 30–31)

In 1987 Davies reiterated these beliefs in "Keeping Faith":

the message of depth psychology is a restatement of an old religious assertion: that God, and the Kingdom of God, is within you, and the enjoyment of God, and entry into His Kingdom, is something you must manage, in the end, for yourself. . . . Gnosticism was so intolerably elitist as to say that salvation was attainable only through an inner journey, an onward struggle, which would, in the end, if successful, bring enlightenment. This ruled out great numbers of people who had no intellectual equipment or spiritual muscle for such a struggle, and the Gnostics accepted cheerfully the conclusion that such people were best suited to the bondage of a church which would keep them out of mischief, but could not enlighten them. . . . Yet here, in the twentieth century, we have Freud and especially Jung saying in effect what the Gnostics said nineteen centuries ago. (190)

Given these strongly expressed tenets, Davies's depiction of the conjunction between religion and the inner journey is less explicit in his pre-Cornish novels than one would expect. Indeed, the Salterton and Deptford trilogies provide only very general indications of this congruence. For instance, in A Mixture of Frailties Monica Gall's self-discovery comes in part through her experience with Bach's St. Matthew Passion, which Davies describes — along with Handel's Messiah — as "marked by a strength of religious feeling which has never since been equalled in music" ("Music for Holy Week"). Monica perhaps also benefits at the unconscious level — her conscious mind is otherwise preoccupied — from Dean Knapp's final Bridgetower Memorial Sermon at the cathedral. In the more Jungian novels of the Deptford trilogy, Dunstan Ramsay pursues his search for self by investigating the saints and exploring religious art, while David Staunton finally discovers those intense feelings so important to his recuperation in a cave that once served as a chapel for ancient bear worshippers. Similarly, Peter Macadam in *Question Time* is guided through his "personal Arctic" by a shaman (8).

The Gnostic notion of the inner light and its exclusivity is present in the pre-Cornish novels, but only in a desultory fashion and never directly linked to the Jungian search for self. The Dean's final sermon in *A Mixture of Frailties* explores the differences among the revelations heralding Christ's birth and then types all of mankind according to these three paradigms: the shepherds *"needed an angel and a multitude of the heavenly host to call it to the[ir] attention . . . that something out of the ordinary had happened"* (375); *"the Wise Men needed no more than a hint, a new star amid the host of heaven"* (376); and Simeon, having *"the rarest"* sort of apprehension, knew the Lord as *"one who was open to the promptings of the Holy Ghost. . . . outwardly passive but inwardly illumined by active grace, through whom much that is noblest and of most worth has been vouchsafed to the world . . ."* (378–79). Davies comments on these ideas to Gordon Roper:

> I really meant quite a lot by that passage. . . . There are people who see things because they have marvelous revelations that are sort of gifts to them; then there are people who see things because they study and get wise; and then there are just wonderfully saintly people who get it because they've got it. (*Conversations* 55)

Mary Dempster is one example of those "wonderfully saintly people who get it because they've got it." After her benefaction in the gravel pit, which confers salvation on another at the price of her own social damnation, Dunstan Ramsay observes: "She knew she was in disgrace with the world, but did not feel disgraced; she knew she was jeered at, but felt no humiliation. She lived by a light that arose from within . . ." (52).

The Deptford trilogy also recognizes the converse ramification of the elitism characterizing this introspection. Ramsay concedes that there will be no awakening for Leola Staunton, neither through an innate shining forth of her inner light — as accorded to Simeon and Mary Dempster — nor through an arduous self-searching, such as he and later her son David undertake. Even Dr. Coué's elementary system of auto-suggestion — continuously stating, " 'Every day in every way, I am getting better and better' " (154) — fails her: "Poor

Leola did not get better and better because she had no idea of what betterness was. . . . I don't think I have ever met such a stupid, nice woman" (155). In *World of Wonders*, clients ask the fortune-teller, Mrs. Constantinescu, " '[H]ave I had all the best that life is going to give me? . . . [I]s this all life holds for me?' " (115–16). Addressing their uncertainty in an interview with Tom Harpur, Davies avers:

> I think a lot of people feel that. They have unreasonable expec-
> tations because they never stop to consider what life actually has
> to offer them. They're always looking for some great epiphany
> from the skies. They never stop to consider that fact which
> human beings find hardest to recognize: "Maybe I'm not worthy
> of an epiphany." (*Conversations* 160)

These Jungian-Gnostic concerns emerge in Davies's pre-Cornish fiction either as very generally religious, or as considerations that appear religious only after an exploration of both Jungian theology and Davies's nonfictional statements. Taken exclusively within the context of the novels, the transcendent elements of the search for self are so obscure that Sam Solecki understandably contends: "Davies' pronouncements on the self and religion tend to sound like good news for modern man, secular (because psychologized) assurances about vaguely spiritual matters" (47). Dennis Duffy correspondingly argues in his assessment of *Fifth Business* that "Davies' creations gravitate toward . . . religion emptied of objective content . . ." (5). Only by first referring to Davies's own statements about Jung — statements such as, "I not only accept his views on religion but I've found them to be true in practice, which is something else" (*Conver-sations* 66) — and then consulting the psychologist's works them-selves, can we conclude that the inner journey exploring the arche-types forms the objective content Duffy sees to be lacking. Likewise, Jung's writings reveal that the ultimate archetype sought in this introspective quest — by, for instance, David Staunton in *The Manticore* — is the self, and since this is identical with the image of God, which is the god within, Davies's good news for modern man is ultimately not as secular as Solecki assumes.[1]

---

1 Similar recourse to Jungian psychology — which very specifically relates such concepts as "totality" and "wholeness" to the archetype of self and thus to the inner god — lends greater credence to a spiritual interpretation of the advice

The Cornish trilogy marks a change from its predecessors, as internal evidence within these novels more clearly delineates the religious side of introspection — although the reader still requires external sources to establish the full Jungian significance of this. Indeed, the conjunction of the inner search and religion reaches a sort of zenith in this trilogy largely because Simon Darcourt, its central quester, is a clergyman — by far the best developed in a series of clerics Davies offers as figures of wisdom. Even more so than his predecessors — Dean Jevon Knapp, Padre Ignatio Blazon, and Father Gervase Knopwood — Darcourt holds a privileged position as a character whose spiritual discoveries are central to the trilogy in which they are presented.[1]

Blazon is Darcourt's most obvious precursor since he, too, is both a heterodox cleric and a Jungian searcher for self. David Dooley justifiably calls him "a most unusual priest":

In his account of [Blazon's] formation, we can see Davies re-shaping Jesuit principles to make them accord with psycho-analytic theory: "Jesuit training is based on a rigorous reform of the self and achievement of self-knowledge. By the time a man comes to the final vows, anything emotional or fanciful in his piety is supposed to have been rooted out" [Fifth 176]. The long and arduous process of formation which a Jesuit undergoes is supposed to make him a soldier of God, disciplined to subordinate his own self so that he may be used as God's instrument. Davies subtly alters the end in view, so that knowledge of self becomes the objective instead of knowledge and service of God. (119–20)

Ramsay gives Boy Staunton in Fifth Business: "Boy, for God's sake, get to know something about yourself. . . . I'm simply trying to recover something of the totality of your life. Don't you want to possess it as a whole — the bad with the good? I told you once you'd made a God of yourself, and the insufficiency of it forced you to become an atheist. It's time you tried to be a human being. Then maybe something bigger than yourself will come up on your horizon" (264).

1 This is not to suggest that all of Davies's clergymen are figures of wisdom; however, those who are not, such as Sidney Beamis and Amasa Dempster, are relatively minor characters who serve as foils to their sagacious counterfigures. Also worth noting is that some of the historical figures Davies most admires are wise but in various ways heterodox men of the cloth: for example, Casanova de Seingault, Sidney Smith, Ronald Knox, R.H. Barham, and François Rabelais.

Of course, being a Jungian quester — notice the similarity with Jung's account of "rigorous self-examination and self-knowledge" as essential for "religious experience and immediate relation to God" (*The Undiscovered Self* 100–01) — Blazon does not draw this final distinction between self and God.

Like Blazon, who seeks " 'a Christ who will show me how to be an old man' " (*Fifth* 176), Darcourt pursues a very personal Jesus and characterizes his search using key Jungian concepts:

> Having discovered how hard it is to save the souls of others (did I ever, in my nine years of parish work among both poor and not-so-poor, really save anybody's soul?) I wanted to give all the time I could spare to saving my own soul. . . . Murray would call me selfish. But am I? I am hard at the great task with the person who lies nearest and who is most amenable to my best efforts, and perhaps by example I may persuade a few others to do the same. . . .
>
> Gradually it came to me that the Imitation of Christ might not be a road-company performance of Christ's Passion, with me as a pitifully badly cast actor in the principal role. Perhaps what was imitable about Christ was his firm acceptance of his destiny, and his adherence to it even when it led to shameful death. It was the *wholeness* of Christ that had illuminated so many millions of lives, and it was my job to seek and make manifest the *wholeness* of Simon Darcourt. (*Rebel* 55–56; emphasis added)

Davies further emphasizes Jungian elements when Darcourt later states that "without any intention of becoming a Gnostic I found myself greatly taken up with the Gnostics because of the appeal of so much that they had to say" (235). This inspires him to quest after Maria, a type of the Gnostic Sophia: "For me Maria was *wholeness*" (236; emphasis added).[1] Darcourt employs other keywords when responding to a question about the liturgical calendar: " 'Do you do much about Lent, Simon?' " With an answer that would have satisfied neither my parents nor religion teachers, who generally encouraged the abnegation of tasty morsels, movies, or television sports — in short, everything that made a child's life worth living —

---

[1] Maimas echoes this in *What's Bred in the Bone* when he argues that knowing the anima makes *"a complete and spiritually whole man"* (149).

Darcourt declares: " 'What I usually do is take on a program of introspection and self-examination — try to tidy myself up a bit' " (252).[1]

Not only does Davies bring the association of religion and the search for self into sharper focus in the Cornish trilogy, but he concurrently depicts the culmination of an inextricably related concern. In earlier novels, Davies's characters often spiritually mature outside Canadian borders: Monica Gall is rescued from a philistine existence in Salterton and sent to England; Dunstan Ramsay receives his profound vision on a Belgian battlefield and undertakes his subsequent investigations of religion in general and saints in particular in Europe and Latin America; David Staunton journeys to Switzerland for his cure; and Magnus Eisengrim absorbs much of his magian worldview in Europe.

Yet, elitist as this introspection may be, and far flung the places it is achieved, Davies has expressed growing confidence in the virtues of Canada as a place where this quest for self can be pursued. In his 1959 review of Hugh MacLennan's *The Watch that Ends the Night*, he asserts: "Our climate sets its mark on us, making some of us moody and introspective in a fashion which is akin to the Scandinavians, or the Russians, and when we dig deep into ourselves we find matters which are very much our own" (*Well-Tempered* 213). Davies's 1977 essay, "The Canada of Myth and Reality," identifies a practical application of this climatic advantage in response to Douglas LePan's poem "Coureurs de bois":

The Canadian is the *coureur de bois* who must understand — understand, not tame — the savage land. And is it the savage land of rocks and forests only penetrable by the patient explorer? Only in the sense that this is a metaphor for that equally savage land of the spirit — "the desperate wilderness behind your eyes, / So full of falls and glooms and desolations, / Disasters I have glimpsed but few would dream of . . ." The Canadian voyage, I

---

1 The trilogy reminds us in other ways of the congruence between the search for self and religion. Francis Cornish, of course, finds his soul through painting a picture of a traditionally religious subject. In *The Lyre of Orpheus*, Schnak, presumably a quester at a much earlier stage of her journey than Darcourt or Cornish, asks Geraint Powell: " 'How can anybody live God?' " He retorts: " 'By living as well as they can with themselves. . . . Truth to yourself, I suppose you'd call it. Following your nose' " (416).

truly believe, is this perilous voyage into the dark interior of which the poet speaks. (*One Half* 285)

In the 1980s, while he was illustrating these ideas in the Cornish trilogy, Davies pursued the same argument wielding the Jungian terms "extroversion" (or "extraversion") and "introversion":

In psychological terms, the U.S. is the most extroverted country in the world. . . . [N]uminosity, and the world of the unseen, cannot be conquered by extrovert means. Is it fanciful to suggest that the enthusiasm for space exploration reflects a refusal to face what is nearest to the soul. . . . Canada is in a psychological mess from which it can extract itself only by taking thought. Canada is not an extrovert country. Its history and its settlement by refugees from various sorts of oppression and betrayal dispose it toward introversion. . . . Canada nevertheless persists in aping the extroversion of the U.S., because to do so requires no thought — only intellectual submission and peonage. ("Keeping Faith" 192)

Among the Cornish novels, this theme is most obviously echoed in *What's Bred in the Bone*. Here, being of an earlier generation than most of the other characters in the trilogy, Francis Cornish needs to pursue his personal search, in part, outside of Canada, as yet still an artistic and intellectual fledgling. In Europe Cornish's mentor, Tancred Saraceni, without mentioning Jung by name, explains to him the distinction between Jung's two terms:

"During those three centuries, to measure roughly, that we call the Renaissance, the mind of civilized man underwent a radical change. A psychologist would say that it changed from extra-version to introversion. The exploration of the outer world was partnered by a new exploration of the inner world, the subjective world. And it was an exploration that could not depend on the old map of religion. It was the exploration that brought forth *Hamlet*, instead of *Gorboduc*. Man began to look inside himself for all that was great and also — if he was honest, which most people aren't — for all that was ignoble, base, evil." (272)

Cornish's lover, Ruth Nibsmith, elucidates the immediate conse-quences of this distinction for a Canadian and notes the ultimate potential it offers. Like Davies, she asserts that Canadians are a " 'psychological mess. For a lot of good reasons . . . Canada is an introverted country straining like hell to behave like an extravert. Wake up! Be yourself, not a bad copy of something else!' " (376). That Cornish accedes to her insight and embraces his national predisposition to introversion is apparent from his painting *The Marriage at Cana*: through it, he has " 'made up [his] soul' " (479), *"got his soul under his eye, so to speak"* (480).

Simon Darcourt truly brings Davies's vision to fruition: like Francis Cornish, he avoids kicking against the pricks trying to embrace extroversion; unlike his friend, he successfully pursues the path of an introvert entirely within Canada. Guided in Toronto by Mamusia's tarot cards — which Jung speculates are "distantly descended from the archetypes of transformation" (*Collected* 9.1: 81) — Darcourt comes to perceive his personal myth: as the Fool, he embodies the "cheerful rogue on a journey" (*Lyre* 295), "the footloose traveller, urged onward by something outside the confines of intellect and caution" (296). Reaffirming the religious aspect of this discovery is the narrator's comment: "He was a priest of the type of the mighty Rabelais. But was not Rabelais a true priest and also a Fool of God? Was he, Simon Darcourt, . . . really a Fool of God? He was too modest a man to greet such a revelation with a whoop and a holler" (297).

In Darcourt we also encounter Davies's most extended examination of a character after that individual has determined his or her personal myth and achieved some degree of self-recognition. This crucial epiphany occurs approximately two-thirds of the way through *The Lyre of Orpheus*: "Simon Darcourt was a changed man. Not a wholly new man, not a man one jot less involved in the life of his duties and his friends, but a man with a stronger sense of who he was" (301). As I noted at the beginning of this chapter, in his review of *The Undiscovered Self* Davies argues that "To reform the world, each man must make a beginning with himself" (*Enthusiasms* 175), and in *A Jig for the Gypsy* Richard Roberts maintains that if a man looks within he can "be of the greatest possible value to his fellow-creatures" (85). Thus, Davies's own statements, both fictional and nonfictional, validate William James's dictum that we must "judge the religious life by its results exclusively" (35). Consequently, as we shall see, the newly enlightened Darcourt provides a particularly good subject for illustrating the merits of this search for self.

In Davies's work prior to the Cornish trilogy, those *"fruits for life"*

(James 191) produced by the inner quest are undoubtedly impressive, but they still seem deficient. Certainly introspection yields striking artistic and intellectual results, varying from Dunstan Ramsay's books on saints and Monica Gall's music, to Francis Cornish's painting and Magnus Eisengrim's magic. These are indisputably a benefit to humanity. Father Blazon best articulates this with respect to his work as a hagiologist: " 'I am a pretty useful person' " (*Fifth* 176). Yet on a more personal level, although David Staunton becomes, in Dr. von Haller's words, " 'a much pleasanter, easier person' " (*Manticore* 237), Ramsay and Eisengrim remain petty and vindictive, while Cornish dies a miserly, dirty recluse. Altruism is not a strong suit of these characters, which is particularly troubling in the case of Ramsay, since he is a teacher. While not expecting a Mother Teresa to emerge from every inner quest, the reader becomes increasingly nagged by a suspicion that the implicit peril of the search for self may be its potential for degeneration into solipsism. In other words, religious though it is, the quest may produce or intensify . . . well . . . selfishness.

That Davies was aware of this danger as early as 1943 is apparent from his review of *The Imitation of Christ*:

Thomas à Kempis was a monk, and it may be argued that by removing himself from the world he made it easy to live a good life; the argument will not bear too close inspection, for a retired life may easily degenerate into the most useless and selfish sort of existence. (*Enthusiasms* 120)

The problem, as we have seen, is that most of his subsequent comments stress the opposite risk, the risk of ignoring one's inner self, as the following typical example reminds us:

A Canadian will work, or fight, or give money to philanthropic causes readily enough, but he will not think if he can possibly, at whatever cost, get someone else to do it for him. . . . There is a reason for this surrender. Good works are cheap in comparison with solitary psychological hard work. ("Keeping Faith" 192)

Indeed, prior to the Cornish trilogy Davies sometimes seems to be ridden by the very tiger he creates in his strenuous promotion of selfishness. He articulates his most extreme position in a 1977 interview with Peter Gzowski:

You help weak people and you've got them and they're on top of you and you're carrying them. And it's very, very hard to shake them. . . . They're always back for more and pretty soon you find that you're sort of a psychological and financial and spiritual and energy-producing milch cow. . . . It is against a great deal of our modern culture and particularly against the Christian ethic, which is to help everybody. . . . [C]ompassion has become almost a disease in our society. . . . If you help somebody, they never can get enough. Sometimes you're almost driven mad with their demands.

To Gzowski's reply, "Well, I'll never help anybody again!", Davies, recognizing the position to which his rhetoric has forced him, reconsiders: "Oh, don't do that. Don't say that. There must be some middle way" (*Conversations* 167–68).

Davies appears cognizant of this dilemma as he stakes out this "middle way" in the Cornish trilogy through Simon Darcourt; however, no doubt wary of compromising his fundamental emphasis on selfishness, he effects this very, very carefully, first ensuring that his protagonist has the requisite selfish credentials. Early on, therefore, we behold Darcourt's rejection of the social-worker approach to religion in favour of the solitary quest for self-discovery (*Rebel* 55–56), and his appropriate firmness towards Urky McVarish and John Parlabane. About the latter, Darcourt maintains that

some measure of what might be called cynicism, but which could also be clarity of vision, tempered with charity, is an element in the Simon Darcourt I am trying to discover and set free. . . . Paul tells us that Charity is many things, but nowhere does he tell us that it is blind. (57–58)[1]

In *The Lyre of Orpheus*, Darcourt advances the obligatory statement about egocentrism when Arthur Cornish calls his wife, Maria, " 'the person I love more than myself.' " In an elaboration of Liesl's earlier admonishment of Dunstan Ramsay, " 'How can you be really good to anybody if you are not good to yourself?' " (*Fifth* 226). Darcourt retorts:

---

1 cf. also p. 99 where Darcourt regrets an act of kindness-gone-wrong towards Parlabane.

"Bullshit! . . . The person you love best is Arthur Cornish, because he's the one God has given you to make the best of. Unless you love him truly and deeply you are not fit to have Maria as your wife. . . . [Y]our value to Maria and the rest of the world depends on how you treat Arthur." (232)

Establishing his protagonist as a credibly selfish person allows Davies to illustrate how effective this makes him as a dispenser of good deeds during his inner quest. Immediately before the exchange cited above, presenting what arguably constitutes his credo, Darcourt tells Arthur:

"I'm not Christ, Arthur, and I can't love like Him, so I settle for courtesy, consideration, decent manners, and whatever I can do for the people I really do love. And you are one of those. I can't help you by weeping with you, though I respect your tears. The best I can do is to bring a clear head and an open eye to your trouble." (227)

This "clear head" and "open eye" are crucially important, since Darcourt's advice to Arthur puts his friend on the way to becoming a magnanimous cuckold, and subsequently, when Geraint Powell's remorse over his tryst with Maria lands him, intoxicated, in the hospital, Darcourt attends, proving a firm but efficacious confessor.

His efficacy is enhanced after he achieves some success in his individual quest by discovering his personal myth. Darcourt refuses to permit the Cranes, professional lilies of the field, to foist their troubles on him and obtain accommodation: "There had been a time, before he recognized himself as the Fool, when he would have been badgered into assuming full responsibility for these Babes in the Wood. But as the Fool he had other things to attend to" (328). Then he enlightens Arthur and Maria Cornish about the superficial, hypocritical nature of their pity towards the justly punished Wally Crottel (332–33). Further, by unyieldingly resisting Schnak's customary abuse, he assists in her socialization and, indeed, eventually comes to stand as the figure most sympathetic to her personal troubles. When everyone else remains oblivious to her hopeless infatuation with Geraint Powell — including Powell himself — Darcourt notices it and declares his concern (374–75). The priest is also the one character the embarrassed Schnak approaches for a demonstration about curtseying. Illustrating the grace inherent in even small acts of kindness, Darcourt overcomes his initial uncertainty and protesting body to teach his petitioner "one of the minor accomplishments of a public performer" (424) — much to the delight of a hidden group of stagehands that applauds from above. When she legitimately warrants it, even Mabel Crane (Muller) receives his charity: in a foreign country and ignored by her boyfriend Al, she would have been entirely alone in the Stratford hospital delivering her stillborn baby in the early morning, but for Darcourt sitting with Gunilla Dahl-Soot in the waiting room. Gunilla — whom Darcourt advises on finding her soul — aptly summarizes his effectiveness throughout: " 'You seem to be the one who is expected to do something when real trouble comes up' " (382).

Because the search for self yields this well-rounded, exemplary individual, Davies decisively eradicates any vestigial doubts the reader may harbour about the worthiness of the quest. We have Darcourt's libretto for *Arthur of Britain, or the Magnanimous Cuckold* and his contributions to scholarship with the identification of the origin of *The Marriage at Cana* and his biography of Francis Cornish — all impressive accomplishments of the sort associated with Davies's other questers. However, valuable as these unquestionably are, only when they are coupled with Darcourt's clear-sighted and frequently shared loving-kindnesses — to use the psalmist's term (25.6, 84.49) — do we see the full splendour of "saving [one's] soul" (*Rebel* 55).

Murther and Walking Spirits reaffirms and summarizes many elements of the introspective search depicted in Davies's previous works. The wisdom figure here, while not a clergyman, is the closest thing to it: Hugh McWearie is an excleric and the *Colonial Advocate*'s religious columnist, so Connor Gilmartin, the novel's narrator and central self-seeker, applies to him for advice about fundamental moral and metaphysical questions. To bring the congruence between religion and the inner quest into sharper focus, Davies draws in a general way upon the sentiments he expressed over thirty years previously in that 1959 review of *Journey into the Self*, in which he remarked the elements of *The Pilgrim's Progress* present in the Jungian journey towards individuation. For Gilmartin's funeral McWearie insists on the inclusion of Bunyan's hymn, which "was a favourite of mine, and of Hugh's" (16):

Hobgoblin nor foul fiend
Can daunt his spirit;

144

He knows he at the end
Shall life inherit. (17)

Perceiving its relevance to his quest, Gilmartin accepts as "a splendid compliment" the song's assertion of *"His first avowed intent / To be a pilgrim"*: "the hymn told of what I had meant in my life, whenever I could collect my thoughts together enough to discover a meaning. I had wanted some self-recognition, as a path to — to what? In what path had I been a pilgrim? Was I now to find out?" (17).

The ensuing endeavour "to find out" occurs within a familiar framework, since art — in this case a series of films — initiates and subsequently informs Gilmartin's journey. This continues posthumously what in life had been a rudimentary introspective experience:

> When I went into a movie house to see something made by [a great director], I felt that the half-darkness, the tunnel-like auditorium, spoke of that world of phantasmagoria and dream grotto of which I was aware as a part of my own life, which I could touch only in dreams or waking reverie. But film could open the door to it, for me. . . . (31)

In keeping with Davies's increasing emphasis on Canada as a setting conducive to the inner search, Gilmartin's journey occurs exclusively in this country, although he witnesses events transpiring elsewhere. Thus, when he weeps, he weeps in Canada; when he falls in love with one of his forebears, he falls in love in Canada — in fact, his discovery of himself transpires entirely in Toronto, Ontario.

The novel also features the by now familiar preaching of selfishness. We have, of course, already seen the very best of egocentricity in Simon Darcourt, who tempers its espousal and practice with charity; in this work, more than in any previous novel, Davies shows the dangers of charity untempered by selfishness. The narrator's Methodist ancestor, Janet Gilmartin, devotes her life to indulging her ne'er-do-well relatives, their ever-multiplying offspring, and her frequently dejected husband. Fittingly, one of her favourite songs is "Do Something for Somebody Quick":

> *When you're heavy at heart*
> *And your world falls apart,*
> *Do not pity yourself, I implore you.*
> *No, up with your chin,*

Meet bad luck with a grin,
And try this infallible trick:
It never will fail you,
Whatever may ail you —
DO SOMETHING FOR SOMEBODY QUICK!

. . . .

Don't fret about you
There's a Good Deed to do —
DO SOMETHING FOR SOMEBODY QUICK!* (146–47)

For a brief instant Janet's altruism is extremely appealing:

Dear Janet! I find myself falling in love with her — yes, with my own great-grandmother — as I watch these scenes, where her bravery and sweet temper keep afloat this household of raving optimist brother, dispirited mathematician-turned-tailor husband, her sister-in-law Polly — a soft machine for replenishing the earth and not much else — and nine children, clamorous and egotistical as children are and must be if they are to save their souls in an adult world. (146)

Yet for a reader who should by this time in this tenth novel be convinced of the importance of the individual quest, her behaviour is more disconcerting than its direct antithesis — the selfishness sometimes unmoderated by loving-kindness of Francis Cornish, Dunstan Ramsay, and Magnus Eisengrim. In her lack of attention to legitimate personal concerns, Janet risks being consumed in the maelstrom of ever-increasing demands on her time and energy. Her great-grandson, while attracted to her, swiftly perceives the dangers of her behaviour; he has, so to speak, read his Robertson Davies: "She thinks as little of self as a human creature can do — which, as everything has to be seen from the watch-tower of self, and as every action is a demonstration of self, is not as great a victory as the dear soul hopes it is" (147).

While all of this may be familiar fare, Davies exploits a new theme in *Murther and Walking Spirits.* He usually insists that organized religions, with their emphasis on good works and second-hand experience of the numinous, are poor substitutes for the hard, solitary work of introspection. However, several years before he published this novel, Davies presented Methodism as an exception; in his view it facilitated an immediate, personal encounter with the spiritual world:

146

The Methodist Church, however it might have laboured in social causes, never forgot John Wesley's emphasis on personal holiness and the need for private prayer and examination of conscience, and in this way it left the path open for numinosity to enter the life of its members. ("Keeping Faith" 188)

Because this Wesleyan conception is so fundamentally congruent with Davies's own preoccupation with self-examination, it is of key significance in *Murther and Walking Spirits*, where Davies devotes more effort to exploring elements of orthodox faith than anywhere else in his canon. In this novel he describes Methodism at its best:

Wesleyans wanted, and found, a deeply personal faith that the Established Church of England no longer gave. The tone of their worship was —

> *He left His Father's throne above —*
> *So free, so infinite His grace —*
> *Emptied Himself of all but love,*
> *And bled for Adam's helpless race:*
> *'Tis mercy, all, immense and free;*
> *For, O my God, it found out me!*

It found out *me*, it placed *me* in direct touch with God, it made *me* and my salvation the driving force in life. (137–38)

Thus, even the standards of her own church rate Janet Gilmartin's near-total self-abnegation undesirable.

Curiously, however, Davies relates rather than shows the numinosity the Methodists experienced. Never does he depict the Wesleyan equivalent of the transcendence associated with David Staunton's metamorphosis in the cave, or Dunstan Ramsay's vision on the European battlefield. Even when *Murther and Walking Spirits* portrays Wesley Gilmartin's baptism (108–09), it emphasizes the external setting and ritual rather than any sense of the numinous that the boy feels. Much as Davies may embrace Methodism as a potential avenue to the world of the spirit, he skirts illustrating specifics because, ironically, this might diminish the credibility of his overall message. Although he constantly stresses the importance of our emotional faculties, the personal spiritual experiences of Methodism were often so excessively emotional — as we see from accounts of their enthusiastic revival meetings — that Davies remarks on their "uncouth raptures" in his discussion of Ronald Knox's *Enthusiasm* (*Enthusiasms* 81). A full depiction of these experiences might, therefore, compromise the stature of some of the novel's otherwise attractive characters. At most, *Murther and Walking Spirits* provides a passage associating Wesleyanism with the romantic rather than the neoclassical movement, emphasizing its emotional over its intellectual appeal (137–38).

However, Davies unequivocally expresses his conviction that even a religion that initially insists on individual experience can degenerate into a tarnished replica of its former self. William McOmish's congregation indicates the extent to which mass organization can corrode the ideal of individual holiness. Davies portrays these latter-generation Methodists at some length, depicting them as excessively materialistic and concerned with external shows of faith. The attitude of their pastor is typical:

> *Of course* the church must have a mortgage for, as the Reverend Wilbur Woolarton Woodside very wisely said, a church without a mortgage is a church without a soul. Without a mortgage to be paid off, how could the congregation be spurred to organize all the bazaars, fowl suppers, home-talent concerts, and other affairs that would raise money, and also generate Christian enthusiasm? If people cannot be goaded into doing something for the church, they may quite probably lose their zeal for the church. As the pastor put it, they might be at ease in Zion, and nineteenth-century Protestantism had no use for ease. Not a particle. Stress and struggle was [sic] what was needed to keep people alive in their faith. . . . People must be kept at the job of raising money, or they may forget Christ. (187–88)

Juxtaposed with this institutional debasement of the individual's apprehension of the divine is Connor Gilmartin's extended quest for self. Because Davies accepts the possibility "that after death there might be another period of preparation for the next move on" ("Canada"), in this novel he significantly expands the metaphysical boundaries of the introspective search, illustrating its potential for transcending mortal existence. Thus, the inner pilgrimage not only provides the spiritual key to living well in this world, but also to entering successfully into the next: "what happens to the man in my book after his death is a kind of summing up before he's ready to go on to something else. At the end of the book there's a strong hint that he's found out something extremely vital" ("Canada").

That Gilmartin's posthumous endeavour has a Jungian foundation — and is thus ultimately a search for the *imago Dei* — is indicated by his finally meeting with the *"woman in the man,"* his "dear companion" (*Murther* 356, 357). This marks a crucial step in the inner quest, since for men the anima personifies the unconscious (Jung, *Psychology* 35). In addition to the underlying religious dimension implicit in the Jungian search for self, Davies explicitly couches his protagonist's exploration within a theological framework. Gilmartin's afterlife experience constitutes the logical culmination of his many discussions of the hereafter with Hugh McWearie — invariably conducted along religious lines — and more generally of the concern with spiritual matters manifested by almost all of his ancestors. Furthermore, his pilgrimage squares with Davies's notion of religion as the awareness of those "things which are infinitely greater than yourself, and in the face of which you and your desires and your hopes are trivial" (*Conversations* 95), since a transcendent filmmaker(s) directs Gilmartin's journey, forcing him to watch the movies that constitute the transforming dynamic of his experience. Gilmartin perceives his helplessness before this filmmaker during his viewing of a particularly painful clip from which he wishes to depart: "Whatever power was showing me this film was determined that I should see it all" (59).

The unequivocal sense here of a transcendent presence guiding the inner search stands as Davies's most explicit championing of selfishness and his strongest affirmation that real egocentrism falls within the purview of religion. What originated in the 1940s as a number of desultory exhortations to avoid the pull of the multitude has blossomed into an expansive, coherent statement of principle. Nothing less than salvation — not just earthly but now also eternal — hangs in the balance.

SEVEN

Towards a New Revelation: Into the Next Millennium

These, then, constitute the central principles of Robertson Davies's religious vision: a belief in God but a reluctance to circumscribe this superior being (or force) too rigidly; an unrelenting insistence on not only the existence of evil but also its presence as both external to and inherent within humans; a corresponding recognition that evil can often lead to good, or even be produced by a seeming good; a steadfast conviction that Christianity must accommodate women; and finally, a recipe for salvation that stresses an individual and introspective approach to spiritual deliverance. In addition to comprising those "brass tacks" that the "investigation of religion by orthodox theological means" never yielded for him (*Conversations* 81), these principles constitute the essence of a larger vision.

Davies has long feared that current religious practice is becoming increasingly irrelevant. In fact, statements dating from his earliest writings reflect the very concerns he outlined in later years. In his 1940 review of Franz Werfel's *Embezzled Heaven*, Davies recognizes the spiritual problems faced by contemporary men and women, maintaining that

> the author leaves us high and dry. He has convinced us that a great part of the world's ills are the result of modern man's denial of the spiritual domain. But where do we go from there? Certainly not backward to a kind of warmed-over medieval religious feeling, as Mr. Werfel tacitly suggests. Attempts to retrace old paths have never been of any value to mankind. ("Salvation")

Decades later, in 1982, he compared the condition of our religious belief today with that of the ancient Romans "two or three hundred years before the birth of Christ," arguing that "[t]heir religion had failed them, just as ours has, rather, lost its strong driving power" (*Conversations* 234). His most recent assertion of this point I have cited in an earlier chapter, but it bears repeating in the present context:

Two very big world wars have shaken the popular notions of religion very gravely and I think upon the whole advantageously because religion had reached a point where it needed a substantial rethink. I am talking now of course of the Christian-Judaic tradition . . . which I think has tremendous virtue and tremendous strength but it had become a little bit set in its ways and [required] some new thinking about it and a new application of it to the life that faces us in a world which is the world of the atom bomb [not the world] which my father remembers, which was the world of the horse. (Interview, *Imprint*)[1]

Particularly striking is Davies's censure of those writers who offer hopelessness in response to the decline of traditional religion. For instance, "What About a Show of Courage?", his 1957 review of Albert Camus's *The Fall*, rebukes Camus for "a graceful despair much too juvenile for an author of forty-three." After noting that "Camus rejects religion — it is 'out of style' says Clamence,"[2] Davies states:

If I were asked to give counsel to the modern intellectual school of novelists I should bid them to look into their own hearts and cultivate the Cardinal Virtues there, beginning with Fortitude, for they seem in the main to be a whining, hopeless lot, worse than the Romantics. A show of courage, a recognition that despair is neither new nor incurable, would work wonders for them. (20–21)

Similarly, in the 1976 Larkin-Stuart lectures, Davies maintains that because "the literature of our day. . . . dwells so much on damnation, without any prospect of blessing, I have called it by T.S. Eliot's

---

1 Similarly, Jung asserts: "Today Christianity is devitalized by its remoteness from the spirit of the times. It stands in need of a new union with, or relation to, the atomic age, which is a unique novelty in history" (*Collected* 18: 1666).

2 Jean-Baptiste Clamence is the main character of *The Fall*.

phrase, Thunder Without Rain" (*One Half* 247). He then describes its prevailing atmosphere of spiritual despair:

> Those among you who are accustomed to keeping up with the modern novel are aware of the atmosphere of Existentialist gloom, of malice against mankind, of the concentration on misfortune, and the delight in gallows-humour, that characterizes so much of the work of even the most talented of our writers. There are no gods, they seem to say, but there is a Lurking Something that acts against mankind, to render his works futile. The people in these novels rarely love, but if they do their love is complex and productive of pain and disillusionment. . . . Guilt and dread are what we find in the most up-to-date exercises in the age-old art of story-telling, where they are cloaked as revelations of the inner life of man. (*One Half* 248–49)

Davies's approach is much more optimistic. Far from dismissing all religion as no longer tenable and filling his novels with the concomitant horrors, Davies, like William James (*Varieties* 257–59), recognizes that beliefs change over the centuries, a point he affirmed in such early pieces as "Night of the Witches" and "New Gods for Old." Simon Darcourt best articulates Davies's views when, in reaction to the extremely conservative creed of Elias Schnakenburg (Schnak's father), he insists to Arthur and Maria: " 'Real religion, my friends, is evolutionary and revolutionary . . .' " (*Lyre* 69). Faith is not static and therefore currently withering into irrelevance; instead, it reacts to cataclysmic events and is being continually reconstructed. Consequently, we live not in a moribund age of dying religion but in a vibrant time of transformation and rebirth. In his review of *Embezzled Heaven*, Davies affirms: "We must go forward, trusting to find something in the future which will be better than what we have lost. What we must not do is regard our troubled place in time as an excuse for spiritual nullity" ("Salvation"). Years later, pondering the "age of superstition" in which we live, Davies told Louise Lague: "I think that we're probably going to see the rise from the midst of all this queer, superstitious searching for something, a new religion. Perhaps not an entirely new religion, but at least a new form of religion" (*Conversations* 162, 163).

The Platonic aeons of astrologers and alchemists, each comprising approximately 2,000 years, provide another context for Davies's comments on this impending change:

It is one of those coincidences that makes astrology such an uncomfortable study for people who despise it that long before the Christian era, the zodiacal sign of Pisces — the Fishes — had been assigned to it, and that the name given to Jesus by his Greek followers — Jesus Christ, Son of God, Saviour — proves, when you look at its initials, to be an acroustic [sic] of the Greek word for fish. . . . [I]f we continue the line of speculation in which Aeons are relevant, we must squarely face the fact that whatever the future of Christianity may be, the Aeon of its inception is waning, and either a new interpretation of Christianity, or a new aspect of faith, must be expected. . . . Aquarius — if the sign runs true to astrological form — should bring a great new advance in the spiritual consciousness of man, because Aquarius is, among other things, The Awakener. ("Christmas")

He reaffirms this later in response to Tom Harpur's question, "Talking about the future of religion, do you see changes coming?":

Yes I do. I think a very decisive, radical change is imminent, because in the psychological history of mankind there has been something which you can call a new revelation about every 2,000 years. The 2,000 years of Christianity, what might be called the Age of Pisces, is running out, and something will come to replace it; and perhaps to build upon it, as the Age of Pisces built upon the earlier, tremendous intellectual probing of the Greeks and also the extraordinary moral force and authority of the Hebrews. I think we are headed for something new. (*Conversations* 210)

In *The Rebel Angels*, John Parlabane exclaims exuberantly: " 'The world is drawing near to the end of one of the Platonic Aeons — the Aeon of Pisces — and gigantic changes are in the air. [My] book is probably the first of the great books of the New Aeon, the Aeon of Aquarius, and it foreshadows what lies in the future for mankind' " (240). Strip away the braggadocio and what remains is a fairly accurate analysis of the religious dimension of Davies's novels. Jung argues that "We are living in what the Greeks called . . . the right time — for a 'metamorphosis of the gods,' i.e., of the fundamental principles and symbols" (*The Undiscovered Self* 123); correspondingly, in Davies's notion of God the old certainties regarding His metaphysical nature are no longer relevant — they have been replaced, instead, by a quest for another vision that extends throughout his canon. Concomitantly, Davies urges his readers to undertake this search individually rather than communally, a point Jung also believes is essential to future change. In *The Undiscovered Self*, the essay in which he most advocates individual spirituality and depreciates the prevailing emphasis on collective worship, Jung maintains:

I am . . . convinced that it is not Christianity, but our conception and interpretation of it, that has become antiquated in face of the present world situation. The Christian symbol is a living thing that carries in itself the seeds of further development. It can go on developing; it depends only on us, whether we can make up our minds to meditate again, and more thoroughly, on the Christian premises. This requires a very different attitude towards the individual, towards the microcosm of the self, from the one we have had hitherto. (74–75)

Jung also argues that in the Age of Aquarius "It will . . . no longer be possible to write off evil as the mere privation of good; its real existence will have to be recognized" (*Collected* 9.2: 142) — a recognition, of course, that underlies all of Davies's beliefs about evil and the two devils. Further, Davies's literary compensation for the inadequate presence of the feminine in western belief presages a more widespread accommodation of women in the future: "I think that we're due for a new religious revelation. It will build on what we have, Christianity, and a lot of it will be concerned with women and women's place in society . . ." ("Conversations").

Thus, although by contemporary standards Davies at first appears to be a conservative and traditional author — comparisons are made between his work and that of Shaw or Dickens — his religious vision surely qualifies this perception. Certainly he does look back and eclectically espouse the monotheism of the Jews and Christians, the Marianic emphasis of the Roman Catholics, and the strenuous introspection of the Gnostics. However, he also breaks with established convention — and, indeed, with many of his secular contemporaries — by reworking these or synthesizing them with each other and with contemporary psychological belief, in order to offer a vibrant new vision that will carry us forward into the next millennium.

APPENDIX I

Davies and Christ

It may seem ironic that Davies's views about the central figure of Christianity are relegated to a brief appendix. However, the relative paucity of comments about Jesus in Davies's work would indicate that he regards Him to be of secondary importance to the other issues explored in this study. When he does discuss Christ, Davies rejects "the Christian claim that Jesus is the unique Messiah for mankind" and states: "It seems to me that Jesus as an ethical teacher and Jesus as the symbol of the best in man are different creatures. When they're mixed up together you get some bad results." For the ethical instructor Davies offers immediate praise: "the teaching . . . must be realized as that of a man of an astonishing degree of insight" (*Conversations* 139).

About the symbolic Christ of legend, whom he distinguishes from the historical figure (139), Davies is more ambivalent. He believes that stories of the virgin birth, the visit of the Magi, and the miracles, for instance, are not literal fact but "very important myth":

> Myth grows [because] people want marvels and when they were describing the life of Christ they wanted marvels, and they got marvels and of course they got something very fine as well; but I wonder how much historical accuracy there is about those accounts of miracles, raisings from the dead, the curings of the sick and this, that, and the other. (Interview, *Harpur's*)

While somewhat enigmatically asserting the "infinite value" of the "myth that grew up around Jesus after His lifetime" (*Conversations* 139), Davies expresses reservations on two accounts. First, he argues that misunderstanding the significance of this myth can be detrimental and illustrates his belief by describing Jung's attitude towards trying to live someone else's myth:

He says that a great many people are told that they should attempt to live out the life of Christ in their own lives; *The Imitation of Christ* is the name of one of the very great books of devotion. What does that mean? That you walk around in sandals and mooch your food off your rich friends and then abuse the rich and get yourself into trouble with the authorities and eventually hanged or electrocuted. . . . That is an absurd way to conduct your life; it doesn't make any sense at all and I think that Christ would have laughed himself sick if he heard about it. . . . [W]hat Jung points out is that Christ lived true to his own nature and his own destiny and the true imitation of Christ is doing the same thing [cf. *Collected* 11: 521–22; *Memories* 280] and it may lead you to lead a life which is not very full of events, not full of great public goings on, that does not form the foundation of a great religion, but which is a completion and a reality of yourself. . . . One of the reasons that the Christian church is in such trouble, and it is in very great trouble, is that they [sic] have forgotten all about that and they have become so externalized: being Christian is doing good to other people. (Interview, *Harpur's*)[1]

Davies's second reservation concerning Christ as a symbol of the best in humanity pertains, ironically, to what he considers the inherent limitations when Jesus represents flawlessness. His unease on this point is longstanding, beginning in his youth:

As he remembers it, Jesus was presented as a "big softie who loved everybody and forgave everybody." Davies hated "the pictures of that bearded lady in a nightie being wonderful to everybody." Hymns like "Tell me the stories of Jesus" with its lines

> Words full of kindness,
> Deeds full of grace,

---

1 Simon Darcourt echoes these sentiments in *The Rebel Angels* (56–57). An instance of a different misuse of the myth about Christ is Boy Staunton's endorsement of Jesus as an aristocratic socialite and capitalist whose materialism seems to have left Him oblivious to the poor and downtrodden (*Fifth* 120–22).

All in the lovelight,
Of Jesus' face

almost made him "throw up." (Grant, *Robertson Davies: Man of Myth* 104)

His sentiments as an adult — though less colourful — are similar. In the 1976 Larkin-Stuart lectures, in which he explores the crucial importance of evil in both life and literature, Davies states:

The idea of complete perfection, even when it is an attribute of Christ himself, has been known to cause disquiet in some souls, who long for wholeness in the Redeemer of Mankind, and who see wholeness as including human attributes of which the Biblical Christ knows nothing. (*One Half* 266)[1]

Elsewhere he protests that "Christianity's focus is entirely on the achievement of perfection and I don't think that is either a possibility or indeed, perhaps, desirable, because perfection is inhuman" ("Conversations"). Surely this deficiency in the symbolic value of Christ makes Him a supernumerary player in the religious vision of a writer who insists so tenaciously on the importance of the evil in all humans.

---

1 Jung states that "the Christ-figure is not a totality, for it lacks the nocturnal side of the psyche's nature, the darkness of the spirit, and is also without sin" (*Collected* 11: 232). It is certainly because this symbol lacks the necessary component of evil that Father Blazon exclaims: " 'The Devil knows corners of us all of which Christ Himself is ignorant' " (*Fifth* 249).

APPENDIX II

Biblical Allusions and Quotations in Davies's Fiction

Although Davies's religious beliefs are hardly those of an orthodox Christian, the Bible has remained of crucial importance to him since boyhood — albeit, not for doctrinal reasons. For instance, in 1941 he commends "the magnificence of the King James Bible," explaining:

> It is important in this present age, when millions of words are written every day with a haste which makes for slovenly, faulty writing, that we should have some standard of great English, and I cannot think of any better standard than the pure and noble English of the Bible. Shakespeare is the only possible alternative, and his vocabulary is too personal and his manner too highly colored to serve as a model for everyone. But in the Bible we have a perfect model of suitable, eloquent English used with supreme style and skill. If our newspaper reports, for instance, were written as simply as the stories of the Prodigal Son or the Good Samaritan what magnificent reading they would make. . . . [L]et us strip as much of the outmoded trappings and taboos from the Bible as we can, but let us maintain our Authorized Version in its purity. ("Cap and Bells")

That this is a strongly held conviction is apparent from its longevity, for in a 1988 interview Davies informs Robert Fulford that

> every day of my life from the time I began to go to school as a little boy, until I emerged from school at the age of 18 or 19, I heard the Bible read to me and that meant that every day of my life I had an example of the finest prose in English read to me first thing in the morning. I didn't think of it as that, but that

was what I heard, and it's amazing how it imposes itself upon you as a standard of exposition and concise expression. (*Conversations* 274)[1]

Coinciding with his enduring praise of the Bible's exemplary prose is Davies's longtime fascination with the stories it chronicles. In the preface to his libretto for the 1993 International Choral Festival's production of *Jezebel*, he states: "I have always admired those Eastern story-tellers who spread their mats in the market places of cities like Baghdad and Alexandria, and cried, 'Give me a copper coin and I will tell you a golden tale.' The Bible is full of such tales . . ." (3). Elsewhere, in words reminiscent of Dunstan Ramsay's,[2] he recalls that

> it used to strike me very, very strongly when I was a small boy that the Bible stories with which I was diverted and instructed, as children were in those days, seemed to me to be just side by side with the stories from *Arabian Nights* and Grimm and Andersen and so forth. They were equally marvelous. They were full of extraordinary characters whom you certainly wouldn't encounter every day but who were very real in another way. (*Conversations* 146–47).

Respecting the Bible as "classical literature of history, poetry, drama, legend, and prophecy" (*Voice* 24), Davies compares it to the works of Homer and Virgil (25). Just as these great mythological works of antiquity united the civilizations that produced them, so

---

1 Magnus Eisengrim affirms this in *World of Wonders*: " 'Big words, said Milady, were a great mistake in ordinary conversation, and she made me read the Bible to her to rid me of the big-word habit' " (241).

2 Compare, for example, the following:

> when the Reverend Andrew Bowyer bade all us Presbyterians to prepare ourselves for the Marriage Feast of the Lamb [Revelation 19.7, 9], it seemed to me that *Arabian Nights* and the *Bible* were getting pretty close — and I did not mean this in any scoffing sense. (*Fifth* 43)

> I read [the New Testament] not from zeal but curiosity and . . . long passages of it confirmed my early impression that religion and *Arabian Nights* were true in the same way. (Later I was able to say that they were both psychologically rather than literally true. . . .) (*Fifth* 71)

did the Bible once inform and unify our own culture. In 1941, after criticizing those by whom the "scriptures were accepted uncritically and their manifest contradictions . . . swallowed whole," and warning that "[p]eople want to read the Bible now with understanding, and without the depressing feeling that they are reading a 'sacred' book," Davies writes:

It is a wicked thing to hedge any book about with so many superstitions and taboos that people cannot read it for the wisdom that is in it. . . . We read the Greek and Latin classics because they contain the distilled wisdom of great peoples; the Bible does the same thing, and it contains the root of all the ethical teaching which has moulded our civilization. ("Cap and Bells")

Almost five decades later, Davies laments the widespread scriptural illiteracy of contemporary times, expressing concern that a society

from which the Bible is disappearing is a society which is moving toward barbarism. Because one of the elements of a civilized society is that it has a congruous body of common knowledge, generally of classic literature. And that is what the Bible was, quite apart from what it had to say on religious subjects, which was another thing. It was a common classical literature which was known to virtually everybody. And it was a literature which had its origin in Hebrew and in Greek, and when you read it in English you were reading perhaps the supreme classic of the English language. And everybody knew the allusions, . . . and when my mother referred to people that she didn't like, as the Tribes of Menassi,[1] I knew exactly what she was talking about. And this meant that there was a common frame of reference for conversation, oratory and opinion, right from the top of society to the bottom, and when somebody in parliament made a biblical reference, he was literally talking to a nation which understood

---

1 The error in transcription here abundantly proves Davies's point about the current lack of biblical literacy. The tribe's name is, in fact, spelled Manasseh, as Davies himself indicates when he incorporates his mother's allusion into *Murther and Walking Spirits* (207); cf. no. 20 of *Murther and Walking Spirits* below.

him, not making a classical allusion which went over the heads of most of the people who might hear him. We have lost that great classic background. And to have lost your classic background is to be very much at sea. (*Conversations* 278–79)

His mother's facility with scripture was, Davies says, often employed ironically: "I was brought up by parents who were always quoting the Bible, not very reverently, I'm afraid. One of my mother's favourite quotations was that about how the dog shall return again to its vomit and the hog to his wallowing in the mire. (Chuckles)" (*Conversations* 228). Similarly, although Davies's novels indicate that the Bible is itself not a humorous text (*World* 70, 79–80, 85–86; *Rebel* 37), as a comic writer he exploits it to invest his own works with wit. This yields a spectrum of allusions, ranging from ill-mannered sarcasm of the kind provided by Urky McVarish, who employs the very words used by Davies's mother; through amusing irreverence, typified by Magnus Eisengrim and Dr. J.A. Jerome, both of whom misappropriate the same passage from the Epistle to the Romans; to unabashed comedy of the type associated, for example, with Humphrey Cobbler, who metamorphoses the sublime vision of the Ancient of Days from the Book of Daniel into an epiphany of a Rotarian God decked out in service club buttons.

Thus, in addition to being a superb model of fine prose, an important mythological document, and a compelling ethical guide, the Bible is valuable to Davies for the considerable and varied humour he is able to derive from it. The extent to which his convictions about the Bible's merit are manifest in his novels is documented in the following catalogue.

In order to prevent this inventory from becoming unwieldy, it is not exhaustive — that is, it does not record *all* of the scriptural allusions in Davies's novels; nonetheless, it is a comprehensive list of most of them. Since this appendix is intended to serve not only as evidence of the importance of the Bible in Davies's fiction, but also as an aid to readers with varying degrees of scriptural literacy, each entry satisfies at least one of the three following criteria:

1) It must be fairly significant to the novel in which it is employed.

2) It must be reasonably obscure in this age in which "Biblical culture scarcely exists" (*Voice* 25).

3) If familiar, it must be at least somewhat difficult to locate in the Bible.

For instance, I felt it unnecessary, indeed potentially cumbersome, to include Davies's very general references to prominent biblical figures. I also omitted briefly rendered allusions to well-known occurrences, such as, for example, the last supper in *Fifth Business* or passing references in *What's Bred in the Bone* to pictures of the nativity and the crucifixion in art galleries.

In keeping with Davies's stated preference, unless otherwise indicated all of my biblical citations are from "the great King James version" (*Voice* 24–25).

I have listed Davies's novels in chronological order.

A. *Tempest-Tost*

1. When explaining Larry Pye's penchant for finding — indeed creating — problems and then solving them, Solly Bridgetower states ironically: " ' "To him that o'ercometh, God giveth a crown" ' " (21).

   ¶ This is taken from a hymn and is probably based on a conflation of two passages from Revelation: "To him that overcometh will I give to eat of the tree of life, which is in the midst of the paradise of God" (2.7); "be thou faithful unto death, and I will give thee a crown of life" (2.10).

2. Davies describes in the following terms Hector Mackilwraith's *modus operandi* as he marks exams: "But there were certain papers upon which he put a cabbalistic word which he had taken over from a teacher of his own younger days. Written always in capitals, and flaming like the Tetragrammaton on the breastplate of the High Priest, the word was TOSASM, and it was formed from the initials of a teacher's heartcry — The Old Stupid and Silly Mistake" (49).

   ¶ The tetragrammaton is the four-letter Hebrew word for God written YHWH or JHVH. According to scripture, the High Priest's breastplate contained not the tetragrammaton but, at God's command, the names of the twelve tribes of Israel (cf. Exodus 28.21; 39.14). However, Josephus documents the presence of the tetragrammaton on the High Priest's breastplate and notes that

Alexander is supposed to have bowed down and adored it (Graves 84).[1]

3. When Hector, the son of the Presbyterian minister, is strapped at school for his fight with the rat-faced Baptist boy, "the shadow of corporal punishment had fallen across a pulpit. In such a community as that, the preachers formed a Sanhedrin, and as they were severe towards others, they were harshly judged when disgrace touched them" (79–80).
¶ Although the Sanhedrin is not directly identified in the King James Bible, according to *The Compact Edition of the Oxford English Dictionary* it was the "name applied to the highest court of justice and supreme council at Jerusalem, and in a wider sense also to lower courts of justice." It was the Sanhedrin before which Jesus stood trial (cf. Matthew 26.57ff.; Mark 14.53ff.; Luke 22.52ff.; John 19) and which later reprimanded his apostles (Acts 4.5–22; 5.17–42; cf. also Hagner 272–73).

4. As he attempts to persuade young Hector Mackilwraith to become a man of the cloth, Reverend James McKinnon distinguishes between the teacher and the minister: " 'The gown and bands may mark the teacher, but it is the working of God's spirit in the heart and mind which marks the minister' " (83).
¶ cf. 1 Samuel 2.35 in which God prophesies the priesthood of Samuel: "I will raise me up a faithful priest, that shall do according to that which is in mine heart and in my mind: and I will build him a sure house; and he shall walk before mine anointed for ever."

5. McKinnon suggests that God may already have spoken to Hector " 'in the watches of the night' " (83).
¶ cf. Psalms 63.6: "I remember thee upon my bed, and meditate on thee in the night watches."

6. In characterizing service to God, McKinnon asserts: " 'His yoke is easy, and His burthen light' " (85).
¶ cf. Matthew 11.29–30: "Take my yoke upon you, and learn of me; for I am meek and lowly in heart: and ye shall find rest unto your souls. For my yoke is easy, and my burden is light."

7. With regard to his role in the production of *The Tempest*, Humphrey Cobbler tells Solly Bridgetower: " 'You have already

---

1 I am indebted to W.J. Keith for bringing Graves's information to my attention.

the harried look of a man who regards himself as the Lamb of God who takes upon him the sins of the whole world. That's silly. . . . Pass the buck' " (139).

¶ cf. John 1.29: "The next day John seeth Jesus coming unto him, and saith, Behold the Lamb of God, which taketh away the sin of the world."

8. When discussing Griselda Webster, Humphrey Cobbler directs " 'a rather delicate phrase from the Prophet Ezekiel' " at Roger Tasset: " 'I deduce that you have already bruised the teats of her virginity' " (175).

¶ cf. Ezekiel 23.2–3: "Son of man, there were two women, the daughters of one mother: And they committed whoredoms in Egypt; they committed whoredoms in their youth: there were their breasts pressed, and there they bruised the teats of their virginity."

9. After seeing Professor Vambrace in long underwear, Solly exclaims: " 'A shocking sight. I felt like the sons of Noah when they had uncovered their father's nakedness' " (253–54).

¶ cf. Genesis 9.20–27. In fact, only one of Noah's sons, Ham, saw his father naked.

¶ cf. also no. 22 of *Murther and Walking Spirits* below.

10. When he believes he is dispatching himself into eternity, Hector utters a prayer that his father, the Reverend John Mackilwraith, had employed when words had otherwise failed him: " 'O Lord, take Thou a live coal from off Thine altar and touch our lips' " (270).

¶ cf. Isaiah 6.6–7: "Then flew one of the seraphims unto me, having a live coal in his hand, which he had taken with the tongs from off the altar: And he laid it upon my mouth, and said, Lo, this hath touched thy lips; and thine iniquity is taken away, and thy sin purged."

¶ cf. also no. 8 of *Fifth Business* below.

B. *Leaven of Malice*

1. One of the crosses that Gloster Ridley must bear as editor of *The Bellman* is a series of letters from a correspondent who deplores

the decline of religion and morals in contemporary society. Now and then the writer relates "a modern enormity to one of the monsters in Revelation" (9).

¶ cf. Revelation 12 and 13.

2. Dean Jevon Knapp suspects that if his parishioners' zeal for their salvation "began to equal their zeal for minding his business, the New Jerusalem would quickly be at hand" (63).

¶ cf. Revelation 21.1ff.

3. Humphrey Cobbler describes his worst fear during his " 'head-long flight from respectability' " (140): " 'Sometimes I have a nightmare in which I dream that I have gone to heaven, and as I creep toward the Awful Throne I am blinded by the array of service-club buttons shining on the robe of the Ancient of Days. And then I know that my life has been wasted, and that I am in for an eternity of Social Disapproval' " (141).

¶ cf. Daniel 7.9 where "Ancient of days" is used to describe God as He appears, resplendent, in a vision: "I beheld till the thrones were cast down, and the Ancient of days did sit, whose garment was white as snow, and the hair of his head like the pure wool: his throne was like the fiery flame, and his wheels as burning fire." This term is also used in Daniel 7.13 and 7.22.

4. Solly explains to Cobbler the peculiarly Canadian traits evidenced by certain Israelites in Charles Heavysege's *Saul*: " 'Does not Jehoiadah behave like a Canadian when he refuses to cheer when his neighbours are watching him? Is it not typically Canadian of Heavysege's Hebrews that they take exception to Saul's "raging in a public place"? Is it not Canadian self-control that David displays when, instead of making a noisy fuss he "lets his spittle fall upon his beard, and scrabbles on the door-post"?' " (189).

¶ The complete story of the irascible King Saul is chronicled in 1 Samuel 9–31. Though Saul certainly indulged in several displays of temper (cf. 1 Samuel 11.6ff; 18.8ff; 20.30ff), the exception taken by his subjects to their public nature indeed seems to be one of Heavysege's Canadianisms.

¶ David's erratic conduct, however, is biblical. While residing with the King of Gath and his servants, he fears for his life; as a means of self-preservation "he changed his behaviour before them, and feigned himself mad in their hands, and scrabbled on the doors of the gate, and let his spittle fall down upon his beard" (1 Samuel 21.13). This public spectacle seems different from the " 'Canadian self-control' " to which Solly refers.

5. During the climactic scene in Gloster Ridley's office, Dean Jevon Knapp affirms: " 'In the Prayer Book you will find a special plea to be preserved from [malice], appointed for the first Sunday after Easter: "Grant us so to put away the leaven of malice and wickedness that we may always serve Thee in pureness of living and truth." The writer of that prayer understood malice. It works like a leaven; it stirs, and swells, and changes all that surrounds it. If you seek to pin it down in law, it may well elude you. Who can separate the leaven from the lump when once it has been mixed?' " (266–67)

¶ cf. 1 Corinthians 5.6–8: "Know ye not that a little leaven leaveneth the whole lump? Purge out therefore the old leaven, that ye may be a new lump, as ye are unleavened. For even Christ our passover is sacrificed for us: Therefore let us keep the feast, not with old leaven, neither with the leaven of malice and wickedness; but with the unleavened bread of sincerity and truth."

C. A Mixture of Frailties

1. Monica Gall begins her musical career singing in the Heart and Hope Gospel Quartet (37).

¶ This group might take its name from Psalms 31.24: "Be of good courage, and he shall strengthen your heart, all ye that hope in the Lord."

2. Regarding Puss Pottinger's disapproval of Pastor Beamis and the Thirteeners, the narrator states: "in her Father's house were many mansions, but some of them were in better parts of the Holy City than others; the Thirteenth Apostle Tabernacle obviously belonged in the slums of the spirit" (42).

¶ cf. John 14.2: "In my Father's house are many mansions: if it were not so, I would have told you. I go to prepare a place for you."

3. Dean Knapp jocularly justifies his "poor opinion" of Pastor Beamis in the following terms: "did not *Leviticus* xxi 18 expressly forbid the priesthood to 'he that hath a flat nose'? And

had not Beamis the flat, bun-like, many times broken nose of the ex-pugilist?" (43)

¶ cf. Leviticus 21.16–18: "And the Lord spake unto Moses, saying, Speak unto Aaron, saying, Whosoever he be of thy seed in their generations that hath any blemish, let him not approach to offer the bread of his God. For whatsoever man he be that hath a blemish, he shall not approach: a blind man, or a lame, or he that hath a flat nose, or any thing superfluous. . . ."

4. Aunt Ellen warns Monica: " 'The Fifth Commandment is sacred: honour thy father and mother' " (69).

¶ cf. Exodus 20.12 and Deuteronomy 5.16.

¶ cf. also nos. 14, 19, and 21 of *Murther and Walking Spirits* below.

5. Giles Revelstoke identifies the " 'enlightening' " of the artist, as distinct from the " 'education' " of the critic, in these terms: " 'It is the spirit we must work with, and not the mind as such. For "the spirit searcheth all things, yea, the deep things of God" ' " (158).

¶ This is taken verbatim from 1 Corinthians 2.10.

6. The part of Bach's *Saint Matthew Passion* in which Monica sings is described thus: "Quickly followed the recitative in the Court of Caiaphas, then the chorale begging for defence against evil, and then — Christ's Silence Before Caiaphas, and the False Witnesses!" (240).

¶ cf. Matthew 26.57–63.

7. When Dr. Cobbett asks Monica to provide her mother's age for the death certificate, she does not know it: "It had always been understood that it was 'bold' to want to know the ages of one's parents; it was like uncovering their nakedness, in the Bible" (283).

¶ cf. Genesis 9.20–27.

¶ cf. also Leviticus 18.7: "The nakedness of thy father, or the nakedness of thy mother, shalt thou not uncover: she is thy mother; thou shalt not uncover her nakedness."

8. At the final Bridgetower memorial service in Saint Nicholas's Cathedral, "[t]he Dean read the lesson for the day . . . *thy voice shall be, as one that hath a familiar spirit.* . . ." Monica applies these words to her own situation: "Like me, she thought; only I have two; Ma speaks to me sometimes, in her very own voice,

so that I'm sure I'm not talking to myself, and today Giles has spoken to me twice, as though he were right behind me" (372).
¶ cf. Isaiah 29.4, from which the italicized words are taken almost verbatim.

9. The Dean's tripartite sermon about the means by which the birth of Jesus was perceived (375–79), refers first to the episode of the shepherds visited by the heavenly multitude (Luke 2.8–15); then to the wise men who saw the star (Matthew 2.1–2, 9–10); and finally to the aged figure of Simeon, "*who knew Our Lord intuitively*" when He was brought to the temple for circumcision (Luke 2.25–35).

10. As a jest, in reference to the birth of the Bridgetower son, the organist, Humphrey Cobbler, concludes the Bridgetower service by playing "*For unto us a child is born, Unto us a son is given*" (379).
¶ cf. Isaiah 9.6, from which this is taken verbatim (via Handel's *Messiah*).

D. *Fifth Business*

1. The hymn "For all the saints, Who from their labours rest" is sung at Dunstan Ramsay's retirement dinner (14).
¶ The title of the hymn is derived from Revelation 14.12–13. Ramsay has a passage from the same source inscribed on the lid of the box containing Mrs. Dempster's ashes (see no. 25 below).

2. Lorne Packer's insulting farewell to Ramsay concludes with this sendoff: " 'You served the school well according to your lights in your day and generation! Well done, thou good and faithful servant!' " Ramsay responds scornfully: "Packer . . . pushes me towards oblivion with tags of Biblical quotation, the gross impertinence of which he is unable to appreciate, religious illiterate that he is!" (14–15).
¶ cf. the parable of the talents in Matthew 25.21: "His lord said unto him, Well done, thou good and faithful servant: thou hast been faithful over a few things, I will make thee ruler over many things: enter thou into the joy of thy lord." This praise is repeated to the other prudent, productive servant in 25.23.

3. When Amasa Dempster refers to Ramsay in his prayers, he describes him as "the stranger within their gates" (40).
¶ cf. Exodus 20.10 and Deuteronomy 5.14, 14.21, and 31.12, from which this expression is taken almost verbatim.

4. In his prayers Dempster requests that God preserve Ramsay from "walking with a froward mouth" (40).
¶ cf. Proverbs 6.12: "A naughty person, a wicked man, walketh with a froward mouth."

5. According to Dempster, "the veneration of saints was one of the vilest superstitions of the Scarlet Woman of Rome" (42). Subsequently, one of Ramsay's peers at Colborne College "thought it his duty to warn me against the Scarlet Woman and demanded rhetorically how I could possibly 'swallow the Pope' " (165).
¶ cf. Revelation 17.3–4: "I saw a woman sit upon a scarlet coloured beast, full of names of blasphemy, having seven heads and ten horns. And the woman was arrayed in purple and scarlet colour, and decked with gold and precious stones and pearls, having a golden cup in her hand full of abominations and filthiness of her fornication."

6. Ramsay states that "when the Reverend Andrew Bowyer bade all us Presbyterians to prepare ourselves for the Marriage Feast of the Lamb, it seemed to me that *Arabian Nights* and the *Bible* were getting pretty close — and I did not mean this in any scoffing sense" (43).
¶ cf. Revelation 19.7, 9: "Let us be glad and rejoice, and give honour to him: for the marriage of the Lamb is come, and his wife hath made herself ready. . . . Blessed are they which are called unto the marriage supper of the Lamb."

7. The young Ramsay is fascinated by Bowyer's descriptions of Gehenna, "the hateful valley outside the walls of Jerusalem, where outcasts lived, and where their flickering fires, seen from the city walls, may have given rise to the idea of a hell of perpetual burning" (46).
¶ In fact, the word "hell" in Matthew 5.22, 29, 30, 18.9, 23.15, 33; Mark 9.43, 45, 47; Luke 12.5; and James 3.6 is a translation of the Hebrew word *geenna*, a valley of Jerusalem used "as a name for the place (or state) of everlasting punishment" (Strong 20).

8. Like the Reverend John Mackilwraith (cf. no. 10 of *Tempest-Tost* above), Bowyer is evidently given to exclaiming: " 'O Lord,

take Thou a live coal from off Thine altar and touch our lips' "
(54).
¶ cf. Isaiah 6.6–7: "Then flew one of the seraphims unto me,
having a live coal in his hand, which he had taken with the tongs
from off the altar: And he laid it upon my mouth, and said, Lo,
this hath touched thy lips; and thine iniquity is taken away, and
thy sin purged."

9. In describing his interest in the Bible, Ramsay says: "I think
Revelation was my favourite book; the Gospels seemed less
relevant to me then than John's visions of the beasts and the
struggle of the Crowned Woman, who had the moon beneath
her feet, with the great Red Dragon" (71). Later Ramsay believes
that he sees this woman in his battlefield vision (77).
¶ cf. Revelation 12.1–9 for the story of the crowned woman
and the red dragon.
¶ cf. Revelation 13.1–18 for the visions of the beasts from the
sea and the earth.

10. George Leadbeater's scriptural exegesis for Boy Staunton (121)
comprises some rather tendentious discussion of the following
biblical episodes:
   i) The woman pouring ointment on Jesus's feet: cf. Luke
   7.36–50 and John 12.3–8.
   ii) The transformation of water into wine at the marriage feast
   in Cana: cf. John 2.1–11 and also no. 18 of *What's Bred in
   the Bone*.
   iii) Jesus driving the moneychangers out of the temple: cf.
   Matthew 21.12–13; Mark 11.15–17; Luke 19.45–46
   (although "moneychangers" are not specifically identified
   here); and John 2.13–17.

11. Ramsay describes his increasing expertise in identifying biblical
scenes in art as follows: "I could spot Jael spiking Sisera, or
Judith with the head of Holofernes, readily enough" (124).
¶ cf. Judges 5.20–31 for the account of Jael and Sisera; the story
of Judith and Holofernes forms the central focus of the Book of
Judith, which is apocryphal for Protestants.[1]

12. The blossoming hagiographer flippantly characterizes his obses-

---

1 Davies describes biblical apocrypha as *"the books puritan scholars decided
to omit, as being more fun than is proper. Very saucy stuff!"* (*Papers* 104n).

sion in biblical terms: "I . . . began to whore after rare and difficult saints . . ." (124).

¶ cf. Deuteronomy 31.16: "And the Lord said unto Moses, Behold, thou shalt sleep with thy fathers; and this people will rise up, and go a whoring after the gods of the strangers of the land, whither they go to be among them, and will forsake me, and break my covenant which I have made with them."

13. Ramsay characterizes Joel Surgeoner's sermon as " 'that cock-and-bull story about the cursing sailor and the widow's mite' " (132).

¶ cf. Mark 12.41–44 and Luke 21.1–4 for the story of the widow's mite.

14. Surgeoner retorts: " 'We come to God in little steps, not in a leap, and that love of police-court truth you think so much of comes very late on the way, if it comes at all. What is truth? as Pilate asked . . .' " (133).

¶ cf. John 18.38: "Pilate saith unto him, What is truth?"

15. Surgeoner describes his release from police custody in Deptford in these terms: "I ran out of that town laughing and shouting like the man who was delivered from devils by Our Lord" (135).

¶ This is a slight embellishment of Mark 5.1–20 and Luke 8.26–39 in which the man is described simply as either beginning to "publish" or having "published" Jesus's actions.

16. Father Regan depreciates Willie Ramsay's alleged return from the dead stating: " 'A few minutes with no signs of life. Well, that's hardly Lazarus, now, is it?' " (138).

¶ cf. John 11.1–44 for the story of Jesus raising Lazarus from the dead.

17. The hunting skills of Orph Wettenhall earn him the sobriquet "the local Nimrod" (162).

¶ cf. Genesis 10.8–9.

18. During the depression, Ramsay asks: "Where shall wisdom be found, and where is the place of understanding? Not among Boy Staunton's ca-pittle-ists, nor among the penniless scheme-spinners in the school Common Room, nor yet at the Socialist-Communist meetings in the city, which were sometimes broken up by the police" (167–68).

¶ cf. Job 28.12, from which the question is taken verbatim.

19. At the College de Saint-Michel in Brussels, Ramsay attempts "to discover how Mary Magdalene had been accepted as the same Mary who was the sister of Martha and Lazarus, and if this pair of sisters, one representing the housewifely woman and the other the sensual woman, had any real counterparts in pagan belief, and sometimes . . . if their rich father was anywhere described as being like the rich men I met at Boy Staunton's dinner parties" (168).
¶ cf. Matthew 27.61, 28.1–10; Mark 16.9–10; and Luke 8.2 for accounts of Mary Magdalene.
¶ cf. also no. 2 of *The Rebel Angels* below.
¶ cf. Luke 10.38–42 and John 11.1–45, 12.1–3 for the story of Mary of Bethany. In the account in Luke, she is negligent concerning household chores, leaving them instead for her sister Martha.

20. Padre Blazon urges: " 'Forgive yourself for being a human creature, Ramezay. That is the beginning of wisdom; that is part of what is meant by the fear of God . . .' " (178).
¶ cf. Proverbs 9.10: "The fear of the Lord is the beginning of wisdom. . . ."

21. When Boy Staunton calls him " 'queer,' " Ramsay mistakenly assumes he is alluding to the " 'Sin of Sodom' " (196).
¶ cf. Genesis 19.

22. When describing Faustina, Liesl asserts: " 'She is of the earth, and her body is her shop and her temple, and whatever her body tells her is all of the law and the prophets' " (221).
¶ cf. Matthew 7.12: "all things whatsoever ye would that men should do to you, do ye even so to them: for this is the law and the prophets."

23. When Boy Staunton is asked to comment on his recent election defeat, he responds: " 'I feel exactly like Lazarus . . . licked by the dogs!' " (235).
¶ cf. Luke 16.20–21: "And there was a certain beggar named Lazarus, which was laid at his gate, full of sores, And desiring to be fed with the crumbs which fell from the rich man's table: moreover the dogs came and licked his sores."

24. Blazon states: " 'I am sure Christ learned a great deal that was salutary about Himself when He met the Devil in the wilderness' " (249).

¶ cf. Matthew 4.1–11 and Luke 4.1–13 for accounts of this encounter in the wilderness.

25. On the lid of the box containing Mary Dempster's ashes is written:

> Requiescat in pace
> MARY DEMPSTER
> 1888–1959
> Here is the patience
> and faith of the saints. (263)

¶ cf. Revelation 13.10, from which the epitaph is taken almost verbatim. This verse describes the reaction of God's chosen at a time of intense persecution from the beast of the sea.
¶ cf. no. 9 above.
¶ cf. Revelation 14.12, which promises the sparing of the holy ones from the torments that will ultimately afflict the beast's followers: "Here is the patience of the saints: here are they that keep the commandments of God, and the faith of Jesus."

26. Eisengrim refers to men of Boy Staunton's ilk as " 'Very important men. Men whom the Crown delighteth to honour' " (263).
¶ cf. Esther 6.6–11, where the phrase "the man whom the king delighteth to honour" is repeated five times.

27. In addition to the above biblical quotations and allusions in *Fifth Business* are the almost inevitable examples of those which have simply become part of the idiom of the language. Some of these are "Good Samaritan" (11; cf. Luke 10.30–35); "Judas" (15); "salt of the earth" (18; cf. Matthew 5.13); "Valley of the Shadda" (105; cf. Psalms 23.4); and "turning the other cheek" (257; cf. Matthew 5.39).

E. *The Manticore*

1. Regarding Boy Staunton's demise at age seventy, Johanna von Haller states: " 'Hardly a premature death. The psalmist's span' " (15).
¶ cf. Psalms 90.10: "The days of our years are threescore years and ten."

2. To von Haller's assertion that " 'All dreams mean something,' "
David Staunton disparagingly retorts: " 'For Joseph and Pharaoh, or Pilate's wife, perhaps' " (19).
¶ cf. Genesis 41.1–36 for the story of Joseph's interpretation of
the Pharaoh's dreams.
¶ cf. Matthew 27.19: "When [Pilate] was set down on the
judgment seat, his wife sent unto him, saying, Have thou nothing
to do with that just man: for I have suffered many things this
day in a dream because of him."

3. David asserts: " 'Love between father and son isn't something
that comes into society nowadays. I mean, the estimate a man
makes of his son is in masculine terms. This business of love
between father and son sounds like something in the Bible.' " To
this von Haller responds: " 'The patterns of human feeling do
not change as much as many people suppose. King David's
estimate of his rebellious son Absalom was certainly in masculine
terms. But I suppose you recall David's lament when Absalom
was slain?' " (48).
¶ cf. 2 Samuel 3.2–3 and 13.1–19.10 for the entire Absalom
story which informs much of *The Manticore*. Later in the novel,
Adrian Pledger-Brown characterizes David's attitude towards his
father as " 'sullen absalonism' " (235).
¶ cf. 2 Samuel 15.14 for King David's estimate of his rebellious
son: "And David said unto all his servants that were with him
at Jerusalem, Arise, and let us flee; for we shall not else escape
from Absalom: make speed to depart, lest he overtake us suddenly, and bring evil upon us, and smite the city with the edge
of the sword."
¶ cf. 2 Samuel 18.33 for David's lament after his son is killed:
"O my son Absalom, my son, my son Absalom! would God I
had died for thee, O Absalom, my son, my son!"

4. David speculates about the tax men as they catalogue the
contents of his father's safety deposit box: " 'Were they conscious
of putting down the mighty from their seat and exalting the
humble and meek?' " (50).
¶ cf. Luke 1.52: "He hath put down the mighty from their seats,
and exalted them of low degree."

5. The poet, Eric Roop, declines the opportunity to write Boy
Staunton's official biography because he " 'had promised himself
a fallow year if he could get a grant to see him through it.' "

David comments wryly: " 'Roop's fallow years were as familiar to Castor as Pharaoh's seven lean kine . . .' " (53).
¶ cf. Genesis 41.17–27 and no. 2 above.

6. Of Doc Staunton's purgations, David states: "On Sunday morning, therefore, I was ready for church as pure as the man from whom Paul drove forth the evil spirits" (80).
¶ I can find no mention of this incident in Acts or in any of Paul's epistles, although Acts 19.12 describes Paul as casting out evil spirits generally.

7. About his putative youthful piety David states: "I suppose I bodied forth some ideal for a lot of people, as the plaster statues of the Infant Samuel at Prayer used to do in the nineteenth century" (83).
¶ cf. 1 Samuel 2.18 and 3.1–10.
¶ cf. also no. 6 of *What's Bred in the Bone*.

8. During the period of his therapy in Zurich, David recalls some of his childhood dreams. In one of these he had seen "Jesus in the sky, floating upward as in pictures of the Ascension . . ." (92).
¶ cf. Mark 16.19; Luke 24.50–52; and Acts 1.9–11.

9. " 'Though he slay me, yet will I trust in him,' expressed half of Netty's attitude toward the Staunton family; the remainder was to be found in the rest of that verse — 'but I will maintain mine own ways before him' " (107).
¶ This is taken verbatim from Job 13.15.
¶ cf. also no. 10 of *What's Bred in the Bone*.

10. Alluding to her age, Netty claims that "she wasn't exactly Methuselah" (116).
¶ cf. Genesis 5.27: "And all the days of Methuselah were nine hundred sixty and nine years."

11. Canon Woodiwiss's yearly sermon to encourage almsgiving from his affluent congregation is based on Jesus's precept that " 'it is easier for a camel to go through the eye of a needle than for a rich man to enter the kingdom of God' " (129).
¶ cf. Matthew 19.24 and Mark 10.25, from which this is taken verbatim.
¶ cf. also Luke 18.25.

12. In his homily, Woodiwiss argues that " 'with God all things are possible' " (129).
¶ He quotes verbatim from Matthew 19.26 and Mark 10.27.

13. Father Knopwood is indignant at the tryst between Boy Staunton's mistress and David, which was arranged by Boy himself: " 'Did she whisper . . . in your ear as Absalom went in unto his father's concubine?' " (184).
¶ cf. 2 Samuel 16.22: "Absalom went in unto his father's concubines in the sight of all Israel." For Absalom, this is an act of defiance against David (16.21).
¶ cf. also no. 3 above.

14. Knopwood concludes the discussion about the consequences of one's actions by citing Paul's advice to the Galatians: " 'God is not mocked' " (188).
¶ cf. Galatians 6.7: "Be not deceived: God is not mocked: for whatsoever a man soweth, that shall he also reap."

15. The Staunton coat of arms proposed by Adrian Pledger-Brown bears the motto " '*De forte egressa est dulcedo* — "Out of the strong came forth sweetness." ' " Pledger-Brown then identifies it as taken " 'from the Book of Judges' " (215).
¶ This forms part of Samson's riddle to the Philistines: "Out of the eater came forth meat, and out of the strong came forth sweetness" (Judges 14.14). (The answer is "a swarm of bees and honey in the carcase of the lion" [14.8, 18].)

16. Davies integrates the story of Samson into David's characterization of his stepmother's domination of his father: "He became an unimaginative woman's creation. Delilah had shorn his locks and assured him he looked much neater and cooler without them. He gave her his soul, and she transformed it into a cabbage" (234).
¶ cf. Judges 16.4–21.

17. David dreams of seeing his father's " 'naked backside.' " He associates this with " 'the passage in Exodus where God promises Moses that he shall see Him, but must not see His face: and what Moses sees is God's back parts' " (239).
¶ cf. 33.18–23.

18. In describing Boy Staunton's reaction to David's reticence with women, Dunstan Ramsay states: "I don't believe you ever knew what a sore touch it was with Boy that you were such a Joseph about women" (253).
¶ cf. Genesis 39.7–20 for the account of Joseph and Potiphar's wife.

1. The verses of Psalm 79, cited early in the novel (24–25), play an important role in effecting Paul Dempster's departure from his home because they remind him of his own tenuous position in Deptford. The many verses of this psalm not quoted in *World of Wonders* make clear that, in its entirety, it is a song pleading for retribution. Thus, it is an appropriate choice for a novel that, in part, explores issues of vengeance.

2. After Paul flees his home for the carnival, he rides a merry-go-round. His mount seemed to him " 'like the horse in Job that saith among the trumpets, Ha, ha' " (26).
   ¶ cf. Job 39.25, from which this is taken verbatim.

3. Magnus Eisengrim (the adult Paul) describes his initial attraction to Willard in scriptural terms: " 'I longed with my whole soul to know what Willard knew. As the hart pants after the water brooks, even so my blasphemous soul panted after the Wizard' " (28).
   ¶ cf. Psalms 42.1: "As the hart panteth after the water brooks, so panteth my soul after thee, O God."

4. Eisengrim employs the New Testament to render the appeal of the magician: " 'But Willard! For me the Book of Revelation came alive: here was an angel come down from heaven, having great power, and the earth was lightened with his glory; if only I could be like him, surely there would be no more sorrow, nor crying, nor any more pain, and all former things — my dark home, my mad, disgraceful mother, the torment of school — would pass away' " (29–30).
   ¶ cf. Revelation 18.1: "I saw another angel come down from heaven, having great power; and the earth was lightened with his glory."
   ¶ cf. Revelation 21.4: "And God shall wipe away all tears from their eyes; and there shall be no more death, neither sorrow, nor crying, neither shall there be any more pain: for the former things are passed away."

5. Regarding the passages about sex he encountered in the Bible, Eisengrim asserts: " 'I knew about men going in unto women, and people raising up seed of their loins, and I knew that my father's voice took on a special tone of shame and detestation when he read about Lot and his daughters, though I had never

followed what it was they did in that cave, and thought their sin was to make their father drunk' " (33).

¶ cf. Genesis 19.30–38 for the account of Lot taken in incest by his daughters.

6. About the sobriquet Deptford bestowed on his mother, Eisengrim explains: " 'I knew only that hoors — my father used the local pronunciation, and I don't think he knew any other — were always turning up in the Bible, and always in a bad sense which meant nothing to me as a reality. Ezekiel, sixteen, was a riot of whoredoms and abominations, and I shivered to think how terrible they must be . . .' " (33).

7. Eisengrim affirms: " 'My father was no brute, and I think he hated beating me, but he knew his duty. "He that spareth his rod hateth his son; but he that loveth him chasteneth him betimes"; this was part of the prayer that always preceded a beating and he laid the rod on hard . . .' " (47).

¶ cf. Proverbs 13.24, which offers this precept verbatim.

¶ cf. also no. 19 of *What's Bred in the Bone* and nos. 10 and 19 of *Murther and Walking Spirits* below.

8. Happy Hannah " 'had collops of fat on her flanks, like the wicked man in the Book of Job' " (64).

¶ cf. Job 15.27.

9. Hannah wielded a " 'large, embracing, Biblical flow of condemnation' " (69). For example, she admonishes Andro the Hermaphrodite: " ' "I know the rock from whence ye are hewn — that no-good bunch o' Boston Greek fish-pedlars and small-time thieves; and I likewise know the hole of the Pit whence ye are digged — offering yourself to stand bare-naked in front of artists, some of 'em women, at fifty cents an hour. So I know it isn't really you that's speaking against me; it's the spirit of an unclean devil inside you, crying with a loud voice; and I rebuke it just as our dear Lord did; I'm sitting right here, crying, 'Hold thy peace and come out of him!' " ' " (70).

¶ cf. Isaiah 51.1: "Hearken to me, ye that follow after righteousness, ye that seek the Lord: look unto the rock whence ye are hewn, and to the hole of the pit whence ye are digged."

¶ cf. Mark 1.23–26 and Luke 4.33–35 for the exorcism episode of which Hannah speaks.

10. While Hannah is being bathed, the poker-playing Charlie,

Heinie, and Willard sing the hymn " ' "Wash me and I shall be whiter than snow" ' " or a parody of it (73).
¶ cf. Psalms 51.7, from which these words are taken verbatim.

11. After being mocked by the others, Hannah " 'had a good deal to say about lasciviousness, lusts, excess of wine, revellings, banquetings, games of hazard, and abominable idolatries, out of First Peter. But she hocussed the text. There is no mention of "games of hazard" or gambling anywhere in the Bible' " (73).
¶ cf. 1 Peter 4.3, from which Hannah's list of sins, with the notable exception identified above, is taken verbatim.

12. Responding to Hannah's futile attempts to derive humour from the Bible (70, 79–80), Roland Ingestree observes: " 'The Bible contains precisely one joke, and that is a schoolmasterish pun attributed to Christ when he told Peter that he was the rock on which the Church was founded' " (85–86).
¶ cf. Matthew 16.18.
¶ cf. also no. 8 of *The Rebel Angels* below.

13. When Rango the orangutan masturbates at his owner's behest, Hannah shouts: " ' "Whoso shall offend one of these little ones which believe in me, it were better for him that a millstone were hanged about his neck, and that he were drowned in the depth of the sea" ' " (89).
¶ cf. Matthew 18.6, from which these words are taken verbatim. cf. also Mark 9.42.

14. The circus people deem Paul a Jonah who brings bad luck to the company (92).
¶ cf. Jonah 1.1–15.

15. Hannah corners Paul, telling him: " ' "I wanta talk mouth to mouth, even apparently, and not in dark speeches" ' " (92).
¶ As she subsequently states, this is taken almost verbatim from Numbers 12.8. It is, perhaps, a measure of her presumption that she uses words originally spoken by God Himself when chastising Miriam and Aaron for having criticized Moses.

16. After Hannah offers several examples from scripture — Genesis 13.13; Deuteronomy 23.10; Leviticus 20.13 — to condemn Paul for his sodomy with Willard, she warns: " ' "You know where that leads, dontcha? Right slap to Hell, where the worm dieth not and the fire is not quenched" ' " (93).
¶ cf. Mark 9.44, 46, 48, from which Hannah's description of

hell is taken almost verbatim.

17. Hannah chides Paul for his love of magic tricks. The boy, however, deflects her ire by quoting directly from Paul's Epistle to the Philippians (3.8): " ' "I count them but dung, that I may win Christ" ' " (94).

18. Regarding the circus audiences, Eisengrim states: " 'They wanted us; they needed us to mix a little leaven in their doughy lives, but they did not like us. . . . But how much they revealed as they stared! When the Pharisees saw us they marvelled, but it seemed to me that their inward parts were full of ravening and wickedness' " (109).
¶ cf. Luke 11.39: "And the Lord said unto him, Now do ye Pharisees make clean the outside of the cup and the platter; but your inward part is full of ravening and wickedness."

19. Eisengrim recalls: " 'As I sat in the belly of Abdullah, I thought often of Jonah in the belly of the great fish. Jonah, it seemed to me, had an easy time of it. "Out of the belly of hell cried I, and thou heardest my voice" [Jonah 2.2]; that was what Jonah said. But I cried out of the belly of hell, and nothing whatever happened' " (111). A few lines later, Paul again quotes from Jonah: " ' "When my soul fainted within me I remembered the Lord" ' " (2.7).
¶ cf. Jonah 1.17–2.10 for the account of Jonah in the fish.

20. Hannah accuses Paul of " 'trying to learn the Evil Eye. . . . She urged me to search Deuteronomy to learn what happened to people who had the Evil Eye: plagues wonderful, and plagues of my seed, even great plagues of long continuance, and sore sickness; that was what was in store for me unless I stopped bugging my eyes at folks who had put on the whole armour of God, that they might stand against the wiles of the Devil' " (119).
¶ cf. Deuteronomy 28. Among the dire consequences with which Moses threatens his people should they "not hearken unto the voice of the Lord thy God, to observe to do all his commandments and his statutes" (28.15) are these:
"the man that is tender among you, and very delicate, his eye shall be evil toward his brother, and toward the wife of his bosom, and toward the remnant of his children . . ." (28.54);
"The tender and delicate woman among you, which would not adventure to set the sole of her foot upon the ground for delicateness and tenderness, her eye shall be evil toward the

husband of her bosom, and toward her son, and toward her daughter" (28.56);

"the Lord will make thy plagues wonderful, and the plagues of thy seed, even great plagues, and of long continuance, and sore sicknesses, and of long continuance" (28.59).

It seems that Hannah has " 'hocussed' " this text also, since she suggests that the plagues are direct repercussions of the evil eye. Deuteronomy 28 clearly indicates that both the plagues and the evil eye result from disobeying God's injunctions.

¶ cf. Ephesians 6.11: "Put on the whole armour of God, that ye may be able to stand against the wiles of the devil."

21. Quoting ironically from Proverbs, Eisengrim renders the " 'delicious satisfaction' " of dominating his one-time master, the now-faltering Willard: " 'If thine enemy be hungry, give him bread to eat; and if he be thirsty, give him water to drink; for thou shalt heap coals of fire on his head, and the Lord shall reward thee' " (131).

¶ cf. Proverbs 25.21–22, from which this is taken verbatim.

22. When discussing his vengeful treatment of Willard, Eisengrim argues: " 'We have shut our minds against the Christ who cursed the fig-tree' " (132).

¶ cf. Matthew 21.18–22 and Mark 11.12–14, 20–24.

23. Eisengrim wonders about Willard's dying look of terror: " 'Was he aware of the lake which burneth with fire and brimstone, where he would join the unbelieving and the abominable, the whoremongers, sorcerers, and idolaters?' " (133)

¶ cf. Revelation 21.8, from which this is derived.

24. Eisengrim explains that at the age of twenty-two, " 'I thought I was the toughest thing going. A verse from the Book of Psalms kept running through my head that seemed to me to describe my state perfectly. "I am become like a bottle in the smoke." It's a verse that puzzles people who think it means a glass bottle, but my father would never have allowed me to be so ignorant as that. It means one of those old wineskins the Hebrews used; it means a goatskin that has been scraped out, and tanned, and blown up, and hung over the fire till it is as hard as a warrior's boot' " (134–35).

¶ cf. Psalm 119.83, from which Eisengrim's statement and the title of this section of the novel are taken verbatim. However, Amasa Dempster is not as well informed as his son suggests. The expression refers "to the drying out and ruining of a wineskin by being left too long near the heat of an open fireplace." Thus it was made weaker, not stronger (van den Born 2583), "brittle and useless" (gloss on this verse in *Saint Joseph Bible 693*). At least two recent translations of the Bible appear to confirm this: "I am shriveled [sic] like a leathern flask in the smoke" (*New American Bible*); "I shrivel like a wine-skin in the smoke" (*New English Bible*).

25. Lebbaeus, or Thaddaeus, the lesser apostle of whom Liesl and Ramsay speak (137, 142; Matthew 10.3) is also identified with the biblical Judas, not Iscariot (Ross).

26. Regarding the plan for a dinner in London which will mend a number of fences, Eisengrim jocularly declares: " 'You see, all things work together for good to them that love God' " (152).
¶ cf. Romans 8.28.
¶ cf. also no. 11 of *What's Bred in the Bone* below.

27. Ramsay comments on Jurgen Lind's artistry: "His films possessed a weight of implication — in St Paul's phrase, 'the evidence of things not seen' — that was entirely his own" (152).
¶ cf. Hebrews 11.1.
¶ cf. also no. 12 of *The Rebel Angels* below.

28. For Roland Ingestree, Sir John's Canadian tour was " 'a personal Gethsemane' " (222).
¶ cf. Matthew 26.36ff and Mark 14.32ff.
¶ cf. also no. 20 of *What's Bred in the Bone* below.

29. Eisengrim again uses Psalms 42.1 to characterize his yearning: " 'I was the kind that knew very little that wasn't tawdry and tough and ugly, but I hadn't forgotten my Psalms, and I thirsted for something better as the hart pants for the water-brooks' " (226).
¶ cf. no. 3 above.

30. Because Milady's eyesight is fading, she has Eisengrim read to her from the Bible (242). The verses from Psalms that she chooses are appropriate:
"Consider and hear me, O Lord my God: lighten mine eyes, lest I sleep the sleep of death; Lest mine enemy say, I have prevailed against him; and those that trouble me rejoice when I am moved" (13.3–4);
"Open thou mine eyes, that I may behold wondrous things out of thy law" (119.18).

31. Milady particularly likes to be read to in French from her " 'chunky old Geneva Bible' ": " *'Je suis le chemin, & la vérité, & la vie; nul ne vient au Père sinon par moi'* " and " *'Bienheureux sont les débonnaires: cars ils hériteront la terre'* " (243). ¶ cf. John 14.6 and Matthew 5.5 respectively.

32. On the Canadian tour Eisengrim was " 'losing, ever so little, my strong sense that every man's hand was against me, and my hand against every man' " (261).
    ¶ cf. Genesis 16.12, in which God warns Hagar about her son Ishmael: "And he will be a wild man; his hand will be against every man, and every man's hand against him."

33. Eisengrim quotes almost verbatim from Psalms 119.83 when he denies murdering Boy Staunton: " ' "I am become as a bottle in the smoke: yet do I fear thy statutes." One of those statutes forbids murder' " (301).
    ¶ cf. no. 24 above.

G. *The Rebel Angels*

1. When Clement Hollier neglects to acknowledge his encounter with Maria on his couch, she silently cries: "abomination of desolation!" (3).
   ¶ cf. Matthew 24.15 and Mark 13.14. In both instances the term refers to the ultimate destruction of Jerusalem.
   ¶ cf. also Daniel 9.27, 11.31, and 12.11.

2. Immediately upon meeting her, John Parlabane notes the significance of Maria Magdalena Theotoky's name: " 'But what a contrast! Theotoky . . . linked with the name of the sinner out of whom Our Lord cast seven devils' " (5). Other references to Mary Magdalene in *The Rebel Angels* appear on pages 104 and 191.
   ¶ According to *The Compact Edition of the Oxford English Dictionary*, *Theotoky* means "the divine motherhood of Mary." The sources of Parlabane's information about Mary Magdalene are Mark 16.9 and Luke 8.2.

3. When Simon Darcourt meets the dying Ellerman, he asks him why he has returned to the university campus. Abruptly, Urky

McVarish interrupts: " 'Surely you ought to know — you of all people, Father Darcourt — that the dog turns to his own vomit again, and the sow to her wallowing in the mire' " (12).

¶ cf. 2 Peter 2.22, which refers to religious backsliding: "The dog is turned to his own vomit again; and the sow that was washed to her wallowing in the mire."

4. At Francis Cornish's funeral, Darcourt observes that Maria "had covered her head with a loose scarf, which most of the women in the chapel had not done, because they are modern, and set no store by St. Paul's admonition on that subject" (17).

¶ cf. 1 Corinthians 11.5–16.

5. Although Darcourt acknowledges the adjuration — which is, in fact, contained in a hymn — "At the Name of Jesus, every knee shall bow," he feels that Parlabane's histrionics at Cornish's funeral are grossly overdone (17–18).

¶ cf. Philippians 2.10, from which the hymn's precept is taken almost verbatim.

6. The choir at the funeral sang: "*I heard a voice from heaven saying unto me, Write: From henceforth blessed are the dead which die in the Lord: even so saith the spirit, for they rest from their labours*" (18).

¶ cf. Revelation 14.13, from which this is derived. Note also that Davies has previously cited this section of Revelation (cf. nos. 1 and 25 of *Fifth Business* above).

7. Parlabane observes that the College of Saint John and the Holy Ghost, "Spook," derives its name from Mark 1.8: " 'I indeed have baptized you with water, but he shall baptize you with the Holy Ghost' " (31).

8. Like Roland Ingestree (cf. no. 12 of *World of Wonders* above), Darcourt observes that the New Testament is not " 'a great book for jokes' " and cites as the exception the pun using Peter's name (37).

¶ cf. Matthew 16.18.

9. Regarding his dislike and distrust of Urky McVarish, Darcourt asks: "Was this charitable thinking? Paul tells us that Charity is many things, but nowhere does he tell us that it is blind" (58).

¶ Although Darcourt is literally correct, one might justifiably argue that the apostle's most famous characterization of charity (1 Corinthians 13) calls for a greater measure of forbearance than Darcourt offers to the admittedly disgusting McVarish.

10. When comparing Ozy Froats's work with excrement to the alchemists' " 'recognition of what is of worth in that which is scorned by the unseeing,' " Clem Hollier offers the " 'Scottish paraphrase — *That stone shall be chief corner-stone / Which builders did despise . . .*' " (82).
¶ The Scots derived this from any (or all) of Psalms 118.22; Matthew 21.42; Mark 12.10; Luke 20.17; or Acts 4.11.
¶ cf. also no. 16 below and no. 5 of *The Lyre of Orpheus*.

11. At Ellerman's funeral, Darcourt recalls two familiar phrases frequently used on such occasions: "*Naked came I out of my mother's womb, and naked shall I return thither . . . Earth to earth, ashes to ashes, dust to dust . . .*" (85).
¶ The first is taken verbatim from Job 1.21; the second is not scriptural but is taken from the Book of Common Prayer.

12. Darcourt is surprised to see Ozy Froats at the funeral: "I knew he had been brought up a Mennonite, but I would have supposed that a life given to science had leached all belief out of him in things unseen, of heights and depths immeasurable" (85).
¶ cf. Hebrews 11.1: "Now faith is the substance of things hoped for, the evidence of things not seen."
¶ cf. also no. 27 of *World of Wonders* above.

13. Uncle Yerko asserts that the three kings brought "Gold, Frank Innocence, and Mirth" to the "Bebby Jesus" (223).
¶ Of course, Matthew 2.11 depicts an equally wealthy, but more sophisticated, sober trio who came bearing "gold, and frankincense, and myrrh."

14. Darcourt cites from the Wisdom of Solomon when describing Sophia: " 'With you is Wisdom, she who knows your works, she who was present when you made the world; she understands what is pleasing in your eyes, and what agrees with your commandments' " (235).
¶ This is almost verbatim from Wisdom 9.9 (New rev. stand. version).

15. The love-smitten Darcourt looks out at the quadrangle of Ploughwright and its fountains remind him of Maria: " 'A garden enclosed is my sister; my spouse, a spring shut up, a fountain sealed' " (244).
¶ cf. Song of Solomon 4.12.

16. Regarding Ozy Froats's excremental research, Darcourt reiterates Hollier's biblical analogy (cf. no. 10 above): " ' "This is the stone which was set at naught of your builders, which is become the head of the corner" ' " (250).
¶ cf. Acts 4.11, from which this passage is taken almost verbatim.
¶ cf. also no. 5 of *The Lyre of Orpheus* below.

17. Darcourt tells Maria that he is " 'a priest forever, after the order of Melchisedek' " (256).
¶ cf. Genesis 14.18–20: "And Melchizedek king of Salem brought forth bread and wine: and he was the priest of the most high God. And he blessed him, and said, Blessed be Abram of the most high God, possessor of heaven and earth: And blessed be the most high God, which hath delivered thine enemies into thy hand. And [Abram] gave him tithes of all."
¶ cf. also Hebrews 5.6–10 and 6.20ff, which characterize Melchizedek as a forerunner of Christ. Darcourt's words are taken verbatim from any of Hebrews 5.6, 6.20, 7.17, or 7.21.

H. *What's Bred in the Bone*

1. Maria informs Darcourt that the Lesser Zadkiel " 'was the angel who interfered when Abraham was about to sacrifice Isaac, so he is an angel of mercy . . .' " (18).
¶ The biblical account of Abraham's attempt to immolate his son does not name the intervening angel (Genesis 22.1–19). In fact, the name Zadkiel does not appear anywhere in the Bible; the only angels identified in it are Michael, Gabriel, Satan, and, for Catholics, Raphael (cf. the Book of Tobit). However, some noncanonical writers do credit Zadkiel with "holding back Abraham's arm when the patriarch was about to sacrifice his son Isaac" (Davidson 324).

2. Among the churches in Blairlogie is a store temple "in whose windows hung gaudy banners displaying the Beasts of the Apocalypse, in horrendous detail" (24).
¶ cf. Revelation 13.1ff.

3. During his conversation with Senator McRory, whose daughter is pregnant out of wedlock, "The Major touched lightly and

tactfully upon Our Lord's behaviour toward the woman taken in adultery . . ." (47).

¶ cf. John 8.3–11.

¶ cf. also no. 23 of *Murther and Walking Spirits* below.

4. In the absence of Francis Cornish's parents, "Aunt Mary-Ben had been given full authority to bind and loose if anything went beyond the nursemaid's power" (84).

¶ These words place the devoutly Catholic Mary-Ben in fairly exalted company. After His famous pun, with which He pronounces Peter the head of His church, Jesus states: "I will give unto thee the keys of the kingdom of heaven: and whatsoever thou shalt bind on earth shall be bound in heaven: and whatsoever thou shalt loose on earth shall be loosed in heaven" (Matthew 16.19). Christ uses the same terms to describe to the apostles the power He is bestowing on them collectively (18.18).

5. The novel describes the attitude of the staunch Presbyterian Victoria Cameron towards the McRorys, her devout Roman Catholic employers: "Judge not that ye be not judged [verbatim Matthew 7.1; almost verbatim Luke 6.37]. Of course, you can't be a Calvinist without judging, but as a Calvinist you know what God's ordinances are, so it isn't really judging. It is just knowing right from wrong" (98).

6. One of the pictures that Aunt Mary-Ben shows young Francis "is the Infant Samuel, wakened from his sleep by God's summons . . . 'Speak, for Thy servant heareth' " (121).

¶ cf. 1 Samuel 3.10.

¶ cf. also no. 7 of *The Manticore* above.

7. The story Mary-Ben relates to Francis about Saint Veronica wiping the face of Jesus as He walked toward Calvary is not scriptural (122).

8. Zadok Hoyle's favourite oath is "By the Powers of Old Melchizedek" (134).

¶ cf. Genesis 14.18–20.

¶ cf. also no. 17 of *The Rebel Angels* above.

9. The "pictures in Aunt's books called *The Entombment*" inspire Cornish to emulate their artistry: "What dignity, what compassion was shown in the faces of those who handled the body of the dead Saviour" (145).

¶ The biblical sources for these are Matthew 27.59; Mark

15.46; Luke 23.53; and John 19.38–42. However, only in John's account does Joseph of Arimathea receive assistance in preparing the body; in the other gospels he works alone. *What's Bred in the Bone* subsequently names Joseph of Arimathea in relation to the legend of King Arthur (191).

10. Victoria Cameron explains her theology to Cornish in these terms: " 'God made me a sinner, and I can't change that. But I don't have to give in, even to Him, and I won't. I won't give it to Him to say. Though He slay me, yet will I worship Him. But I won't throw in the towel, even if He's damned me' " (166).
    ¶ cf. Job 13.15: "Though he slay me, yet will I trust in him: but I will maintain mine own ways before him." David Staunton also uses this passage to describe Netty's attitude about serving his family (cf. no. 9 of *The Manticore* above).

11. In response to the senator's explication of how well " 'Everything has suddenly clicked into place' " for the Cornish trust, Dr. J.A. Jerome jests: " 'All things work together for good for those that love the Lord' " (172). Eisengrim jocularly used almost exactly the same words in *World of Wonders* (cf. no. 26 of *World of Wonders* above).
    ¶ cf. Romans 8.28, from which the Doctor's words are taken almost verbatim.

12. The irreverent Doctor J.A. alters a passage from Lamentations to characterize Marie-Louise and Mary-Ben's complaints about their digestive woes: " 'B'God they make it almost religious. "Behold and see, if there be any acidity like unto my acidity" ' " (244).
    ¶ cf. Lamentations 1.12: Mourning the destruction of Jerusalem, the speaker cries: "Is it nothing to you, all ye that pass by? behold, and see if there be any sorrow like unto my sorrow, which is done unto me, wherewith the Lord hath afflicted me in the day of his fierce anger."

13. The Daimon Maimas urges the Lesser Zadkiel: *"Circumcise yourself as to the heart and not as to the foreskin"* (342).
    ¶ cf. Romans 2.28–29: "he is not a Jew, which is one outwardly; neither is that circumcision, which is outward in the flesh: But he is a Jew, which is one inwardly; and circumcision is that of the heart, in the spirit, and not in the letter; whose praise is not of men, but of God."

188

14. When discussing Jesus's putative indifference to art, Tancred Saraceni affirms: " 'Christ would have had no time for a man like me. Have you noticed how, in the Gospels, He keeps so resolutely clear of anybody who might be suspected of having any brains?' " (395).
¶ The account of young Jesus with the scholars in the temple (Luke 2.42–50) vitiates Saraceni's confident assertion. Davies indicates his awareness of this by subsequently referring to this biblical event (426).

15. Pictures depicting biblical themes are central to Cornish's artistic apprenticeship. In one important instance, Saraceni tells him to study a drawing of the head of the crucified Jesus that is " 'rendered in exquisite, tiny Gothic script in such a way that it depicts Christ's agony, while writing out every word . . . of Christ's Passion as it is recorded in the Gospel of St. John, chapters seventeen to nineteen.' " Saraceni then orders Cornish to " 'do something in the same manner, but your text shall be the Nativity of Our Lord, as recorded in Luke's Gospel, chapter one, and chapter two up to verse thirty-two. I want a Nativity in calligraphy . . .' " (400).

16. The painting *The Harrowing of Hell* (411, 415–16) that Cornish is asked to authenticate in The Hague is based on the apocryphal gospel of Nicodemus.

17. Zadok Hoyle's grave is "in that part of the Protestant cemetery which was called, with Blairlogie harshness, the Potter's Field" (459).
¶ When the repentant Judas Iscariot returned the thirty pieces of silver he had received for betraying Jesus, "the chief priests took the silver pieces, and said, It is not lawful for to put them into the treasury, because it is the price of blood. And they took counsel, and bought with them the potter's field, to bury strangers in" (Matthew 27.6–7).

18. John 2.1–11 provides the scriptural underpinning for Cornish's *pièce de résistance*, his painting *The Marriage at Cana* (469ff). The English translation offered for the caption *"Thou hast kept the good wine until now'* " (474) is taken verbatim from John 2.10.
¶ cf. also no. 10 of *Fifth Business* above and no. 4 of *The Lyre of Orpheus* below.

189

19. Cornish thanks Saraceni for his effectiveness as a teacher: " 'you have been very good to me, and you have not spared the rod.' " To this Saraceni responds: " 'He that spareth his rod, hateth his son' " (479).
¶ cf. Proverbs 13.24, from which Saraceni's words are taken verbatim.
¶ cf. also no. 7 of *World of Wonders* above and nos. 10 and 19 of *Murther and Walking Spirits* below.

20. The novel describes as an "obligatory Gethsemane" the committee debate over Aylwin Ross's appointment as director of the National Gallery (503).
¶ cf. Matthew 26.36ff. and Mark 14.32ff.
¶ cf. also no. 28 of *World of Wonders* above, where Magnus Eisengrim employs a similar biblical allusion to characterize Roland Ingestree's Canadian tour with Sir John Tresize's company.

21. Regarding the government's parsimony towards purchases for its National Gallery collection, Cornish says: " 'The Ark of the Lord seems to have fallen into the hands of the Philistines' " (507).
¶ cf. 1 Samuel 4.10ff.

22. Cornish's affection for his friend is related in Old Testament terms: "In the biblical phrase, his bowels yearned toward Ross" (509).
¶ cf. Genesis 43.30, which describes Joseph's feelings when, unrecognized himself, he sees his brother Benjamin in Egypt after many years of separation: "his bowels did yearn upon his brother: and he sought where to weep. . . ."

I. *The Lyre of Orpheus*

1. In response to a friendly jibe from the fortune-telling Mamusia — " 'Isn't there something in the Bible that tells you to keep away from people like me?' " — Simon Darcourt confesses: " 'In several places we are warned against them that have familiar spirits, and wizards that peep and mutter. But we live in a fallen world, Madame' " (40).

¶ cf. Leviticus 19.31 and 20.6, 27; Deuteronomy 18.11; Isaiah 8.19–22 and 19.3. Of these, only Isaiah 8.19 suggests that the wizards "peep and mutter."

2. In a brief moment of doubt about Mamusia's card reading, a "part of [Darcourt's] mind told him he was a fool to play King Saul, and resort to wizards who peep and mutter" (45).
   ¶ The Bible makes no specific reference to Saul's employing wizards. Darcourt is probably alluding to the doomed King's visit to "a woman that hath a familiar spirit at Endor" (1 Samuel 28.7–25).

3. Anglicans refer to the sort of broad black waistcoat worn by Darcourt as "an M.B. waistcoat, meaning Mark of the Beast because of its High Church and Romanist implications" (121).
   ¶ The beast of the earth, who seals many with his mark, is the subject of Revelation 13.11ff.

4. There is a discrepancy in this novel concerning the translation of the caption accompanying *The Marriage at Cana*: " 'Thou hast kept the best wine till the last' " (258), versus " 'Thou hast kept the good wine until now,' " is the English equivalent of *"Tu autem servasti bonum vinum usque adhuc"* (324). The latter of the two renderings has the multiple advantages of being consistent with what appears in *What's Bred in the Bone* (cf. no. 18 of *What's Bred in the Bone* above), precisely what is present in John 2.10, and the better translation of the Latin original.

5. After his discovery of the picture's origin, Darcourt hums "[o]ne of the metrical psalms":
   > That stone is made head corner-stone,
   >   Which builders did despise;
   > This is the doing of the Lord,
   >   And wondrous in his eyes. (259)
   ¶ cf. Psalms 118.22–23, from which Darcourt's song is derived.
   ¶ cf. also nos. 10 and 16 of *The Rebel Angels* above.

6. Geraint Powell characterizes his cuckolding of Arthur in these terms: " 'This was more than adultery. I was a thief in the night — a thief of honour. It was breaking faith with a friend' " (272). Powell exaggerates a biblical analogy here:
   ¶ cf.1 Thessalonians 5.2: "For yourselves know perfectly that the day of the Lord so cometh as a thief in the night."
   ¶ cf. 2 Peter 3.10: "But the day of the Lord will come as a thief

in the night; in the which the heavens shall pass away with a great noise, and the elements shall melt with fervent heat, the earth also and the works that are therein shall be burned up."

J. *Murther and Walking Spirits*

1. In a sermon at the beginning of the American War of Independence, the Reverend Cephas Willoughby, a loyalist, warns his New York City congregation against the rebels by taking "his text from Jude, the sixteenth verse: *These are murmurers, complainers, walking after their own lusts; and their mouth speaketh great swelling words, having men's persons in admiration because of advantage*" (44).
   ¶ The Book of Jude is applicable to Willoughby's particular circumstances since it judges false teachers and instructs the faithful to remain steadfast. The passage is quoted verbatim from Jude 16.

2. Continuing to cite from Jude, Willoughby refers to the rebellious Bostonians as "filthy dreamers who despise dominion and speak evil of dignities" (44).
   ¶ cf. Jude 8, from which this is taken almost verbatim.

3. Willoughby characterizes the King's enemies thus: "*These speak evil of things which they know not — or rather, which they pretend they know not; but what they know naturally* — which is to say from the impulses of their own dark and greedy hearts — *they know as brute beasts, in those things they corrupt themselves . . .*" (45).
   ¶ cf. Jude 10, from which the italicized portions of the quotation are derived.

4. Willoughby compares the revolutionaries to Cain who "rebelled and struck down his worthy brother Abel. And was not Cain abundant in excuses, saying *Am I my brother's keeper?*" (45–46).
   ¶ cf. Genesis 4.1–15.
   ¶ cf. also where Thomas Gilmartin invokes the story of Cain as part of his endeavour to convert a band of Welsh ruffians to Methodism (*Murther* 100).

5. Davies derives the title of this section of the novel — *"Cain Raised"* — from a phrase Willoughby declaims at his sermon's peroration: *"Cain is raised in our midst!"* (46).
¶ This forms an appropriate conclusion to a homily informed largely by the Book of Jude, since verse 11 states: "Woe unto them! for they have gone in the way of Cain. . . ."

6. After the war has been lost, Willoughby is forced to depart New York City. Psalm 137 provides an appropriate theme for the final homily he will preach there: *"How shall we sing the Lord's song, in a strange land?"* (*Murther* 65; Psalms 137.4).
¶ There is a suitable subtext provided by this short Psalm: several verses later it concludes with a cry for brutal vengeance against the oppressing Babylonians.

7. The third section of the novel, which focuses on the Welsh Methodist element in Connor Gilmartin's heritage, is entitled *"Of Water and the Holy Spirit."*
¶ This title is taken from any (or all) of Matthew 3.11; Mark 1.8; Luke 3.16; or Acts 1.5 and 11.16.
¶ cf. also no. 7 of *The Rebel Angels* above.

8. On the beam of Young Wesley Gilmartin's loom are written, in Welsh, the words, " 'My days are swifter than a weaver's shuttle, and are spent without hope' " (110).
¶ Job speaks these words verbatim in the depths of his misery (7.6). Happily, *Murther and Walking Spirits* indicates that they are not appropriate to Young Wesley's circumstances.

9. As he explains his plan for upward mobility by becoming a servant of the local Earl, Thomas Gilmartin parodies a passage from the Bible: " 'I would rather be a doorkeeper in the house of a lord than dwell in the tents of the Wesleyans' " (113).
¶ cf. Psalms 84.10: "I had rather be a doorkeeper in the house of my God, than to dwell in the tents of wickedness."

10. In order to prevent Young Thomas from fulfilling his ambition, Young Wesley, his father, "beats Young Thomas soundly, for he that spares the rod hateth his son" (113).
¶ Like Amasa Dempster (cf. no. 7 of *World of Wonders* above), Young Wesley relies on Proverbs 13.24 as his Dr. Spock.
¶ cf. also no. 19 below and no. 19 of *What's Bred in the Bone* above.

11. When the rod fails, Young Wesley "exhorts him, but Young

Thomas has a scoffer's way with the Bible, and can quote more Scripture on behalf of the good and faithful servant's life than his father can quote against it" (113).

¶ The most obvious example supporting Young Thomas's position is the parable of the talents in which the master characterizes each of his worthy attendants as a "good and faithful servant" (Matthew 25.21, 23).

¶ cf. also no. 2 of *Fifth Business* above.

12. Eventually, the dissolute Thomas is dismissed from service at the castle. His brother Samuel, to whom he turns for aid, reflects on the conflicting messages offered by the Bible: " 'The wicked are like the troubled sea, when it cannot rest, whose waters cast up mire and dirt.' Isaiah [57.20] said it all. But did not John [1 John 4.20] say: 'He that loveth not his brother whom he hath seen, how can he love God whom he hath not seen?' " (129).

13. Young Thomas's nephew David Gilmartin, who also strays from the Wesleyan path, is eventually forced by poverty to make the homeward journey: "David returns to his father, a prodigal son, for whom Samuel prepared the thinnest and poorest of calves" (134).

¶ cf. Luke 15.11–32 for the parable of the prodigal son.

14. Walter Gilmartin's prospective career in the civil service is ruined (133) and he is eventually impoverished and dispossessed because he obeys the biblical admonition "Honour thy father and thy mother" (136), which, ironically, promises prosperity. In this he differs from Monica Gall, who, in the face of the same adjuration, is still able to pursue her musical education.

¶ cf. Exodus 20.12: "Honour thy father and thy mother: that thy days may be long upon the land which the Lord thy God giveth thee."

¶ cf. also Deuteronomy 5.16: "Honour thy father and thy mother, as the Lord thy God hath commanded thee; that thy days may be prolonged, and that it may go well with thee, in the land which the Lord thy God giveth thee."

¶ cf. also no. 4 of *A Mixture of Frailties* above and nos. 19 and 21 below.

15. When financial insolvency strikes, "Walter sees, as he puts it to himself, the handwriting on the wall. The biblical phrase is not comforting. MENE, MENE, TEKEL, UPHARSIN [Daniel 5.25]: *Thou art weighed in the balance and art found wanting* [5.27].

Yes, indeed: wanting several hundred utterly unobtainable pounds. *God hath numbered thy kingdom, and finished it* [5.26]. This, it appears, is God's reward for a man who has been faithful to a promise given to his dying mother. We must not dispute His will. *Thy kingdom is divided and given to the Medes and the Persians* [5.28]. Certainly this will be so very soon, for the Medes and the Persians of Trallwm, themselves hard-pressed for money, will force the action that will get them at least some of what is owing to them. In short, bankruptcy impends" (153).

¶ cf. Daniel 5: during a feast a man's hand suddenly appeared and wrote the above four words on the palace wall of the Babylonian ruler. After the wise men of the court failed to decipher them, Daniel was called in to explain their meaning to the doomed king. His interpretation is contained in verses 26–28.

16. One of Connor Gilmartin's McOmish ancestors is proprietress of a tavern: "drunkards are warned off, and Mrs. McOmish sears them with biblical admonitions that *wine is a mocker, and strong drink is raging*" (171).

¶ cf. Proverbs 20.1.

17. When William McOmish asks for Virginia's hand in marriage, her father " 'said I'd have to wait. Prove myself. Serve seven years for Rachel, he said; he was full of Bible sayings' " (176).

¶ cf. Genesis 29 for the account of Jacob, Laban, and Rachel.

18. In keeping with Wesleyan notions, William McOmish's Methodist congregation eschews the architect's plan to engrave the Latin "*Ad Majoram Dei Gloriam*" over the pulpit in their great new church (184). Instead, McOmish carves "*The Lord Is In His Holy Temple: Let All The Earth Keep Silence Before Him*," which he regards as " '[v]ery choice and doctrinally correct' " (185).

¶ cf. Habakkuk 2.20, from which the acceptable citation is taken verbatim.

19. It seems that several branches of Connor Gilmartin's genealogy hold to the same Old Testament admonitions (cf. nos. 10 and 14 above). The Vanderlips also believe that "the only way to bring up children is to beat the Old Ned out of them whenever He asserts himself." In this they have clerical concurrence: " 'He that spareth the rod hateth his son,' says the minister, to general approbation, and, lest a few children dare to look resentful, he

adds, 'Honour thy father and thy mother, that thy days may be long upon the land that the LORD thy God giveth thee' " (200).
¶ cf. also no. 21 below, and no. 4 of *A Mixture of Frailties*, no. 7 of *World of Wonders*, and no. 19 of *What's Bred in the Bone* above.

20. McOmish's brother-in-law, Dan Boutell, asks, " 'Ever think of joining the Oddfellows, Will?' " McOmish retorts, " 'Why would I want to get mixed up with that Tribe of Manasseh?' " (207).
¶ This allusion is a slippery one. McOmish clearly means the term to be pejorative, and 1 Chronicles 5.23ff confirms this: many of this tribe "transgressed against the God of their fathers, and went a whoring after the gods of the people of the land. . . . And the God of Israel stirred up the spirit of Pul king of Assyria, and the spirit of Tilgathpilneser king of Assyria, and he carried them away . . ." (5.25–26). However, "In Psalms 4.7 and 108.8 Manasseh is called a most precious possession of God. Ezekiel has a place for the tribe of Manasseh in his picture of the future (Ezekiel 48.4) and John includes the tribe in his vision described in Revelation 7.6" (Schultz).

21. Although young Brochwell Gilmartin "fancies himself to be an atheist, he cannot escape from the indoctrination that bids him honour his father and his mother" (223).
¶ cf. Exodus 20.12 and Deuteronomy 5.16.
¶ cf. also nos. 14 and 19 above, and no. 4 of *A Mixture of Frailties* above.

22. Julia's mad, seminaked grandfather suddenly interrupts a party being held in his home without his permission. Astonished, Brochwell describes the occurrence using a biblical allusion: "we saw his ancient body, yes and even his withered parts, like the sons of Noah beholding their father's nakedness" (258). Brochwell's dead son, Connor Gilmartin, employs the same reference to describe his own feelings at being allowed in the afterlife to observe many of the youthful Brochwell's foibles: "How far was this voyeurism to go? I knew now the shame of the sons of Noah when they beheld their father's drunkenness" (268).
¶ cf. Genesis 9.20–27. Only one son, Ham, saw his father in this drunken, unclad state; the others refused to look.
¶ cf. also no. 4 of *Tempest-Tost* above.

23. Finding it difficult to forgive his wife's deception concerning her age, Rhodri Gilmartin states: " 'Christ forgave the adulteress,

but I don't recall that he ever forgave a liar' " (301).

¶ John 8.3–11 provides the account of Jesus forgiving the woman taken in adultery. The four gospels contain no mention of Christ specifically forgiving a liar; conversely, Revelation 21.8 and 22.15 depict him meting out harsh treatment to liars at the last judgement.

¶ cf. also no. 3 of *What's Bred in the Bone* above.

WORKS CONSULTED

Anthony, Geraldine, ed. *Stage Voices: Twelve Canadian Playwrights Talk about Their Lives and Work.* Toronto: Doubleday, 1978.

"Azazel." *The New Encyclopaedia Britannica: Micropaedia.* 15th ed. Vol. 1. Chicago: Encyclopaedia Britannica, 1989. 755.

Barnstone, Willis, ed. *The Other Bible.* San Francisco: Harper, 1984.

Bonnefoy, Yves, comp. *Mythologies.* Trans. Gerald Honigsblum, et al. Vol. 1. Chicago: U of Chicago P, 1991. 2 vols.

Bonnycastle, Stephen. "Robertson Davies and the Ethics of Monologue." *Journal of Canadian Studies* 12.1 (1977): 20–40.

The Book of Saints: A Dictionary of Servants of God Canonized by the Catholic Church. 6th ed. London: A & C Black, 1989.

Bowen, Gail. "Guides to the Treasure of Self: The Function of Women in the Fiction of Robertson Davies." *Waves* 5.1 (1976): 64–77.

Buitenhuis, Elspeth. *Robertson Davies.* Canadian Writers and Their Works. Toronto: Forum, 1972.

Campau, Dubarry. "There's Magic in Davies' *Fifth Business.*" *Toronto Telegram* 28 Oct. 1970: 58.

Cavendish, Richard, ed. *Man, Myth and Magic: The Illustrated Encyclopedia of Mythology, Religion and the Unknown.* 11 vols. New York: Cavendish, 1985.

Chambers, E.K., and F. Sidgwick, eds. *Early English Lyrics: Amorous, Divine, Moral and Trivial.* London: Sidgwick, 1966.

The Compact Edition of the Oxford English Dictionary. 2 vols. Oxford: Oxford UP, 1971.

Cude, Wilfred. "Historiography and Those Damned Saints: Shadow and Light in *Fifth Business.*" *Journal of Canadian Studies* 12.1 (1977): 47–67.

———. "Miracle and Art in *Fifth Business* or Who the Devil is Liselotte Vitzliputzli?" *Journal of Canadian Studies* 9.4 (1974): 3–16.

Davidson, Gustav. *A Dictionary of Angels Including the Fallen Angels.* New York: Free, 1967.

Davies, Robertson. "Answer to Job." Rev. of *J.B.*, by Archibald MacLeish; and *Answer to Job*, by Carl Gustav Jung. *Peterborough Examiner* 11 July 1959: 5.

———. "The Art of Fiction: Robertson Davies." With Elisabeth Sifton. *Robertson Davies: An Appreciation.* Ed. Elspeth Cameron. Peterborough: Broadview, 1991.

——. *At my Heart's Core*. Toronto: Clarke, 1950.

——. "At the Theatre: Good and Evil Struggle for Little Joe." *Saturday Night* Mar. 1941: 24.

——. "Believe Science Why not Witches?" Rev. of *The Discovery of Witchcraft*, by Reginald Scot. *Toronto Daily Star* 31 Oct. 1959: 31.

——. "Canada: A Disillusioned Daughter." With Peter O'Brien. *Bulletin* [University of Toronto] 16 Dec. 1991: 6.

[1]——. "Cap and Bells." Rev. of *The Bible, Designed to be Read as Literature*, ed. Ernest Sutherland Bates. *Peterborough Examiner* 12 Aug. 1941: 4.

——. "Christmas in the Age of Aquarius." *Vancouver Sun* 24 Dec. 1975: 5.

——. "Conversations with Robertson Davies." *Time* [Canada] 3 Nov. 1975: 10.

——. *Conversations with Robertson Davies*. Ed. J. Madison Davis. Literary Conversations Series. Jackson: UP of Mississippi, 1989.

——. "A Definitive Jung in a Single Volume." Rev. of *The Essential Jung*, sel. Anthony Storr. *Globe and Mail* 18 June 1983: E15.

——. *The Enthusiasms of Robertson Davies*. Ed. Judith Skelton Grant. Toronto: Macmillan, 1979.

*——. "Familiar Spirits and Wizards that Peep." Rev. of *Witchcraft in England*, by Christina Hole. *Peterborough Examiner* 31 Oct. 1945: 4.

——. "Fiction and Seven Deadly Sins." *Toronto Daily Star* 3 Mar. 1962: 27.

——. *Fifth Business*. Markham, ON: Penguin, 1977.

——. *Fortune, My Foe*. Toronto: Clarke, 1949.

——. "From the Critic's Notebook." Rev. of *The White Goddess*, by Robert Graves. *Peterborough Examiner* 28 Apr. 1949: 4.

——. *High Spirits*. Markham, ON: Penguin, 1984.

——. *Hunting Stuart and Other Plays*. New Drama 3. Toronto: New, 1972.

——. Interview. With Tom Harpur. *Harpur's Heaven and Hell*. Vision Television, Toronto, Jan. 1989.

---

1 The articles or reviews marked by asterisks represent early columns written under the signature "Samuel Marchbanks." I have not treated them separately because they are tonally and thematically of a piece with the material written under Davies's own signature at this time, rather than with that written later and attributed to the ever curmudgeonly, caustic Sam. Davies was, no doubt, acknowledging this when he subsequently excluded these from his Marchbanks collections. When discussing the early Marchbanks offerings, Patricia Monk affirms that "Davies does not project Samuel Marchbanks as a personality in his own right in these reviews and discussions. In them, Samuel Marchbanks is merely a label for the reviewer — a pseudonym" (27). In a note to this comment she adds: "I do not mean to suggest that there is no personality in the reviews — on the contrary, they give a clear impression of the reviewer, but the reviewer is Davies, not Samuel Marchbanks" (191).

———. Interview. With Daniel Richler. *Imprint*. TV Ontario, Toronto. 29 Oct. 1991.

———. Interview. With Harry Rasky. *The Magic Season of Robertson Davies.* CBC, Toronto. 27 Dec. 1991.

———. *Jezebel.* International Choral Festival. Roy Thomson Hall, Toronto. 3 June 1993.

———. *A Jig for the Gypsy.* Toronto: Clarke, 1954.

———. "The Joy of Christmas: A Historical Ramble by Robertson Davies." *Chatelaine* Dec. 1978: 23+.

———. " 'Jung and Saint Paul' Fascinating." Rev. of *Jung and St. Paul*, by David Cox. *Toronto Daily Star* 4 June 1960: 34.

———. "Jung's Theories Recall Bunyan's." Rev. of *Journey into Self*, by M. Esther Harding. *Toronto Daily Star* 9 May 1959: 31.

———. "Keeping Faith." *Saturday Night* Jan. 1987: 187+.

*———. "Laski's New Religion." Rev. of *Faith, Reason, and Civilization*, by Harold J. Laski. *Peterborough Examiner* 11 Oct. 1944: 4.

———. *Leaven of Malice.* Toronto: Clarke, 1954.

———. Letter. *Salterrae* [Trinity College, University of Toronto] 20 Jan. 1989: 3.

———. *The Lyre of Orpheus.* Toronto: Macmillan, 1988.

———. *The Manticore.* Harmondsworth: Penguin, 1976.

———. *The Mirror of Nature.* Toronto: U of Toronto P, 1983.

———. *A Mixture of Frailties.* Toronto: Macmillan, 1958.

———. *Murther and Walking Spirits.* Toronto: McClelland, 1991.

*———. "Music For Holy Week." *Peterborough Examiner* 28 Mar. 1945: 4.

———. "New Gods for Old." Rev. of *Biography of the Gods*, by A. Eustace Haydon. *Saturday Night* Apr. 1941: 20.

*———. "The Night of the Witches." *Peterborough Examiner* 31 Oct. 1942: 4.

———. *One Half of Robertson Davies.* Markham, ON: Penguin, 1978.

———. "Of the Human Predicament." Rev. of *The Well Adjusted Personality*, by Phillip Polatin. *Saturday Night* Mar. 1953: 20–21.

———. *Overlaid: A Comedy.* Canadian Playwright Series. Toronto: Samuel French, 1948.

———. *The Papers of Samuel Marchbanks.* Toronto: Collins, 1987.

———. *Question Time.* Toronto: Macmillan, 1975.

———. *The Rebel Angels.* Markham, ON: Penguin, 1987.

———. "Salvation is not Free." Rev. of *Embezzled Heaven*, by Franz Werfel. *Saturday Night* Dec. 1940: 20a.

———. *Tempest-Tost.* Harmondsworth: Penguin, 1980.

———. *A Voice from the Attic: Essays on the Art of Reading.* Rev. ed. Harmondsworth: Penguin, 1990.

———. *The Well-Tempered Critic: One Man's View of Theatre and Letters in Canada.* Ed. Judith Skelton Grant. Toronto: McClelland, 1981.

——. "What About a Show of Courage?" Rev. of *The Fall*, by Albert Camus; and *The Fountain Overflows*, by Rebecca West. *Saturday Night* Mar. 1957: 20–21.

——. *What's Bred in the Bone*. Markham, ON: Penguin, 1988.

——. *World of Wonders*. Markham, ON: Penguin, 1987.

Dombrowski, Theo and Eileen. " 'Every Man's Judgement': Robertson Davies' Courtroom." *Studies in Canadian Literature* 3 (1978): 47–61.

Dooley, David J. *Moral Vision in the Canadian Novel*. Toronto: Clarke, 1979.

Duffy, Dennis. "To Carry the Work of William James a Step Further: The Play of Truth in *Fifth Business*." *Essays on Canadian Writing* 36 (1988): 1–21.

Eliot, T.S. "Tradition and the Individual Talent." *Criticism: The Major Statements*. Ed. Charles Kaplan. New York: Saint Martin's, 1975.

Frye, Northrop. *Anatomy of Criticism: Four Essays*. Princeton: Princeton UP, 1973.

——. *A Natural Perspective: The Development of Shakespearean Comedy and Romance*. New York: Columbia UP, 1965.

Gnoli, Gherardo. "Manichaeism: An Overview." *The Encyclopedia of Religion*. Ed. Mircea Eliade. Vol. 9. New York: Macmillan, 1987. 161–70. 16 vols.

Godard, Barbara. "Writing Paradox, the Paradox of Writing: Robertson Davies." *Robertson Davies: An Appreciation*. Ed. Elspeth Cameron. Peterborough: Broadview, 1991.

Godwin, Malcolm. *Angels: An Endangered Species*. New York: Simon, 1990.

Goldie, Terry. "The Folkloric Background of Robertson Davies' Deptford Trilogy." *Studies in Robertson Davies' Deptford Trilogy*. Ed. Robert G. Lawrence and Samuel L. Macey. English Literary Studies 20. Victoria: U of Victoria P, 1980. 22–31.

Grant, Judith Skelton. *Robertson Davies*. Canadian Writers 17. Toronto: McClelland, 1978.

——. "Robertson Davies." *The Oxford Companion to Canadian Literature*. Ed. William Toye. Toronto: Oxford UP, 1983.

——. *Robertson Davies: Man of Myth*. Toronto: Viking, 1994.

Graves, Robert. *The White Goddess: A Historical Grammar of Poetic Myth*. Rev. and enl. ed. New York: Farrar, 1966.

Hagner, D.A. "Sanhedrin." *The Zondervan Pictorial Encyclopedia of the Bible*. Vol. 5. Grand Rapids, Michigan: Zondervan, 1976. 269–73. 5 vols.

Haines, Victor Yelverton. *The Fortunate Fall of Sir Gawain: The Typology of Sir Gawain and the Green Knight*. Washington: U of America P, 1982.

James, William. *The Varieties of Religious Experience: A Study in Human Nature*. Fwd. Jacques Barzun. New York: NAL, 1958.

Jonas, Hans. *The Gnostic Religion: The Message of the Alien God and the Beginnings of Christianity*. 2nd ed. Boston: Beacon, 1991.

Jung, C.G. *Collected Works*. 2nd ed. 20 vols. Bollingen Series 20. Princeton, NJ: Princeton UP, 1967–79.

——. *Memories, Dreams, Reflections*. Ed. Aniela Jaffe. Trans. Richard and Clara Winston. New York: Vintage, 1989.

——. *Psychology and Religion*. New Haven: Yale UP, 1938.

——. *The Undiscovered Self*. Trans. R.F.C. Hull. New York: NAL, 1958.

Kealy, Seán P. *The Apocalypse of John*. Message of Biblical Spirituality 15. Wilmington, Delaware: Michael Glazier, 1987.

Keith, W.J. *Canadian Literature in English*. Longman Literature in English Series. London: Longman, 1985.

——. "Robertson Davies and the Cornish Trilogy." *Journal of Canadian Studies* 24.1 (1989): 140–45.

Koster, Patricia. "'Promptings Stronger' than 'Strict Prohibitions': New Forms of Natural Religion in the Novels of Robertson Davies." *Canadian Literature* 111 (1986): 68–82.

——. "'A Rum Start': The Redoubled Baptisms of Francis Chegwidden Cornish." *Canadian Literature* 116 (1988): 248–53.

Lovasik, Lawrence G. *My First Catechism*. New York: Catholic, 1983.

LoVerso, Marco P. "Dialectic, Morality, and the Deptford Trilogy." *Studies in Canadian Literature* 12 (1987): 69–89.

Mercatante, Anthony S. *The Facts on File Encyclopedia of World Mythology and Legend*. New York: Facts on File, 1988.

Mills, John. "Robertson Davies (1913–)." *Canadian Writers and Their Works*. Fiction Series. Vol. 6. Ed. Robert Lecker, Jack David, Ellen Quigley. Toronto: ECW, 1985. 21–78. 10 vols. to date. 1983– .

Milton, John. *Paradise Lost, Samson Agonistes, Lycidas*. Ed. Edward Le Comte. New York: NAL, 1981.

Monk, Patricia. *The Smaller Infinity: The Jungian Self in the Novels of Robertson Davies*. Toronto: U of Toronto P, 1982.

Moreno, Antonio, O.P. *Jung, Gods, and Modern Man*. Notre Dame: U of Notre Dame P, 1970.

Morley, Patricia. *Robertson Davies*. Profiles in Canadian Drama. Toronto: Gage, 1977.

Nevo, Ruth. *Comic Transformations in Shakespeare*. London: Methuen, 1980.

The New American Bible. New York: P.J. Kennedy, 1970.

The New English Bible with the Apocrypha. Oxford: Oxford UP, 1970.

Peterman, Michael. *Robertson Davies*. Boston: Twayne, 1986.

Philp, H.L. *Jung and the Problem of Evil*. London: Rockcliff, 1958.

Quispel, Gilles. "Gnosticism: Gnosticism from Its Origins to the Middle Ages." *The Encyclopedia of Religion*. Ed. Mircea Eliade. Vol. 5. New York: Macmillan, 1987. 566–74. 16 vols.

——. "Sophia." *The Encyclopedia of Religion.* Vol. 13. New York: Macmillan, 1987. 416–17.

Radford, F.L. "The Apprentice Sorcerer: Davies' Salerton [sic] Trilogy." *Studies in Robertson Davies' Deptford Trilogy.* Ed. Robert G. Lawrence and Samuel L. Macey. English Literary Studies 20. Victoria: U of Victoria P, 1980. 13–21.

——. "The Great Mother and the Boy: Jung, Davies and *Fifth Business.*" *Studies in Robertson Davies' Deptford Trilogy.* Ed. Robert G. Lawrence and Samuel L. Macey. English Literary Studies 20. Victoria: U of Victoria P, 1980. 66–81.

Roper, Gordon. "A Davies Log." *Journal of Canadian Studies* 12.1 (1977): 5–19.

——. "Robertson Davies' *Fifth Business* and 'That Old Fantastical Duke of Dark Corners, C.G. Jung.'" *Journal of Canadian Fiction* 1.1 (1972): 33–39.

Ross, A.M. "Thaddaeus." *The Zondervan Pictorial Encyclopedia of the Bible.* Vol. 4. Grand Rapids, Michigan: Zondervan, 1976. 713. 5 vols.

Roy, James Charles. *Islands of Storm.* Dublin: Wolfhound, 1991.

Ryrie, John. "Robertson Davies: An Annotated Bibliography." *Annotated Bibliography of Canada's Major Authors.* Vol. 3. Ed. Robert Lecker and Jack David. Downsview, ON: ECW, 1981. 57–279. 8 vols. to date. 1979– .

Saint Joseph "New Catholic Edition" of the Holy Bible. New York: Catholic Book Publishing, 1962.

Schultz, A.C. "Manesseh." *The Zondervan Pictorial Encyclopedia of the Bible.* Vol. 4. Grand Rapids, Michigan: Zondervan, 1976. 63. 5 vols.

Senior, Michael. *The Illustrated Who's Who in Mythology.* London: Macdonald, 1990.

Shakespeare, William. *Henry V.* Ed. J.H. Walter. London: Methuen, 1964.

——. *King Lear.* Ed. Kenneth Muir. London: Methuen, 1963.

——. *The Tempest.* Ed. Frank Kermode. London: Methuen, 1966.

——. *Timon of Athens.* Ed. H.J. Oliver. London: Methuen, 1963.

Solecki, Sam. "The Other Half of Robertson Davies." Rev. of *The Rebel Angels,* by Robertson Davies. *Canadian Forum* Dec.–Jan. 1981–82: 30+.

Stone-Blackburn, Susan. "Robertson Davies, Rebel Angel." Rev. of *The Rebel Angels,* by Robertson Davies. *Essays on Canadian Writing* 28 (1984): 93–101.

Strong, James. "A Concise Dictionary of the Words in the Greek Testament; With Their Renderings in the Authorized English Version." *The Exhaustive Concordance of the Bible.* Peabody, MA: Hendrickson, n.d. 5–79.

Sypnowich, Peter. "Toronto Author: Writers Shouldn't Write for Money." *Toronto Daily Star* 23 Jan. 1971: 59.

van den Born, A. *Encyclopedic Dictionary of the Bible.* Trans. and ed. Louis F. Hartman. New York: McGraw, 1963.

Wilken, Robert L. "Nestorianism." *The Encyclopedia of Religion.* Ed. Mircea Eliade. Vol. 10. New York: Macmillan, 1987. 372–73. 16 vols.

The Wisdom of Solomon. *The Holy Bible Containing the Old and New Testaments with the Apocryphal/Deuterocanonical Books.* New rev. stand. version. Toronto: Canadian Bible Society, 1989.

Woodcock, George. "A Cycle Completed: The Nine Novels of Robertson Davies." *Canadian Literature* 126 (1990): 33–48.

INDEX

imprimerie gagné ltée

PRINTED IN CANADA